GW00381968

Rod & Lu H

THE TRADE WIND FOODIE

Sailing the world discovering and cooking good food

Imray Laurie Norie & Wilson

Published by
Imray, Laurie, Norie & Wilson Ltd
Wych House, St Ives,
Cambridgeshire, PE27 5BT, England.
✆ +44 (0)1480 462114 *Fax* +44(0)1480 496109
Email ilnw@imray.com
www.imray.com
2013

1st edition 2013

ISBN 978 184623 502 3

British Library Cataloguing in Publication Data
A catalogue record for this book is available from the British Library.

Printed by Zrinski in Croatia

Contents

Preface

The days are long gone, if they ever really existed, when sailing folk opened a tin of something for dinner or like Tilman, cooked up a pot of gumbo or burgoo which was added to for weeks until it got too mouldy to eat. Most cruising people eat very well and spend a lot of time thinking about and preparing food. Over the years I've been putting together boat recipes and listening to lots of other cruisers who like good food. Bit by bit this book 'just growed'.

I am not a professional chef. I don't even think I am a great cook. What I like is food and that naturally leads to an interest in cooking good food and once you start there is no holding back. All of these recipes have been cooked on board. We eat well in harbour and on passage without resorting to ready-meals or frozen made-up meals. There are a lot of tasty meals, often quite simple, that you can put together on passage when things are a bit bumpy and you don't want to have a long list of ingredients strewn around the galley. Conversely there are also more complicated recipes here you can cook up in harbour or in calm weather at sea. On passage from the Marquesas to the Tuamotus in the Pacific the ocean lived up to its moniker and we were becalmed on a flat sea. We adjusted the passage plan to arrive a day later at the coral pass and put together a feast while drifting around in the middle of the ocean. And of course a bit of sauvignon blanc in wine glasses – it was that calm.

Whatever sort of boat you are on from the humble to something that has a jacuzzi on the back where you can sip champagne, there is still the whole business of sourcing ingredients and cooking on board. Converting skills from the home kitchen to the boat galley is not always easy and a bit of confidence in substituting ingredients and exploring new culinary areas can make all the difference between a happy ship and mutiny.

There are around 100 recipes at the back of the book plus tips on catching and filleting fish, dealing with crayfish, suggestions on marinades and the mysteries of cooking bread on board. At the beginning of the book I deal with sorting the galley, on water and gas supplies, refrigeration and freezers, on stowing food and fresh fruit and vegetables. Sandwiched in the middle chapters of the book is an account of *Skylax*'s circumnavigation tipped towards cooking and looking for good food around the world.

All the recipes are used on board by us so they do work, although these recipes, in fact any onboard recipes, should be taken as a guide and not absolute instructions set in stone. One of the things most cruising folk get used to is substituting ingredients which look like, taste like, or have the same texture as the missing ingredient. As long as it tastes about right, it will do in the absence of the real thing and who knows, it may taste better.

While much of this book is down to me, Lu is just as good a cook and there are lots of recipes she has made her own or honed for cooking on board. She also has her areas of expertise in the fishy arena and bread making. For some reason I've never had much success baking bread so I'm grateful she is good at it. Lots of friends have made suggestions, provided recipes and best of all, cooked for us on board. Somehow food, even a simple meal, tastes so good on board and at the end of a passage there is nothing quite like a few drinks in the cockpit and dinner with fellow travellers.

The photos of food in the book are all taken of real food. I was a bit shocked to find that many recipe books employ food stylists to prepare the food for photographing. That includes covering it in hair spray so it glistens, using dry ice so it looks like it's steaming, and generally prodding and poking the food into a photogenic arrangement. Well all the food in the photographs here was eaten after the photos were taken. It was for consumption and not presentation.

This is a book about the business of cooking on board. If you are looking for meals that are long on description, the sort of thing where you get a chicken breast stuffed with venison sausage on a bed of samphire and a *jus* of distilled blueberries and balsamic with sweet potato and truffle mash, then look elsewhere. I just made that description up, but I'd be tempted to try it ashore if I was in the money and the restaurant looked good, but it's got little to do with the job of cooking on board that I do. The recipes here have been simplified, have suggestions for alternative ingredients when you don't have the specific ingredient, and should really be treated as broad outlines where you paint in the bits you like. Good food doesn't mean overly fussy although there are a smattering of recipes that are more suited to a harbour or anchorage. After all we spend more time at anchor or tied up than we ever do on passage.

Rod Heikell, London 2012

Acknowledgements

Lu as ever has been shipmate, soulmate and friend on passages around the world. She has contributed important bits to the book and is no mean cook. Other friends on boats have suggested recipes, Anton on *Anatina*, cousin Frank who has been a shipmate in the Indian Ocean, Michael and Linda on *B'Sherrit*, Roy and Irene on *Peggy West*, Peter Seary on *Sayonara* who always carries fine reds and paté de foie gras on the boat, Chrissy for her fish and lentils, Pete and Jan on *Penyllan*, Paul and Marguerite in Antigua, Gill who likes cooking when she goes camping, Alan and Penny on *Penny Pincher* for lures, James on *Kaama* for fishy advice, Sally on *Astra*, Genevieve on *Pi*, Richard in the Médoc and Harry Potts on *Andrea*. Willie Wilson at Imrays has encouraged me in the project and Elinor Cole and Clare Georgy put in long hours making it look as good as it does. To all of you my thanks and may your rice never stick to the bottom of the pot.

Cooking on board: The practical stuff

This introductory section deals with the details of cooking on board, the galley, equipping the galley, water and refrigeration, storing food and looking after fruit and vegetables on passage. Most of us are stuck with what we have on a boat except for equipping the galley. Even then it is possible to make do with the pots and pans and utensils that you have, though I suggest a few items well worth investing in to make cooking easier and more rewarding on board.

Dinner arrives in the San Blas

Cooking duties

I always cook a big meal before we set off on longish passages. It just needs to be warmed up, some pasta, rice or other starch cooked to go with it and you have a meal ready to go for dinner. Usually there is enough for a couple of nights and then after a few days when stomachs have settled down we are ready for something else.

One solution often touted for passage-makers is that you visit the local supermarket and order a pallet of ready-made meals. It's an odd one when you really have a lot of time on your hands on passage and feel you need to resort to a TV-dinner of goo masquerading as meat in a sauce of soya thickener. In any case you just can't buy them in many places in the world.

There is a lot of pre-passage prepping you can do to make life easier in the galley. If you have a freezer then make up some meals or the base for meals. A Bolognese-type sauce (ragu) that can be used as the base for a pasta sauce, lasagne, chilli con carne or a stew. A chicken stew that can be made into a fruity curry, a Thai curry or a Mediterranean stew. You can add the fresh ingredients you have on board to the base dish and that will lift it out of the realms of a frozen meal. In the recipe section I often list alternatives to some ingredients that may be impossible to get so you get a dish that has texture and taste along the lines of the original recipe. After a while this improvisation becomes second nature on board a boat where the ingredient list is limited. On *Skylax* we don't run the freezer as a freezer, more of a cold store, so we don't do frozen base meals. After the pre-cooked passage meal has gone we just make things up depending on say whether the frozen chicken has defrosted or the fresh mushrooms need using. And there is always the chance of landing a fish which usually provides meals for a few days.

Most cruising yachts are crewed by a couple which makes cooking pretty straightforward. Larger crews on yachts require a bit more planning and here cooking base meals that go in the freezer are more important. It's also more important to plan meals that will keep the crew happy and to find out if there are any likes and dislikes. I've had crew that didn't eat raw tomatoes but would eat them cooked, crew who couldn't stand pasta, and vegetarians including a friend who decided he would lapse on passage and thereafter always enquired about the quantities of bacon, salami, chorizo and other meaty things being shipped, just to make sure there would be enough.

Cooking on board is a celebration for your fellow shipmates helping you on passage and a celebration of food. On board *Skylax* everyone has to cook on passage and the cook never washes up. I don't care whether someone cooks a simple omelette or a gastronomic delight, as long as they cook. And after all what better to do than devote some of that long graveyard watch to dreaming up a dinner to titillate the senses.

The Galley

Most of us will be stuck with the galley inherited on the boat we have. Most galley designs provide a secure place to work with somewhere to wedge yourself when cooking. A few do not and a bit of thought needs to go into how to make the galley area more secure. This can be some sort of raised structure to lean against or may be done by beefing up the boat furniture on bench galleys along one side of the saloon, a common arrangement on many modern yachts.

Working in the galley entails a sense of balance and some anticipation of how the boat is moving

One thing I'm personally not too keen on is the sort of galley strap that used to be recommended for working in the galley at sea. A lot of the motion on a monohull at sea is fore and aft pitching or the corkscrew motion of catamarans which mean you need to brace against that as well as against the roll of a monohull. A galley strap makes it difficult for me to do that, though there are no doubt those who swear by them. Try one out before you get a strap made up.

Below are a few tips for making cooking on board safer and easier in a seaway.

Cookers

Most cookers on monohulls are gimballed athwartships to counter heel and any rolling motion. Rolling downwind in the trades can have the cooker thrashing back and forth swinging well beyond the actual heeling angle of the boat as the momentum of the cooker keeps it going beyond the angle of heel. It's worth checking how far a cooker can go before it comes up on its stops so the cooker is not slamming to an abrupt halt as it swings. There needs to be plenty of space for it to swing back and forth without coming to a jarring stop and jolting pots and pans on the top burners off the cooker.

If you are getting a new cooker it's worth taking the dimensions and making a cardboard mock-up of the side dimensions in the galley to see if there is enough room for it to swing before coming to a halt. You need the cooker to swing to at least to 35–40°, a bit more if you have room. There are a couple of other things to look out for as well.

- All modern cookers have or should have flame failure devices and be certified for marine use. If you don't have a remote solenoid cut-off for the gas supply then it's worth fitting one. The solenoid cut-off is mounted in the gas locker and the switch (with a nice red light to remind you the gas hasn't been turned off after use) mounted handy to the cooker.

- The cooker should have a good fiddle around the entire top, at least 4–5cm high. Pan holders should be easily adjusted to keep pots and pans from flying off, not just from the rolling but also when the boat is pitching. Often you can wedge the kettle or another pot on the top to keep pans from sliding around with the motion of the boat.

- If you are getting a new cooker it's useful to do the roast chicken test. Many ovens marketed for yachts are not high enough to get your average chicken in for roasting. We wandered around a supermarket and measured the height of a 1½–2kg chicken which is around 15cm. It's surprising how many ovens are too small to get your chicken in unless you spatchcock it.

Checking the maximum angle of swing on the new stove

Four burner stoves don't really work unless very big. Here the kettle is wedged in to hold everything in place, but you can't really use that fourth burner

- A grill is useful, but not used as often as you might think. Personally I would always want one, but I have survived happily on other boats without them. If you like toast there are cheap conical or flat toasters that sit on a burner and work well. We use one.
- If you are splashing out on an all-singing-and-dancing cooker don't make the mistake I did of getting a four-burner cooker. Your average boat cooker is not big enough on the top for four burners and you just can't physically get pots or pans on all four burners. Get a three-burner cooker.

Equipping the galley

Fire extinguishers and blankets You need to have at least one in date extinguisher close to the cooker but not in the immediate vicinity. If there is a fire on or in the cooker the extinguisher should not be so close you can't get to it without being burnt. Arguably more useful than an extinguisher is a fire blanket. Smothering the flames can be a lot more effective than using a relatively small extinguisher, something I know from having used one on a neighbouring boat that was on fire.

Non-slip mats Non-slip mats on the work surfaces are essential to stop everything sliding around. You can buy ready-made mats, but pop into a hardware shop or some supermarkets or search the internet and you can find rolls of non-slip for less money. Cut them up to fit the work surfaces.

Apart from stopping things slipping around when you are cooking, it will stop mugs of hot drinks sliding about. One of the most common injuries on a boat is burns from boiling water from the kettle or spilt from a mug. Any mugs of hot drinks should only be two-thirds full or the motion of the boat will splash scalding hot water out whether in the galley or up in the cockpit.

Pots and pans No less an authority than Uffa Fox said throw away all your aluminium pots and pans and use something else. At the time Uffa may have been right, but nowadays very good thick-base pans with a good non-stick finish are made in aluminium and I suspect most of us use them. On *Skylax* we use a mixture of aluminium with non-stick and stainless pots and pans. Don't skimp on buying some good pans. They will last and are a joy to cook with compared to thin-bottomed cheap pans.

Pressure cookers A pressure cooker is always cited as a 'must have' in the galley and I have had one on most of my boats, the latest a very nice stainless Prestige. A pressure cooker is useful because it uses less water, it has a lid which is fastened down, and uses less cooking gas compared to your run of the mill pot or pan. They do have a few drawbacks and, I think, a few semi-true stories attached to them. The following points should be kept in mind.

- In general a pressure cooker cooks food in ONE-THIRD of the time of a conventional pot or pan, so you can reduce cooking times to one third of that given in the recipes. In practice I find it needs a little more time than this so just open it up, have a taste and cook it a bit longer if necessary.

- A pressure cooker is quite a high unwieldy beast and on a few trips bouncing to windward I've had to hold it on the cooker with a bungee cord over the top – and yes the cooker did have fiddles and pot-holders. That was on the 31ft *Tetranora* and seems not to be such a problem on larger boats.

- Pressure cookers are sometimes touted as a device you can bake bread and cakes in. In my experience the end-product has been less than tasty, unevenly cooked with a mushy interior, and the pressure cooker itself gets unseemly hot. Personally I've never really had any luck trying to cook bread in a pressure cooker, but others say they have.

- For me a pressure cooker is useful for some stews, cassoulet, and as a large pot for pasta when friends are over for dinner, though in the latter use it's really just used as a large pot without pressure.

- In the recipes at the back any suitable for pressure cookers are marked as such.

High-sided pan This is my most used pan, effectively a high sided frying pan with a lid also called a chef's pan. A good thick base spreads the heat evenly and get one with quality non-stick. A lid is useful. You need to pay a bit for a good one.

Frying pan Definitely needed for the traditional fry-up and for a few other frying jobs. We don't have one of the square frying pans, but I have given them as presents and they seem to do a good job without taking up all the cooker top as a normal round pan does. I've bought mesh spatter guards to go on top of the pan when frying, but they rarely last more than a year before rusting to bits.

Pans We have a selection on board including a set of three stainless pans that have a detachable handle and stow inside each other to save storage space. You can get these off the internet or through some catalogue suppliers.

A high sided pan like this is the most used cooking pot on *Skylax*. The high sides and lid stop food slopping over

Other cooking implements

Knives and other implements A blunt knife is a danger in the galley. Buy at least one good stainless cutting knife and get one of those awful ceramic wheel things to sharpen it. Two good stainless knives of different sizes won't go amiss and on *Skylax* we have four or more good knives. A good high carbon steel knife is a delight, but they will rust on board unless cleaned and oiled regularly.

I favour wooden spatulas for stirring in non-stick pans, but any soft plastic spatula or spoon will work. You also need all those other utensils like a plastic serving spoon, kitchen tongs (good for spaghetti, turning things like sausages, and BBQs), plastic fish slice, and any other stirrers and shakers you might need.

Kitchen scissors A good pair of kitchen scissors are useful for all sorts of chores like cutting up bacon into bits, opening stubborn plastic packets especially the vacuum sealed type, gutting fish, cutting up herbs like parsley and basil, even cutting small cordage and trimming stick-on sail repair patches when allowed out of the galley.

Salad whizzer This may seem a bit excessive, but we managed to find a small one in New Zealand that is used a lot on board. Otherwise resort to a tea towel to dry off salad greens after they have been washed.

Lemon squeezer. You don't want to get lemon pips into your dish or it will have a sour pectin flavour and this gadget makes squeezing the lemon or lime dead easy

Dog bowls so essential for eating on passage. These American ones have a rubber ring around the bottom to stop them slipping

Lemon squeezer You may laugh at this, but they do make life easier. It's easy and it stops the pips getting into the food. Lemon pips cooked in any of the recipes here will give a bitter almost tannin taste to the food and you need to make sure that pips do not fall into the food when you are cooking, whatever way you get the juice out.

Grater Needed for cheese, especially fresh Parmesan and also for carrots, radish and any other vegetables that need grating. We have a flashy flat chef's stainless grater, but any flat grater will do.

Tableware While we have some melamine dog bowls for eating in rougher weather, most of our plates, side-plates, bowls and salad bowls are ceramic or something similar. Likewise mugs for coffee and tea are also ceramic pottery. We have some of those cheap thin wooden bowls where something like bamboo is glued together in a plaited pattern that you can buy almost anywhere and are amazingly durable. Most of our glasses are plastic with the exception of a few shot glasses and some boxed-up wine glasses for use in harbour and at anchor. After quite a lot of miles the only ceramic items we have broken have been in harbour or an anchorage in a dead calm.

Cockpit tables

A lot of the time you will be eating in the cockpit where there is a bit more breeze to cool things down and the views are better. Cockpit tables come in all shapes and sizes and a lot of production cruisers now have a built-in cockpit table as standard. You can retrofit a cockpit table but do make it easy to operate or put together.

On *Skylax* we have a standard table in teak sold in lots of chandlers. It attaches to the binnacle crash bars and folds down with the two-hinged leaves folded in. With the leaves open there is plenty of room for two, four is a squeeze but possible, more than four and some of the guests or us are eating with a plate on their knees or the coaming. Importantly it doesn't have a leg to support the forward end and relies on two locking supports which fold up when it goes down. Fold-out legs are a magnet for my own legs with catastrophic results.

Skylax's cockpit table is a retrofit job and works well for up to four people

Gas

Gas safety

Gas installation rules vary around the world, but there are some basic ground-rules that, though obvious, need to be briefly stated here.

- Gas bottles should be stored in an outside locker, usually in the cockpit, with a bottom drain overboard. Some older yachts get around this by storing the bottles outside, commonly secured on a platform on the transom or beside the mast. The problem with outside storage is that sea water takes it toll on steel bottles fairly quickly in such an exposed position. With aluminium or FRP containers this is less of a problem. Regulators and connectors also suffer badly from salt water damage.

- Gas lines to the cooker are commonly rigid copper tube with armoured flexible pipe to the cooker at the end. Armoured pipe and any flexible pipe is date-stamped and should be renewed when the date is up.

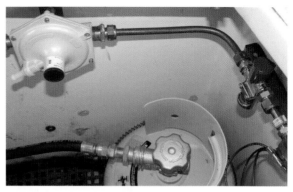

Bubble tester and remote
solenoid in the gas locker

Universal regulator
with fitting for NZ
gas on the bottle

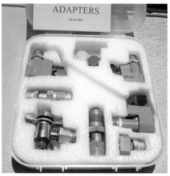

A gas fitting kit like
this from Haywards
means you can
connect to any gas
bottles in the world

- Within a gas locker a solenoid cut-off valve is a good safety factor (see above under *Cookers*). A bubble tester for leaks is also a useful device on the gas line.
- Gas regulators should be of marine quality or alternatively carry a number of back-up regulators.

Getting cooking gas around the world

One of the problems that doesn't usually get a lot of thought when arriving in a new country is how easy, or not, it is to get gas bottles filled. In a significant number of countries you effectively need to get a new gas bottle that conforms to the regulations in that country so you can have gas on board. The reason for that is that to get an old bottle certified can be next to impossible and even if you manage it, the cost of certification will often be more than the cost of a new bottle.

Most cookers will run happily on propane or butane, but you need to make sure the regulator will work with both. Propane cookers running on butane will give out slightly less heat than when on propane, but for the most part you won't notice the difference. Butane is stored at a lower pressure than propane so you should never fill a butane bottle (such as Camping Gaz bottles) with propane. In lots of places, Tonga and New Zealand are examples, the gas is actually a mix of propane and butane.

Once you have a new bottle then there is the matter of connecting it. The fittings for bottles in different countries vary and the chances are that you will not have a fitting for the local bottle. We use the kit that Hayward (www.whayward.com) makes for cruising boats which has a permanently mounted marinised regulator that can cope with propane and butane and a fittings kit with all the connectors you are likely to come across around the world.

You can siphon gas from a local bottle into your own as long as you have the fittings for both bottles. Not surprisingly you should do this outside in a well ventilated area and away from any naked flame. Hoist the full bottle upside down on a tree or whatever, connect the fittings to take the hose and connect the two bottles. Open the valves and the gas will slowly, very slowly, drain into the empty bottle. It takes a good few hours and you rarely get a full bottle. It's not a bad idea to know the full weight of your own bottle just in case it does over-fill.

Water

Water on a long trip is liquid gold and you need to hoard it. On a three week trip from the Red Sea to Cochin in the 31ft *Tetranora* two of us still had water left from 60 gallons total, though we could have done with more showers. On Atlantic crossings of around three weeks, three of us have had lots of water left from 100 gallons total. Forty gallons on board a yacht with two crew should be augmented by at least four five gallon jerry cans and you might want to think about installing another tank somewhere. Two

Four 20 litre cans of water on *Skylax*. In lots of places you are going to have to ferry water to the boat using cans

of the jerry cans should be strapped to the guardrails in case of the awful prospect of abandoning ship in which case you can sling them into the liferaft or the water (and they should float in the denser salt water). We also carry around a dozen five litre bottles of drinking water for emergencies should the water in the main tanks become undrinkable for any reason and remember a lot of tinned goods have water in them as well.

Watermakers A watermaker is often cited as an essential bit of equipment for ocean passages. There is no doubt that a watermaker is a useful bit of kit, especially in

Hygiene

Watching the water consumption you do get to shower now and again, probably every 3–4 days on passage, but there is no possibility of showering every day without very large tanks or a watermaker. Most people don't and the saving grace is a reserve of baby wipes. Moreover they can be used when the boat is too uncomfortable to shower which is more often than you think, especially in big trade wind seas when you roll about all over the place and showering becomes a slippery exercise in holding on.

Water economy on board mostly entails not leaving a pressure tap running. When you clean your teeth turn the tap on when needed. When showering once you are wet turn the shower off and shampoo your hair. Wash the shampoo out and turn the shower off again. Lather up your body and shower off again. This all saves lots of water and even in a house I can't leave a tap running when I clean my teeth.

While a lot of yachts carry watermakers, it is not necessary for a long trip – after all yachts were crossing oceans long before watermakers were around. And they are not always reliable as per my comments above. In most places in the world you can find water and you can also collect rain to augment your supplies. The easiest way is to get hold of a small plastic tarpaulin, about 1½m by 1½m should do (around 5ft by 5ft) and put a simple screw skin fitting in the middle and tie it up on the foredeck with a bit of hose to the water tank. It doesn't need to be flashy, any old bits of string will do to tie it up so there is a hollow around the skin fitting, and you will be surprised how much water you can catch in the Tropics. In Tonga during downpours enough water was collected in under an hour to fill the tanks and the jerry cans.

The great bottled water myth

It is a curse of seas around the world that they are peppered with empty plastic water bottles bobbing around, collecting in trash gyres where currents meet, washed up on beaches and casually disposed of ashore. Even if they are taken ashore to be disposed of they invariably end up being burnt on a rubbish dump somewhere releasing all sorts of toxic compounds into the environment. Plastic bottles are mostly made from polyethylene terephthalate (PET), but also contain traces of plasticizers, phthalates, antioxidants, heavy metals, fillers, and anti-static agents. PET can be recycled, but not by burning it in an open air rubbish dump.

Plastic water bottles pollute the seas everywhere and wash up on even quite remote beaches. This is inside a cay in the San Blas

Here are the reasons why it is pointless to carry all that bottled water on board – apart from the very obvious matter of pollution in the sea and on the land.

Most bottled water is not required to comply with the sort of standards and rigorous testing that is applied to municipal water supplies. You get a list of the 'ingredients' in terms of *x*% or PPM sodium, potassium, calcium nitrates, sulphates, nitrites, etc., but these do not have to conform to the levels set by the government for drinking water from the tap. I well remember the MD of Perrier being put on the spot in a TV interview and asked if he would give his small child Perrier or tap water to drink. He replied tap water, though rather sheepishly.

Drinking bottled water is not going to keep you away from any perceived nasties in the local tap water. What do you clean your teeth with? Do you eat ashore? If you do then what do you think the ice in your drink is made of? What do you think the glass is washed up in? And the plates you eat off and the utensils you use? What do you think the salad ingredients are washed in?

You cannot insulate yourself from the local water unless you never eat or drink ashore, never clean your teeth except with bottled water, never touch the stuff.

Water in another country will have some benign bacteria of a slightly different strain to that your gut is used to at home and maybe it will cause a slight upset for a day or so. Your gut will then adapt to the

somewhere like the Red Sea or parts of the Pacific and Atlantic Oceans, but essential, it is not. In fact there are a not a few yachties stuck in various ports around the world who would disagree after trying to get the watermaker repaired or just waiting around for spares. While a watermaker is a useful bit of kit on board, large numbers of yachts make long passages without one. There are a few drawbacks to watermakers.

While watermaker reliability has greatly improved, they can be temperamental to say the least. I have helped lots of boats take out their new or nearly new watermaker for it to be collected yet again by an agent so it can be returned to the manufacturer for repairs or replacement. To be fair there are owners who have had few if any problems with their chosen make of watermaker. Do some research amongst users to see what recommendations come up for different makes and also choose a manufacturer who will give good after sales service. If you are thinking about getting a watermaker the following is worth thinking about.

- Watermakers like to be worked so if you are leaving the boat for more than two weeks or so then you need to go through the complicated procedure of cleaning 'foreign' bacteria and you won't experience any more problems in the normal course of events. And you get to eat ashore.

So don't buy all those bottles of water. It is an affectation you can do without. And you will be doing yourself and the environment a favour as well.

As a caveat to all this the following may be useful. As George Carlin quipped: 'Ever wonder about those people who spend $2 apiece on those little bottles of Evian water? Try spelling 'Evian' backward.'

- *Chlorinating water* If you are worried about the local water add some bleach solution (around a 0.5% sodium hypochlorite solution) to the water in the tank. This effectively chlorinates the water which will get rid of most of the nasty bacteria and any single cell organisms. Generally around 20ml to 200 litres (20ml is a bit over a tablespoon) is recommended. The exact dose is dependant on the water quality, an unknown, so I generally splosh a bit more into the tank if I am worried. Don't put too much in though.

- While local water is often perfectly OK to drink, in some places it is heavily chlorinated. We use a Brita water filter jug to filter water for tea and coffee and fill water bottles to go in the fridge for drinking water. It gets rid of any taste in the local water, especially chlorine, and costs very little compared to bottled water.

- *Sea water* On *Tetra* with just 50 gallons in the way of fresh water and two of us on board we used to wash up in a bucket of sea water in the cockpit. The trouble is you need to rinse the plates off with fresh or they feel salty-sticky and the stainless cutlery starts to rust. With more water we rarely bother and wash up with fresh down below. You can try adding salt water to fresh for cooking pasta, potatoes, rice, that sort of thing, but my estimate is to use a measly 10% of salt water or everything tastes really salty. Maybe it's all the other things in sea water, but even adding very little to cooking water imparts an odd flavour to the food when I've used it.

A Brita water jug at least gets rid of chlorine and other tastes for coffee and tea and drinking water

out the pipes and membranes and then washing them through with the chemical wash and preservative provided by the manufacturer. Before starting them up again you need to wash them through again.

- Watermakers do not like dirty water with silt and other debris in it. They really need to be run in clean anchorages or at sea.

- Depending on the size of the watermaker you will need to run a generator or for smaller models have a good source of amps for a 12 or 24 volt system.

- If you need spares then getting them to where you are can be an expensive business. It's not only the matter of getting spares somewhere, but also of extracting them from the local customs. It usually works out to be hundreds of dollars not tens.

If you leave the boat for more than a couple of weeks at times then you may, like us, decide that it is not worth the bother and time, let alone expense, of keeping your watermaker going. In our case we got rid of the watermaker after several expensive repair stops and manage on tank water and jerry cans. It's surprisingly liberating.

Refrigeration

There are few yachts out there which don't have a refrigerator on board, though by no means all and I know of a number of boats that have cornered the globe without refrigeration on board. The following brief points should be considered.

- Most refrigerators these days are 12 or 24 volt. Older engine driven compressors are rarer with the increased efficiency of DC powered fridges. If it is going to draw power from your batteries it may be necessary to upgrade your amp hour capacity. For medium sized yachts (35–45 ft) 500 AH is probably about right. You will also need to revise your charging methods – a refrigerator is estimated to use around 50–60% of total power consumption on most yachts. Smaller yachts without an auxiliary generator usually fit a solar panel or two or a wind-powered generator to supply the much-needed amps.

Most yachts have a top opening fridge set into the work top. *Skylax* has a fridge and freezer compartment next to each other

- Heat-absorption and thermo-electric types do not work well in the high ambient temperatures in the Tropics. There is really no alternative to having a compressor working off the batteries (high current drain) or off the engine (very annoying when you need to run it just for the fridge). Holding (eutectic) plates are pretty much essential if you are running a freezer and dramatically reduce the time a compressor will have to run to keep things frozen.

- Get a top-opening refrigerator so that the cold air does not fall out every time it is opened. As a general rule, most refrigerators do not have adequate insulation – 10cm (4in) should be the minimum.

- On *Skylax* the fridge/freezer has a compressor running off the engine with holding plates in the 'freezer' compartment and a 12 volt compressor with a normal cold plate in the fridge. For the approx size fridge/freezer unit we have on *Skylax* we would need 150 AH a day if running off the batteries alone. For a 6 cubic foot fridge and 2 cubic foot freezer the requirement is 80 AH a day. All figures are from Richard Kollman (www.kollmann-marine.com/selecting.html) who gives no-nonsense advice on boat refrigeration and I know from previous boats that these are the sorts of figures you are looking at for 12 volt systems. On passage on *Skylax* we need to run the engine driven compressor for an hour in the morning and an hour or more at night to freeze the two holding plates down in the freezer compartment. For the record the fridge and freezer have 11cm (4½ inches) of enclosed foam insulation and the coolant for the engine driven compressor is water-cooled as opposed to air cooled. When the sun is shining directly onto the side of the hull where the fridge/freezer is located even running the engine and compressor for two hours a day can have the freezer struggling to keep up. See below for why we don't run the freezer as a freezer.

The freezer trap

In the 31ft *Tetranora* it took us three weeks hard on the wind to get from Yemen to Cochin on the bottom of India. All sorts of things had conspired to a late departure and we were in the wrong season with the north-east monsoon blowing straight out of where we were headed. Distance sailed 2,100 miles to cover a rhumb line route of 1,400 miles, all of it hard on the wind on port tack dipping right down into the doldrums before we could curve back up towards India. We anchored off the Taj Malabar Hotel in Cochin and after clearing in we cleaned up and went ashore for dinner. I can still clearly see the bottle of Kingfisher Ale the waiter brought, the condensed drops running down the outside of the green glass, still taste even now the cool amber liquid, still remember how Frank and I looked at this apparition from heaven with awe and something approaching reverence. You see *Tetra* didn't have a fridge and anyway we don't drink much on passage. And can you remember what the last beer you had tasted like with this sort of simple clarity?

In truth I would have liked a fridge and most of my other boats have had them of varying types. Freezers are another matter. On *Skylax* we have a freezer but I don't treat it as such. It is more of a very cold fridge and I have good reasons for keeping things this way. In all sorts of different parts of the world I've come across cruising boats where the skipper or crew are effectively imprisoned on board to monitor the freezer.

The bottom line here is that I'm not prepared to spend the resources or the time to ensure my freezer is keeping everything in it frozen. I remember being at anchor in Ao Chalong in Thailand on *Tetra* sipping evening drinks in the cockpit with a bunch of friends until we decided solids would be useful and we should go ashore to eat. 'Sorry,' said one couple, 'but we need to go back to the boat to run the generator to keep everything frozen, but would we like to come for some Turkish steak out of the freezer'. The answer was a polite 'no' – the rest of us were going ashore for some wonderful Thai food. A freezer can hold you prisoner on board. There are things to do ashore, restaurants and bars to visit, trips inland for a couple of days or a week to explore a country. And if the beer gets a bit warm and the butter melts in my absence, then it's not a disaster.

On passage a freezer can be a boon and I well remember hearing a conversation on SSB in the Atlantic going east where a dry American was asked if he was stopping at Bermuda. 'Nah,' he said, 'I've still got half a cow and a couple of chickens in the freezer so we'll just keep plugging on.' At the time we would have liked a bit of his cow, but we had lots of other interesting things to cook and when we got to the Azores there is a wonderful restaurant there where the meat couldn't have tasted better.

Rubbish

Modern food packaging generates large amounts of rubbish. On *Skylax* we do the following when on passage. On short passages of 2-3 days there should be no problem storing most rubbish on board and disposing of it when you arrive.

Organic By this I mean vegetable peelings, egg shells, tea bags, old fruit and stale bread, that sort of thing. We keep a separate organic rubbish bin in the galley area and all of these things which will decompose in the sea are put in it. We then empty it over the side every day when out at sea. On shorter passages some items like banana skins and melon rind are kept as they seem to just float around the surface.

Plastic All plastic should be kept until you arrive on the land and disposed of there.

Tins We used to put holes in the bottom so they sank and throw them in the sea. Now we crush them on the basis that there is so little oxygen in the bottom layers of the sea that they take longer to decompose than on the land. And some of your landfalls will have recycling facilities anyway.

Glass On longer trips we still fill glass containers with water so they sink and dump them over the side. Glass is basically silica with some other naturally occurring oxides. This means that it should break up into natural compounds, basically silica or sand. I have a theory that the pressure at depth will explode most bottles which always contain small bubbles of gas from the manufacturing process which will compress under the huge pressures at depth. I'm not really sure how viable this theory is, but it's comforting in an eco-sense.

Storing food

Dry goods

All packs of pasta, rice, couscous, flour, etc. should be packed into zipped plastic bags. Just put the original packet into the zipped bag, fold it over to get rid of the air inside and zip it up. This is simply to guard against weevils in any one box or bag of dry goods getting out and into others. Weevils are just a fact of life in hot climates and the eggs or larvae will often already be in a box of pasta, rice or flour. Sometimes you just have to live with it if the outbreak is not too bad. Flour is the worst offender and often will have a weevil outbreak in weeks.

And whatever did we do without zipped plastic bags? The ones you seal together by running your thumb and forefinger along the top work OK as well.

What did we do before zipped plastic bags. Pasta, biscuits, all sorts of stuff goes into them to keep bugs in or out

Tins

Nobody varnishes tins these days and I've never taken the labels off and used a felt tip pen to write what a tin contains on it. In any case most tins have labels printed onto the tin these days. As long as you don't stow tins in the bilge there is no need to do anything. Some tins will have a use-by date on them, though I'm not too sure why. The only precaution I take is to check that the tin is not blown, usually easily seen because the top and bottom will be distended outwards, and to smell the contents when I open it. If a tin is blown then don't open it or you will have the contents all over the galley and yourself. The only problems I've had with blown tins are tomatoes, tomato paste, and mushrooms. The latter always worry me as some years

Galley stowage with commonly used items to hand.
The stretchy keeps bottles and stuff from tumbling out

ago I remember one person dying and another being rescued from a yacht in the Indian Ocean after a tin of bad mushrooms had been used for a meal. Botulism miles out in the ocean is not something you need.

Aluminium cans of drinks can be kept in the bilge, though preferably a dry bilge as the aluminium will oxidise, though hopefully not before you have imbibed all that beer. Even aluminium cans sometimes leave a rust stain which is confusing as I always thought aluminium just oxidised to white crumbly dust.

Tins of some food items have been replaced by Tetra Paks which makes stowage a lot easier and solves that eternal problem of a tin rolling around somewhere and keeping you awake at night. Things like chopped tomatoes, passata, tomato paste, coconut milk and probably a few others can now be found in Tetra Paks.

Canned drinks stowage in the bilges

Tinned vegetables Tinned (or Tetra Pak) chopped tomatoes, passata and tomato paste are essential and apparently tinned tomatoes have as many anti-oxidants in them as fresh ones. In addition we carry a reasonable supply of tinned peas, green beans, mushrooms, spinach and some mixed vegetables. No one would ever argue that tinned vegetables are better than fresh, but at times they can be a life-saver and in parts of the world you just cannot get some items that add to the overall recipe.

Tinned beans and pulses Canned beans are easy to use on board compared to soaking beans which often need to be soaked overnight. We carry a good selection including cannelloni, borlotti, kidney, broad, haricot and some tins of four bean mix. And baked beans. Tinned lentils are a useful addition to a vegetable stew, but we carry dried lentils too.

Tinned fish Tinned tuna is always on board *Skylax* and is used in a number of recipes in the book. Of course if you catch a fresh tuna the difference between fresh and tinned is chalk and cheese. Tinned sardines are useful for grilling on toast and in sardine dip. Tinned anchovies are good for some dressings and in a salad niçoise. Tinned fish like mackerel and others in tomato sauce are not to my taste with a flavour somewhere between old fish and ketchup, but if you like them then stock up.

Tinned chicken bits in a sort of curry sauce are widely available in SE Asia. You get a lot more sauce than chicken

Tinned meat Some boats carry tins of corned beef and spam. Personally I'm not fond of the stuff and hardly ever use it. I have included a recipe for corned beef hash in the book, but it took four attempts to get to something tasty. Tinned sausages are an abomination and tinned ham not to my taste. In places you can get canned meatballs and these can be good. The best I have come across are Greek canned meatballs in a light tomato sauce. You can make up a tomato-based sauce and put the meatballs in towards the end for a satisfactory spaghetti with meatballs, a good rough weather meal.

This is only part of the total provisioning for a transatlantic

In most parts of the world you can get powdered milk to make yoghurt or milk for mashed potato or pancakes. It works OK in tea and coffee as well

In Southeast Asia you get tins of chicken curry and other things that are serviceable when you need them. There is generally more sauce than chicken, but they can be useful combined with other ingredients.

Tinned fruit We carry a modest selection of tinned fruit, really just some fruit salads, apples including apple sauce, pineapple and apricots. Most of it is for breakfasts with cereals and yoghurt when we have run out of fresh or cannot get fresh fruit.

Dairy products

Milk Fresh milk can be kept in the fridge for four to five days. UHT milk has a long shelf life, often six months or more, so check the use-by date when you buy it. It only needs to be kept in the fridge after it has been opened. The alternative is powdered milk which if mixed properly works reasonably well. Even if you are not partial to powdered milk it is useful for recipes that use milk and works well for yoghurt making (see below).

Cream Long life UHT cream can be found in handy 200ml or so Tetra Paks that will keep for six months or more. Again check the use-by date when you buy it. It can also be found in small tins. In some places the cream is sweetened for use in desserts so check on the label.

Cheese All sorts of hard cheeses like Gouda, Emmenthal, Edam, Cheddar, Monterey Jack, can be

16 THE TRADE WIND FOODIE

Coffee and tea

We are inveterate tea drinkers and like good coffee as well. After a bout of bad weather there is nothing like a hot cuppa to calm nerves and restore a feeling of normality to things.

Tea We drink a lot of tea on board. Tea bags are easiest and kept in zipped plastic bags will last for a good year or more. Choice of the type of tea will depend on what you can get in different parts of the world and sometimes even the same brand and type tastes different when packaged for overseas sales. We usually buy up a lot of tea bags, Earl Grey usually, and take them back in baggage. They don't weigh much and you can usually squish them into your bag.

Coffee Instant coffee is another variable around the world. You just have to experiment and see what the stuff tastes like. We make real coffee in a stainless cafetière that is insulated and so keeps the brew hot for a second mug. The Italian espresso makers with a wasted shape make excellent espresso, but are notoriously unstable when the boat is bouncing around. Good in harbour but I ban them on passage. Vacuum packed ground coffee keeps well though its best kept in the fridge once opened. In places you never imagined you can get excellent coffee, in Panama, the Galapagos and Australia where it's grown in the highlands above Cairns.

Lists If you have new crew or more than two crew on board you may need to post a list with who has what in tea and coffee. On a trip to Southeast Asia with three of us on board I had tea black with half a sugar and coffee with milk and no sugar, Frank had tea with milk but no sugar and coffee black with two sugars, and Colin tea with milk and sugar and coffee black with one sugar. It can get confusing and add in a few more crew and you really do need a list.

bought in vacuum packs and keep well in the fridge for weeks. Hard cheeses with a wax covering like Edam or Manchego will keep for months out of the fridge. Friends kept a large Manchego for something like six months and still pronounced it perfectly edible after that amount of time. Parmesan or Grana Padano in a vacuum pack will keep for months in the fridge. It's not a bad idea to get some ready grated parmesan as well even if it is not really like the real thing grated. Processed cheeses like Philadelphia and Chesdale also keep well, often for a month or more in the fridge. You can also get some softer white cheeses such as Camembert and Brie tinned or vacuum sealed. Tinned white cheese will have a use-by date on them. Some white cheeses such as feta, halloumi and mozzarella are vacuum packed in brine and will have use-by dates of six months or more and are a handy stand-by. Several recipes here use feta or you can always make a Greek salad. All these cheeses except any with an outer wax covering or tinned cheese will need to be kept in the fridge.

Cheese can be kept in oil, vegetable or olive oil, in sealed jars, but this is a messy business and for me and most people is too much bother compared to keeping cheese in vacuum packs in the fridge.

Strange cheese

Beating up the Red Sea I was making slow progress, around 60M made good for every 24 hours. Worse I had a crew member who had cracked up on the trip and refused to take watches, was drinking heavily and wouldn't cook as the boat slammed her way north. In India I had bought a little stock-pile of that strange French processed cheese, *La Vache qui rit*, that comes in foil wrapped segments and however it is made, would survive a nuclear holocaust. There was no refrigeration on the boat so it was the only cheese that could survive the Tropics and the Red Sea heat. On night watch I took to eating *La Vache qui rit* on Ritz-type crackers and on board I've become addicted to it. I never eat it ashore, but on the boat I must have *La Vache qui rit*, no other brand will do, a token that all is right with the world.

I managed to get the crewman on board a flight from Hurgadha and sailed into the Mediterranean on my tod, slowly becoming human again, snacking on *La Vache qui rit* through calms and gales.

Processed meat

Bacon In most places in the world you can find vacuum packed bacon that keeps for two weeks or more in the fridge. If you have a freezer you can freeze it though it doesn't seem to last that long when thawed. In some countries, notably Muslim countries like Indonesia, Malaysia, the Middle East and Red Sea it can be more difficult to find although with persistence you will locate it in the larger tourist spots in Indonesia, Malaysia and even Egypt.

Salami Again widely available though not in all Muslim countries. Proper unrefrigerated salami will last for months without refrigeration, but often it is kept in a fridge, especially in the Tropics, and the safe option is to put it in the fridge.

Chorizo Can be found outside Spain and keeps for months unrefrigerated, even in the Tropics.

Hams Keeps well unrefrigerated, although a whole ham is a big chunk of meat and you will probably find you get sick of it after a while. If you have a bigger crew, four or five, then it will get finished before everyone gets sick of ham with everything. In some places you can buy vacuum packed smaller chunks of ham, though they often have a fair amount of fat in them. These keep well in the fridge for two months or so. Vacuum packed sliced ham will keep for several weeks in the fridge, though check use-by dates when you purchase them.

Sausages Vacuum packed sausages keep for 8–10 days in the fridge depending on use-by dates. Tinned sausages are truly horrible and I've thrown them away after a year or so when no one really wanted to eat them.

Fresh poultry and meat

Chicken In most parts of the world you can find frozen chicken. You can often get bags of frozen chicken bits, wings, thighs, and some unidentified bits, as well. On passage we normally take a frozen chicken or two on board, wrap it in several layers of newspaper and pop it in a plastic bag and then put it in the bottom of the fridge/freezer. In a fridge it will slowly defrost and will be ready to use in 5–6 days. In a freezer it will last for a month or so.

Duck In places you can buy vacuum packed duck breast. Well worth it though it will only keep in the fridge for a few days.

It's surprising how many places in the world you can find duck breast. Just sauté until just cooked and serve with a salad

Beef, lamb and pork With the partial exception of pork in Muslim countries, you can find fresh or frozen meat in most parts of the world where there are a few shops and a bit of a population. In the Tropics much of the meat you will come across will be frozen and if you have a good freezer then you stick it in a few plastic bags and a zipped bag just for safety and stick it in the bottom of the freezer. Even if you don't have a freezer most frozen meat will keep a couple of days in the bottom of the fridge. When it has defrosted then you have to use it.

Fruit and vegetables

I remember asking a good friend, on her second circumnavigation, what she did about washing fruit and vegetables before a passage. Barb replied that she was always 'bloody seasick for the first four days so she didn't give a damn what hubby and the kids ate, and by that time half the fruit and vegetables had gone off so what the hell, why wash them now?' I love that Kiwi directness, but you can prolong the shelf life of fruit and vegetables with a bit of initial prep and sensible storage on board.

Vegetables

Tomatoes Get some medium ripe and some green and keep them in the fridge. Any green tomatoes you want to ripen put under the front of the sprayhood where the sun will get to them, a sort of makeshift greenhouse to ripen them. If you don't have a fridge put them individually into cardboard egg boxes and stow carefully with plenty of air. I've kept tomatoes in egg boxes up to two weeks without refrigeration in the Tropics and though they get a bit wrinkly, they taste OK.

If you can get fresh fruit and vegetables from the local market these will keep a lot better than chilled fruit and vegetables

Green peppers Keep them in the fridge. If you keep them outside the fridge they will shrivel up a bit, but I've kept them for nearly two weeks this way and they still taste good.

Aubergines (Eggplant) Will keep for 8–10 days in a cool dark place if in good condition.

Potatoes When you get them clean any loose dirt off and make sure they are dry. Store in a cool dark place and sort through every 3–4 days. Will last a month or more.

Onions Store in a cool dark place and sort every 3–4 days. Will last a month or more.

Lettuce Keep in the fridge. Take off rotting leaves every day. It is useful to keep lettuce in an open plastic bag just to stop old leaves falling into inaccessible parts of the fridge.

Cabbage Wrap in several layers of newspaper and keep in a cool dark place (not the fridge). Every 2–3 days replace the newspaper and throw the old away which will have absorbed some of the moisture that would otherwise rot the cabbage. You can keep them at least two weeks like this.

Carrots (and other similar root vegetables) Normally don't keep well, especially if they have been refrigerated. Wrap individually in newspaper and change it every 2–3 days. Should last 5–7 days like this.

Courgettes Keep in the fridge. Will last without refrigeration for 4–5 days.

Bok/Pak choi (Chinese cabbage) Will last a week or more in the fridge and for 4–5 days in a cool dark place.

Green beans Keep in the fridge and use in 3–4 days max.

Vacuum bagging

You can buy vacuum sealing machines to seal up whole meals or the base ingredients for meals and freeze. This all assumes you have a freezer. Vacuum sealed meat and poultry will last for a good month or so when vacuum sealed in the freezer, though you need to make sure the freezer is kept freezing. That might sound silly, but for most will entail running the generator or the engine to make sure things really are kept frozen. In some parts of the world you can get cuts of meat vacuum packed for freezing at the butchers or purchase packs ready frozen.

Apart from meat it's useful to vacuum pack 'base' meals. The bolognese or ragu base works well to make a whole range of meals. Vacuum sealed sliced onions, carrots, beans and all sorts of other vegetables can be handily extracted in the quantities you need. Some full 'ready-meals' can also prove useful.

We don't use a vacuum sealer on *Skylax* and I'm in a bit of quandary over why you need to vacuum seal food to freeze it when at home you just stick things in a tub or a zipped bag and freeze it anyway. I've eaten cooked meals like this that have been frozen for months and they seem just fine. Most landlubbers and a lot of cruising folk I know with freezers do the same and just freeze food by putting it in the freezer without vacuum packing it.

Some cruisers also recommend vacuum sealing dry goods like flour, rice, pasta, etc. to stop any weevils and the like inside

getting out, but in my experience putting it in a zipped plastic bag without vacuum sealing it works just as well.

It may be that vacuum sealed items put in the freezer last longer than simply using zipped bags. The point is how long do you want to keep items in your freezer. If you are leaving the boat for any length of time then the freezer is going to have to be emptied. I suspect that keeping things in a freezer for a year or more in a vacuum sealed bag may be practical in that it will still be OK after a year, but not all that practical in that many people will lay-up the boat after a year to visit family and friends or to check on how a business or stocks and shares are ticking over. The point is do you really want to keep food frozen for a year or even for six months or so?

One practice sometimes mooted with vacuum sealed meals is that you just take it out and pop it into a pan of boiling water until it is cooked. I'd recommend emptying the contents into a pan to cook them for two reasons. The first is that you need to open the packet or put a hole in it to let the expanding meal ventilate and getting a packet with a hole in it out of a pan of boiling water can be dangerous. The packet itself is really hot and you may spill part of the hot meal when trying to get the packet open. The other reason is that when it is in a pan you can give it a stir to make sure it is properly defrosted and thoroughly heated through.

Celery Keep in the fridge. Invariably it will have been refrigerated somewhere along the line, but in the fridge celery can last 8–10 days and even out of it will last a surprisingly long time.

Chillies Keep in the fridge. Will generally last for several weeks. Outside the fridge they should last up to a week and although they shrivel up a bit, are still OK. A word of warning: some types of chilli like jalapeño in Central America and prik kee noo (literally 'mouse shit' chilli) in Thailand can be wickedly hot. It pays to taste test a small bit before using and adjust quantities accordingly.

Ginger and garlic Keep in a cool dark place (not the fridge). Lasts for months.

Squash Keep in a cool dark place. Will last for months.

Avocado Buy some green and keep them in a cool dark place. Will last up to a week or more.

Most vegetables need little attention before stowage apart from taking the dirt off potatoes and you can also wipe tomatoes and green peppers with a 5% bleach solution to get rid of bacteria that might cause decay.

Fruit

Bananas Don't buy a whole bunch on a stalk. They will all ripen at once and you will end up throwing them away. Buy a couple of decent hands with some green and some riper. Put them in a bucket of sea water for a few minutes so any nasties (like cockroaches) will have to swim for it and you then empty them overboard.

Oranges and other citrus Wipe over with a 5% bleach solution and let them dry. Store in a cool dark place. Will last at least two weeks if picked through carefully every 3–4 days. Grapefruit, especially pamplemousse, last well.

Limes You usually don't need to do anything. The skins will often go brown, but inside the lime is still juicy. Last three weeks easily.

Apples So often refrigerated that they will seldom last longer than 5–6 days before going mushy, if they are not actually a bit mushy on purchase.

You really don't need a whole huge bunch of bananas or they will all ripen at once

Pears Seem to last better than apples and will last a week. Don't refrigerate.

Peaches, apricots and nectarines Store in a cool place. If a bit green will last up to a week. Pick through carefully for any going off so the others are not encouraged to follow suit.

Melons I've had too much watermelon as a free dessert over the years so we rarely buy watermelon. Honeydew and Rock melons keep for 4–5 days. Once cut you will need to keep the rest of the melon in the fridge if you haven't finished it all.

Pineapples Though they look solid, will usually only last 4–6 days. On a trip in the Indian Ocean Frank and I used to have a whole pineapple each for breakfast as they were going off that fast – and these were unrefrigerated good ones from Cochin. Dunk in sea water to get rid of nasties.

Passion fruit Keep in a cool dark place. The skin will often go wrinkly but inside the fruit will still be good. Last up to three weeks plus.

Kiwi fruit Usually refrigerated so keep in the fridge. Will last a week.

Mangoes and papaya Go off in 4–5 days when nearly ripe and around 6–8 days when green. If bruised will go off quicker. Papaya can taste a bit 'sicky', but squeeze lemon juice over it and it's delicious.

Green coconuts Surprisingly these go off in a couple of days and the juice inside ferments and can build up a fair head of pressure – beware!

Storing fruit

It's common boat lore that a hanging net is a good place to keep fruit. It has never worked for me with the net banging around as you roll downwind and somewhere in the middle of the fettered fruit an orange or somesuch goes off and starts dribbling over whatever is below. We prefer to wedge bowls in various places for fruit that is ready to be eaten and keep a bulk store in a plastic tub with newspaper separating the different fruits. Fruit ripens by releasing ethylene gas so the further apart you can store unripe fruit from ripe the slower it should ripen. Hence storing tomatoes (technically a fruit) in egg-boxes if not in the fridge.

COOKING ON BOARD

Yoghurt

Yoghurt can be used for all sorts of things on board. On cereal with a dribble of honey on top. As a dressing on something like a lettuce and avocado salad: just put a dollop of yoghurt on the top with a drizzle of sweet chilli sauce. Finely chop a little onion and add to yoghurt with some mint sauce to make a really passable raita. Use it instead of cream in curries, ragu, chilli sausage pasta, in fact in most dishes where you need cream including desserts.

Years ago, in more penurious days, I used to make my own yoghurt using skimmed milk powder and a wide-mouthed vacuum flask. Somewhere along the way the flask broke and I reverted to commercially made yoghurt in those deceiving little tubs. Apart from Greek yoghurt, most of this stuff is saturated with sugar and it's only when you go back to making your own yoghurt that you realise how much sugar, artificial sweetener and other compounds from some organic chemistry lab go into the commercially made yoghurts. I know this because we have gone back to making our own yoghurt on board. From *Easy-Yo* we got the wide-mouthed Thermos flask and the plastic screw-cap jar that fits inside. *Easy-Yo* make packets of dried milk powder with the yoghurt culture (good bacteria! including acidopholus) mixed in. Mix the packet with fresh drinking water in the yoghurt jar and screw the lid on firmly. Boil a kettle and fill the flask up as far as the internal baffle. Put the yoghurt jar inside and stick it somewhere warm. The outer container, the flask with the boiling water, keeps the inner container with the milk/yoghurt culture warm. We put it in a shelf above the engine though almost anywhere would be warm enough in the Tropics or Mediterranean summer. It will make yoghurt overnight and then you just stick the screw-top jar in the fridge: *viola*, one litre of yoghurt.

A small investment in an *Easy-Yo* yoghurt maker ensures fresh yoghurt supplies on passage or at anchor

You don't need to keep using the *Easy-Yo* packets of dried milk and bacteria culture. Once you have one batch, just mix up dried milk powder and add a couple of tablespoons of the old culture. Keep some back-up packets in case your culture gets a bit old or you have a no-yoghurt period and need to start it all over again, though you can also do this with any live yoghurts from the grocery shop though not with some of the sterilised sugar solutions passing themselves off as yoghurt.

Apart from yoghurt with honey and cereal for breakfast you can also use it for:
Yoghurt dressing. A cup of yoghurt, two tablespoons of olive oil, a tablespoon of honey, salt and pepper, two tablespoons of lemon juice, a tablespoon of Dijon mustard or less of the powdered kind, a squirt of balsamic and mix it all up. Experiment with other things like a bit of sesame oil, chopped parsley/coriander/basil, white wine vinegar, a squirt of hot chilli sauce, etc. Make it up.
Stir some yoghurt into curries, stews, ragu, etc. in place of cream. Use on desserts in place of cream.
And apparently *Easy-Yo* do an ice-cream pack though I haven't tried it.

Libations

I don't have any effective religious leanings or practice any rituals that give obeisance to a god or gods. I quite like Thai Buddhism which is really a mix of Buddhism and animistic beliefs. Those little shrines dotted around Thailand with offerings of fruit, pastries, little bowls of rice, are for the Buddha. I like the contradictions of Zen Buddhism, the 'one hand clapping' take on life. But none of this is serious and nor are the libations we make when sitting in the cockpit of *Skylax* of an evening with a glass of wine.

Libations in ancient Greece were a serious matter. They are mentioned in the *Iliad* and the *Odyssey* and had a ritual process to them. Here is Achilles in the Iliad doing the business.

... his handsome, well-wrought cup. No other man would drink the shining wine from its glowing depths, nor would Achilles pour the wine to any other God, none but Father Zeus. Lifting it from the chest he purified it with sulphur crystals first then rinsed it out with water running clear, washed his hands and filled it bright with wine.
And then, taking a stand before his lodge, he prayed, pouring the wine to earth and scanning the high skies and the God who loves the lightning never missed a word...

In Aeschylus' play The Libation Bearers we have the serious business of paying obeisance to the dead, in this case Clymenistra to the murdered Agamemnon. It's interesting that Aeschylus' Trilogy, of which The Libation Bearers is one play, was first presented at the Festival of Dionysus These festivals, to the god of wine, could be pretty hedonistic with lots of wine flowing and no doubt a goodly number of libations to the god for providing the fermented stuff. Nothing to do with Aeschylus and his

bloody and tragic trilogy of course. But that is way beyond what happens on *Skylax*.

When the wine is poured we simply pour a libation into the sea for Aeolus and Poseidon, gods of wind and sea. After all they are the ones who influence what happens to us on the sea. I'm not sure how that goes down with the Polynesian gods in the Pacific, does Tangaroa get a bit pissed that we have introduced Greek gods to his domain. Growing up in New Zealand we were always warned about the Taniwha, a monster that lives in deep pools and rivers and will pull you in and devour you if you stray near his lair. Well anyway the Greek gods worked in the Pacific and Indian Ocean and certainly work for us back here in the Mediterranean.

And we also pour a little libation to *Skylax*, mole (the autopilot) and Yanni (the engine who is getting on a bit) as well. Ritual is not so bad for life as long as you don't take it too seriously. After all look at what happened to Achilles when he got serious about it.

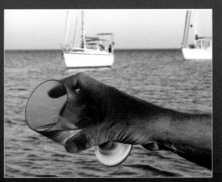

Libation to the gods, whichever gods those are, for fair winds and safe landfalls

Glass or plastic

Where possible it's best to get goods in plastic containers rather than glass. I'm talking about things like mayonnaise, sauces, honey, spreads, etc. There are a lot of things you are unlikely to get in plastic and that's just the way it is. Where possible getting plastic instead of glass is partly a matter of weight and for safety as plastic is unlikely to break if it falls out of a locker or a hand on passage. There are very good squeezy bottles that are useful for things like honey, salad dressing, sauces and the like that are a lot easier to use than pourers on passage.

I don't really like advocating plastic on eco-grounds, but it does have it's place on board. You will need all sorts of plastic containers, 'Tupperware' type stuff, to store the open packs of biscuits on the go, the goody box for night watches, dried fruit and nuts, leftovers to go in the fridge, any number of items. Like zipped plastic bags, how did we ever survive on board without Tupperware?

Drink around the world

Whatever your tipple it is not always straightforward stocking up on ship's stores around the world. The following list of countries should help when deciding on what to get where.

Spain and the Canaries Beer is good value and widely available. Spirits, especially local spirits are worth stocking up on though remember you are heading towards the rum islands on the other side of the pond. Wine is a mixed bag. There is excellent Spanish wine, usually bottled, and some truly appalling stuff in boxes. Try some before you buy in bulk. In the Canaries although there is less duty and VAT is less than on the mainland, prices seem about on a par with Spain.

Leeward and Windward Islands Rum and local beer are good value. Wine is reasonably priced on most of the islands though not always widely available. St Maarten is duty free and a good place to stock up on drink as well as food.

Panama In the supermarkets beer and spirits are relatively cheap. So is wine which is often from Argentina or Chile and is perfectly quaffable in bottles or cartons. Just remember that you will likely be checked by customs in French Polynesia where the amounts you are allowed to bring in are meagre.

French Polynesia Alcohol is not cheap, even in the supermarkets, This policy of relatively high priced alcohol is designed to cut down on an alcohol problem amongst the Polynesians and probably a few Europeans as well, so you will just have to swallow it as it were. The alcohol limits are basically 2 litres of spirits and 2 litres of wine per person, but see the section on Ashore in Tahiti for more.

Tonga Most alcohol is imported from New Zealand and attracts a premium because of this. You can buy local rum flavoured with vanilla here which is surprisingly good. And kava is also for sale if you happen to like the muddy mixture (personally not my tipple) which has a slightly narcotic effect on drinkers.

New Zealand Alcohol is moderately priced here as it is fairly highly taxed. There are also 'dry' areas in New Zealand where it is difficult or impossible to buy alcohol and it cannot be consumed in public. Beer, spirits and wine are available in 'Bottle Shops' and supermarkets. New Zealand produces excellent wines, especially whites, though good ones are relatively expensive. You can buy duty free alcohol when you clear out of New Zealand.

New Caledonia Again as part of French Polynesia alcohol is fairly highly priced.

Australia Beer, spirits and wine are moderately priced and available from 'Bottle Shops' or supermarkets. Australia produces excellent wines, especially reds though some find them a little 'thick' and they are high in tannin. Good whites are also produced. You will need to stock up here for Southeast Asia and it's probably worth getting in some box wine to augment supplies, not just for Southeast Asia but for the Indian Ocean as well. Again like New Zealand there are 'dry' areas and restrictions on drinking in public in places.

Singapore You can find alcohol in the supermarkets though prices are relatively high.

Malaysia This is a Muslim country and there are prohibitions on alcohol in some places. The exception is Langkawi which is a duty free island and beer and spirits are cheap. *Tiger* and *Anchor* (brewed in Singapore) are both quaffable lager types. Wine is moderately priced. You will need to stock up here for the trek across the alcohol desert of the Indian Ocean. Not until you get to South Africa or the Mediterranean will alcohol be easily accessible again.

Thailand Alcohol is moderately priced but you are well advised to pop back down to Langkawi to top up supplies. Beer is relatively cheap with *Singha* and *Chang* beer being the most popular local brands. Thai whisky is relatively cheap though it bares little resemblance to whisky. It's made from sugar cane syrup and is more like a rum, though not a very good one. Wine is comparatively expensive.

Sri Lanka Alcohol is relatively expensive except for the local beer *Lion*. They make very good peppery ginger beer here.

India Alcohol is relatively expensive. There is a wide range of beers and although brands like *Kingfisher* are well known, there are many others that are just as good. Spirits and wine are expensive.

Mediterranean Needs little introduction. Good lager type beer is brewed in most countries. Spirits can be expensive if imported, but locally produced spirits are relatively cheap. Wine is good and relatively inexpensive from Greece through to Spain.

Cockroaches and other unwanted guests

When you bring fresh fruit and vegetables and packaged goods, especially anything in cardboard, on board, you stand a chance of introducing cockroaches and other creatures to your ship where they will readily make themselves at home. Over the years I've had various creatures on board with cockroaches being the worst and Rhino beetles the most curious. I've also had a selection of spiders that we have nurtured even though they persist in building webs outside, usually on the pushpit, which is not the best place for a spider to be when it's wet and windy. Weevils are also commonplace arriving in all sorts of packaged goods and to my surprise they can even gnaw their way through zipped plastic bags. Probably the most surprising guests we had were a couple of geckos that somehow made their way on board in Panama. We named them Fat Bastard and Slim for pretty obvious reasons and they stayed with us until Tahiti. Slim was getting slimmer all the time so probably didn't make it, but I suspect Fat Bastard skipped ship in Papeete.

Below are a few suggestions on dealing with unwanted guests.

Cockroaches Cockroaches often lay their eggs in the glue that holds cardboard cartons and boxes together so it pays to get rid of cardboard containers as quickly as possible. Otherwise stick cardboard or paper wrapping in a zipped plastic bag. They can also wander aboard from the quay or other boats if you are alongside. If you get an infestation the best way of getting rid of them is to buy a bug-bomb or two. You can buy them in various places, in the USA, Australasia and Southeast Asia and a few other places. You open up everything below, cover or put away food items like fruit and vegetables, let it off and then get out as quickly as possible closing all the hatches and ports. They usually take four hours or so to work. You can also get cockroach poison or bait in little plastic 'homes' that you distribute around the boat which give them severe indigestion and death. If you see any bombs in your travels it's worth getting a few on the off chance you might need them. Cockroach poison or bait you can buy almost everywhere.

Weevils Weevil eggs often arrive in packets of flour, rice, pasta. Putting a couple of bay leaves in rice and flour seems to deter them. Otherwise make sure these dry goods are in zipped plastic bags and maybe a solid Tupperware container as well.

Other creepy-crawlies In dried nuts and dried fruit you may occasionally get the eggs of some flies. Keep them in a solid Tupperware container.

Dried fruit and nuts

Keep well in a Tupperware box with some things like nuts in separate small zipped plastic bags. It's useful to have a selection of dried apricots, currants, raisins, dates, walnuts, blanched almonds, and pine nuts. Walnut bits and blanched sliced almonds are generally more useful. Pine nuts can be a bit on the expensive side so use pepitas, dried pumpkin seeds, which when toasted are a passable substitute.

Eggs

I don't know anyone who covers eggs in petroleum jelly or similar to keep them fresh. Eggs will keep OK without refrigeration if you use the egg-box method below.

In truth most people just keep eggs in the fridge. Even if you are keeping them in the fridge it's useful to get some plastic egg-boxes. Drill a small breather hole in the top of each egg bubble on either side and the eggs will be a lot less likely to go mouldy if you keep them like this. Turn the egg boxes once every 3–4 days.

If you keep eggs outside the fridge try to get unrefrigerated eggs (difficult these days) and put them in plastic egg boxes with holes in the top of each 'bubble'. Keep them in a cool dark place and turn every 3–4 days. I've kept them unrefrigerated like this for up to a month in the Tropics.

Drill holes in the 'bumps' of the egg box to let the eggs breathe

Condiments

You will need basic herbs and spices and sauces for the recipes here. The following should be regarded as a basic list only.

Oils Our everyday oil is usually an extra virgin olive oil. It is easy to find good olive oil in the Mediterranean and in Australia. Elsewhere it is usually available but will be expensive. We also keep a vegetable (rapeseed) oil for frying, and sesame oil for stir-fries and noodle dishes.

Herbs Dried herbs should include oregano, bay leaves, basil and rosemary. Fresh herbs are infinitely preferable but hard to come by. Fresh basil, coriander (cilantro), parsley and mint can be found in Europe, America, Australasia and Southeast Asia, though you will have to hunt around a bit sometimes. If you can't get fresh herbs some chopped vegetable greens can be used. Try celery tops, spring onions tops or something similar can be used at a pinch.

Spices Cumin, coriander, turmeric, medium curry powder, chilli powder or crushed chilli (or harissa powder as used in the Maghreb for heat in a dish), cinnamon (sticks if possible), nutmeg (whole with a little grater if possible), mustard seeds, coriander seeds, paprika, and five spice. In different parts of the world all sorts of fresh spices can be found. Nutmeg in Grenada. Cinnamon sticks and five spice in Southeast Asia. Cinnamon sticks, curry leaves, cumin and tumeric, in fact a whole selection of fresh spices in Sri Lanka. Not to mention the spice stalls in India.

Sauces Soy sauce, sweet chilli sauce, hot chilli sauce (use it to heat things up a bit), teriyaki sauce, Worcester sauce, tomato ketchup, balsamic vinegar, white wine vinegar, bottled lemon and/or lime juice.

Other Dijon mustard, Easy Garlic paste (so easy to use instead of crushing garlic at sea), curry paste (if you can find it), sun dried tomato paste, sun dried tomatoes, pickled ginger, mayonnaise, French or Italian salad dressing, mint sauce, wasabi powder or paste, brown or demerara sugar, Tetra Pak UHT cream, Tetra Pak or tinned coconut milk. And salt and black pepper. We use a lot of freshly ground black pepper and even carry a back-up pepper mill.

Caribbean sauces and chutneys. A single bottle of Caribbean hot sauce (read very hot) is useful for adding a bit of chilli taste to some dishes. Measure the amount in drops rather than glugs

Essential condiments

Everyone has likes and dislikes. The list below is of condiments I like to have on board, special things I stock up on when I can.

Easy Garlic Goes by all sorts of names, but is essentially a jar of pulped garlic that is so much easier to use at sea compared to using garlic proper, getting the dried outer skin off and pulping the cloves. I still use real garlic as well, but getting a teaspoon of Easy Garlic out when the boat is rolling around makes life easy.

Mint sauce Mint can be surprisingly hard to come across around the world. Using a dollop of mint sauce works a whole lot better than dried mint. And you can use it for that lamb as well.

Sun-dried tomatoes Keep well in oil in a bottle and can be used for salads and lots of other dishes.

Sun-dried tomato paste Such an intense flavour. Use a teaspoon with plain tomato paste when recipes call for it.

Brown sugar White refined sugar will work OK but brown or demerara sugar has that malty richer flavour.

Pesto Pasta pesto is one of those good standby dishes when it's rough, but you can use it in all sorts of other things as well like marinades and dips.

Sesame oil Can be added to Asian and oriental dishes.

Sweet chilli sauce Used in some of the recipes here and good with things like sausages.

Hot chilli sauce Useful to add a bit of heat to some recipes. It varies a lot in strength, some Caribbean hot chilli sauce is lethal, so experiment carefully to see if you need four or five drops or a bit more.

Salad drizzles You can find these in the States, Australasia and a few other places. They are usually quite sweet, essence of wine, various fruits or other things, with a bit of balsamic or other vinegar. I often put a small drizzle over a salad and then oil, balsamic or lemon. I've had a small bottle of Cabernet drizzle and fig and orange drizzle on board for years, you don't need much.

Balsamic vinegar Useful for all sorts of recipes and in a simple dressing.

Dijon mustard Or any whole grain French mustard. Keeps well.

Seasickness

A large number of people get a feeling of queasiness at the start of a passage, butterflies in the stomach, slight nausea and a general listlessness. This is quite normal and you shouldn't worry too much about it unless it gets worse and goes on for more than a couple of days. It's one reason why a ready-cooked passage meal, all up and ready to go, is a good idea as you don't need to fuss around chopping and cooking to get something on the go. Just heat up the pre-prepared meal and usually some starch of choice to go with it. By the time a few days have gone by and your body has settled into the rhythm of the sea most people recover.

For those who are not so fortunate the following may be of some help. There is the awful old joke told to me by someone who had circumnavigated on the cure for his quite chronic seasickness for the first few days. I always carry a lot of tinned pineapple he said, because it tasted as good on the way up as on the way down. It's a terrible old saw, but contains an important element and that is that it is important to try to eat something even when you are feeling a bit grim.

Tablets A number of antihistamines are on the market: Avomine, Dramamine, Marzine RF, and Stugeron. Of these Stugeron is widely accepted as the most effective. They all cause drowsiness to some extent, though Stugeron to a lesser extent than others. These pills must be taken before setting sail, sometimes up to four hours before going to sea, their effect is minimal once someone begins to feel seasick. Other tablets such as Phenergan, Kwells, and Sereen contain hyoscine hydrobromide which has a sedative effect and leaves the sufferer drowsy.

Scopoderm disk A small elastoplast disc which is stuck behind the ear four hours before sailing. It contains hyoscine hydrobromide which is released slowly into the bloodstream and is said to reduce the sensitivity of the inner ear without causing undue drowsiness as it does in tablet form. The disk will work over two to three days and tests seem to indicate a good success rate. It is available only on prescription, cannot be used by young children, and for a minority does have some side effects such as minor drowsiness and one or two reports of mild hallucinations!

Homeopathic cures A number of homeopathic treatments are available: Nux Vomica 6, Coculus Indicus 6 and Ipecac 6 tablets. I have not tracked down any results from these. A number of old salts swear by natural remedies such as ginger, glucose and Vitamin B12. Ginger seems to be the favourite.

Sea bands Elasticated bands with a small plastic knob sewn into them can be purchased and when slipped over the wrist the knob is supposed to press on the nei-kuan pressure point, an acupuncture point that reduces nausea. The problem is hitting exactly the right point – something an acupuncturist spends years learning to do.

Someone who is seasick should be kept warm, but should stay in the cockpit if possible. Watching the horizon seems to have a curative effect, while down below, apart from the absence of a horizon, any odours, diesel, cooking food, will be enough to induce vomiting. When seasick try to eat something like dry bread or crackers, and drink plenty of water as vomiting causes dehydration. Someone who is mildly nauseous can be given something to do: operating a winch or even helming can reduce the feeling of seasickness.

There can be occasions where seasickness becomes so debilitating that you will need to divert to somewhere or return to port to get treatment.

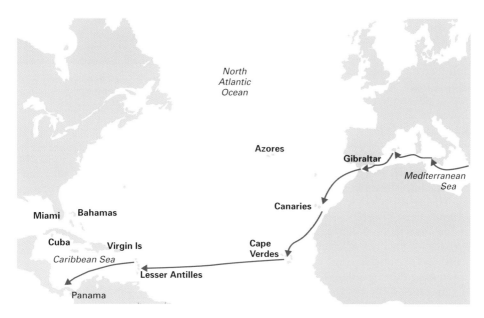

Twenty years from now you will be more disappointed by the things that you didn't do than by the ones you did do. So throw off the bowlines. Sail away from the safe harbor. Catch the trade winds in your sails. Explore. Dream. Discover. *Mark Twain*

Gibraltar was and to a lesser extent still is the departure point from Europe for boats heading across the Atlantic. A lot of yachts from northern Europe, from the United Kingdom, France, Scandinavia, Holland and Germany coast hop down to here before setting off for the Canaries. Yachts from the Mediterranean coast hop to Gibraltar before pointing the bows into the Atlantic. And tens of thousands of tons of merchant ships chug in and out of the Mediterranean through the Strait of Gibraltar entering and leaving the Mediterranean. It's a nautical Clapham Junction with ships everywhere you look.

Waiting under the Rock of Gibraltar for a weather window

In the different ports and anchorages along the way you get to recognise the yachts southbound for the Canaries. It's a great 'wildebeest' migration with yachts heading south to newer pastures and all along the way the numbers of migrating yachts are swelled as others join in on the route. For many the passage to the Canaries will be the longest passage they have made and everyone is checking and re-checking gear and stowage on board. After a while you start meeting up with other boats and swap stories, anecdotes and passage plans, all the while contemplating this nautical rite of passage out into the ocean.

The Rock of Gibraltar. It's 'once seen never forgotten' aspect marks the passage in or out of the Mediterranean

It has probably always been thus. When the Phoenicians, the Greeks and the Romans passed through the Pillars of Hercules, they were voyaging into the unknown with every possibility that if the sea didn't claim their cockleshell boats, then the uncivilized hordes that inhabited the coasts would attack them when they landed for supplies or trade. For the Greeks the Pillars of Hercules marked the uttermost ends of the world, though what they meant a little huffily was the ends of the known civilized world. Outside of the Greek Mediterranean were the Barbarians, the ones who when they spoke sounded like 'Ba-Ba-Ba', though a trader could just about put up with that if valuable trading commodities were to be had.

On his first voyage in 1492 Columbus sailed from Palos in the Gulf of Cadiz just up around the corner from Gibraltar. The Spanish were already familiar with this stretch of water and indeed the Canaries were the only sizeable colony Spain had until Columbus set off on his first voyage and claimed huge swathes of the New World for his Spanish sponsors. And though he didn't find the fabled Spice Islands, he changed the face of European cuisine forever by introducing all those vegetables and fruits we now regard as essential: tomatoes, chillies, peppers, potatoes, squash, maize, pineapples and lots of others. Vasco da Gama was also familiar with the waters and the Portuguese had explored the coast of West Africa and claimed the Cape Verdes for Portugal before da Gama sailed around Africa to India.

On *Skylax* sitting in Gibraltar in early November we are scanning the internet for weather information looking for a weather window that will give us an easy run down to the Canaries. It's early winter and in Gibraltar you are not yet down into more settled trade wind conditions just 700 miles south. Setting off on any ocean passage leaves me with a dry taste in the mouth, a storm of butterflies in the stomach and a lot of mentally ticking off checklists. *Skylax* is packed from stem to stern with enough food for four trans-Atlantics. We have enough spares to fix just about anything on board, though Sod's Law dictates that the one spare we do need will be the one we omitted. It's kind of endearing that, how ever many times we get ready for an ocean passage, it is still a daunting experience setting off into the open ocean on a small boat. The nerves get to you every time and the bravado on the dock is notably muted.

Provisioning before you leave Europe

Gibraltar is not the place it once was for provisioning and you will get a better selection of goods in the Spanish supermarkets. If you are in Gibraltar then cross over the border to La Linea where there are big supermarkets not far away. Alternatively stock up on non-perishables in the Spanish Mediterranean or in Atlantic Spain when you are in a sizeable town. Any of the big supermarket chains will have good supplies of tinned items, flour, pasta, couscous and pulses, as well as Spanish specialities. If you haven't provisioned fully in Spain don't worry too much as there are large supermarkets on the main islands in the Canaries and you can get most things there at similar prices.

In Gibraltar the Morrisons supermarket has a good selection of items including a lot of English goodies you might need like Branston Pickle or Marmite, but these days you are just as likely to find those, or at least a close approximation, in a large Spanish supermarket.

In Spain take a look at the following:

Hams (Jamon) You can get a shoulder of cured ham which will keep well without refrigeration for the passage and beyond. Get a muslin or light cotton cloth (a pillowcase will do fine) to keep it covered while it is hanging. Decades ago when refrigerators on board were not a common feature, cruising yachts always bought a shoulder of ham in Spain. Even a small shoulder is a lot of ham and most boats with just a couple on board will be sick of the stuff by the time they get across to the Caribbean. Larger crews will be fine. You can buy vacuum packed hams in smaller chunks, but it does tend to be a bit salty and some of the cheaper vacuum packed hams are poor quality with a lot of fat. You can also buy vacuum packed sliced ham that needs to be stored in the fridge – buy some *Jamon Iberico* for special lunches mid-Atlantic.

Bacon Spanish bacon, similar to streaky, is good.

Vacuum packed meat Many of the supermarkets have vacuum-packed beef, lamb and pork that you can freeze.

Chorizo Keeps forever out of the fridge and is useful for all sorts of dishes like risottos and stews as well as in sandwiches. Can be a bit greasy depending on the quality. We bought chorizo in mainland Spain and used the last of it some six months later in Panama and it was just fine, even stored in a locker without refrigeration.

Salamis Like chorizo, keeps well without refrigeration, though it should be used within a couple of months. You can also get vacuum-packed sliced salami, often assorted types, that must be kept in the fridge.

Cheese There is a large selection of Spanish cheeses both hard and soft as well as imported varieties. The excellent hard-cured Manchego keeps well on board and is a very more-ish cheese.

Tinned fish and shellfish You can get excellent tinned chunk tuna in Spain though you need to pay a bit more for it. It is far superior to the common-place tinned brands which look a bit like mush when you open the can. You can also get tinned smoked or plain mussels and oysters which are great for nibbles when having a drink in the evening. It's also worth getting some mussels in jars or tins of brine for quick spaghetti and mussels with a tomato sauce.

Strong flour and yeast Spanish supermarkets will usually have strong flour for bread making and packets of dried yeast. If you can't get it in Spain you will likely find it in Morrisons in Gibraltar.

Vacuum packed pittas Spain is one of the few places I've found vacuum packed pittas (usually six to a pack) that will last several months or more without refrigeration depending on the use-by date. Great filled for lunch.

Olives and capers Lots of different sorts of bottled olives and capers. I usually get some chopped olives for cooking – saves having the little beggars running around the chopping board while you try to chop them at sea.

Alcohol You can get good wines in Spain, but box wine is of variable quality and often disappointing. If you can get Chilean or Argentinean box wine this is superior to most of the Spanish box wines. Beer and alcohol is reasonably priced in the supermarkets. Alcohol, especially spirits and beer, is the one area where Gibraltar wins hands down. Gibraltar is a duty free zone and alcohol is very reasonably priced. You do need to be based in Gibraltar as if you get caught driving over the border with a boot-load of alcohol you will be fined. If you are berthed in Gibraltar then there are no problems loading up the boat with alcohol.

In Gibraltar the Levanter has been blowing half a gale for days and despite the fact that it's blowing in the right direction to whoosh us out of the straits, no-one wants to leave in half a gale. There is a whole gaggle of boats waiting for a weather window and most of us know that if there is half a gale in Gibraltar then its blowing old boots at Tarifa and we are going to get a pasting. Twenty-five knots in Gibraltar means 40 knots plus out in the strait.

The early voyagers, Columbus, Vasco de Gama, and a whole host of others where neither the captain or the navigator or even the name of the ship are remembered, were intrepid souls, though many of them were reluctant sailors, pressed to make the trip by necessity of one sort or another. Columbus had to make do with an intransigent crew and contrary commanders on his other two ships. When Columbus set off on his first voyage in 1492 there were three ships in the fleet. The flagship *Santa Maria* was 87 feet and around 100 tons. The *Pinta* and the *Nina* were caravels of 74 feet and 65 feet respectively and around 80 and 55 tons. These were not fast boats, probably averaging around 4 knots on passages or around 90–100 miles a day. If you compare *Skylax* at 14m (46 ft) we expect to do 130–150 miles a day depending on the wind and can do 180 plus mile days. Even better, when the wind drops, we have an engine to make some progress. Compared to Columbus' three boats, *Skylax* is likely to complete passages nearly twice as quickly.

On Columbus' boats by the time spares like cordage and timber, cannon, shot and powder, and all the other items to make the ships self-sufficient had been loaded there was little room for food and water. The crew slept on deck or in the hold if there was room and meals were taken from a communal wooden bowl. Cooking in the galley was over a fire which was strictly regulated and guarded and had to be doused in bad weather. Conditions for the crew were hard in the extreme with fouled food and unpalatable slop served for meals. The officers had better fare and ate separately from the crew, though they suffered as well on voyages.

And would the crew have loved to have got their hands on the foodstuffs you get in a Spanish supermarket these days? In the 15th century foodstuffs were kept in wooden barrels and frequently went off. Meat, fish and vegetables were heavily salted and usually of poor quality. Vinegar was carried in large quantities to dress the food when it was cooked and was often added to water to disguise the putrid taste. Is this where the British inclination to put vinegar on fish and chips comes from? Victuals on a Spanish or Portuguese ship would have some of the following: salted beef, pork and mutton, salted sardines, anchovies and later salted cod (bacalao), cheese and butter in oil, flour, pickled vegetables, typically carrots, cabbage and beets, potatoes and onions, dried pulses like haricot beans and legumes, dried ships biscuit, and wines and beer. Even on short passages the meat and fish would spoil, the flour and pulses would be full of weevils, and the wine

Sailors' Salad

In Gaeta on the western coast of Italy, Anna who runs Base Nautica Flavio Gioia, told me about a dish she called Sailors' Salad or Captain's Salad. It resembles Panzanella, a salad made from old dried bread. Anna's version is made from fresella, a crunchy dry bread that you can buy in Gaeta and other parts of Italy, it keeps for months and I suspect is a hygienic modern version of ship's biscuit.

Recipe for Sailors' Salad

Moisten the fresella with water in a bowl until it is softened but not mushy. Add olive oil, olives, basil, and chopped fresh tomatoes and toss lightly. Leave for an hour for the bread to absorb all the flavours.

The Strait of Gibraltar on a good day

would go off and the beer go sour. There seemed to be amongst sailors a perverse aversion to fresh vegetables with crews simply refusing to eat them. In later years under Captain Cook crews had to be threatened with punishment if they did not eat sauerkraut or lime juice, both of which contain Vitamin C and alleviate the worst effects of scurvy.

On passage the supplies deteriorated rapidly and the food was infested by weevils, maggots and rat faeces. Ships biscuit, also called hardtack and pilot bread, was a flour and water mixture baked to the consistency of concrete and was usually dipped in vinegar or the communal gruel to soften it. As the passage went on weevils would create enough perforations in the biscuit to make it easier to eat. The salt pork and beef was frequently of poor quality and contained much gristle and fat. Fresh fish was caught, though it appears not that often. Columbus recorded on Monday the 17th September that '… they saw many tunnies, and the crew of the *Nina* killed one.' Presumably the fish was divvied up and cooked over the open fire or made into some sort of stew, something the Spanish were good at.

We slipped the lines at Marina Bay at 0630 and it's still dark. Bill and Sharon on *Sunrise*, a beautiful Sabre 452, are leaving with us. We make our way out into the roadstead and weave our way through all the anchored ships, ferries zooming off to Morocco and bumboats going back and forth to the anchored ships. Gibraltar is still a busy place. We put three reefs in the main and motorsail towards Tarifa in light winds. Bill comes out in *Sunrise* and puts everything up. Maybe I'm being a bit over-cautious, but I stick with the reefs.

By Tarifa the wind is kicking up and *Sunrise* is starting to round up. Just after Tarifa it's up to 35 knots and it's not long before I've got 40 knots on the clock and we are doing 7–8 knots under a triple reefed main and nothing else. Bill tries to wrap up the genny, gets it in a muddle but finally rolls it up and puts three reefs in the main.

We fly downwind with a Force 6–7 and more in the gusts until midnight. It's usually like this on this trip to the Canaries. Come out of Gib like a cork out of a bottle and then once you are off the African coast and a little bit around the corner then the wind dies away to a gentle Force 4 or so and there you are putting up more sail to keep you moving comfortably through the Atlantic swell.

We have been slowly sailing downwind for the last four days. Sometimes with the wind on the quarter, sometimes wing and wing straight downwind. The days drift by in a relaxed fashion as the miles are clocked off, nothing spectacular at

4th Nov Midday. Levanter is still blowing 25 —30 knots and gusting over the Rock.

Day 1

6th Nov 0630. Slipped lines at Marina Bay and motoring gently into Gib Bay.

6th Nov 1200. Wind E7 —8. Speed 7·8. Big seas. Third reef only. Sunrise out on port beam.

Day 2

7th Nov 0930. Wind NNE4. Speed 6·3. Shaken reefs out. Beautiful trade wind morning.

Day 3

8th Nov 0300. Wind ENE2 —3. Speed 5·5. Slatting around so motor-sailing for a bit. Phosphorescence around dolphins at bow. Starry night - again.

8th Nov 2100. Wind N4. Speed 4·8. Gentle sailing under full main and genny. LBCs (little black clouds as opposed to BBCs, big black clouds) with occasional small squall.

Day 4

9th Nov 1800. Wind NNE4. Speed 4·9. Rolling gently downwind under experimental poled out jibs in roughly the right direction.

Day 5

10th Nov 0600. Wind NE4. Speed 5·5. 1 ship. Sunrise on radio and heading for Las Palmas (generator trouble).

10th Nov 2120. Anchor down on S side of Graciosa. Night entrance a little hairy with yachts with no anchor lights on.

147/132/123/127 miles from noon to noon, but not too bad either in the light winds. We see a few ships and bizarrely keep nearly bumping into *Sunrise* for the first three nights. Bill and Lu have a radio schedule so they are nattering away in the evening.

Our first stop in the Canaries is Graciosa, a small island above Lanzarote where some of the spirit of the Canaries still survives. The Canaries are a moonscape vision of volcanic peaks and dusty plains where little grows. There is little water and to cope with the needs of the huge numbers of tourists that come to the islands for winter sun a number of desalination plants have been built. Graciosa is no different to the other islands and in the approaches a number of greyish-brown volcanic peaks rise up from umber lowlands.

The main islands are spread out in a ragged chain from Lanzarote and Fuerteventura near the African coast and extending out to Gran Canaria, Tenerife, Gomera and La Palma further out in the Atlantic. The Romans visited the islands and then they became somewhat 'lost' until the Middle Ages and the later expeditions of the Spanish and Portuguese. Wines were exported up until the 19th century which would indicate that these dry dusty islands had a more benign climate before the arrival of Europeans and livestock and more intensive farming methods. Prior to Columbus the islands had been subdued and Spanish settlements established. After 1492 the islands were an important stepping stone for Spanish and other sailing ships catching the trade winds to the Americas, just as they are for today's sailors. One of the largest ocean rallies in the world, the Atlantic Rally for Cruisers (ARC) congregates in Las Palmas in November before more than 200 yachts set off for St Lucia in the Caribbean.

Graciosa off the top of Lanzarote does not have the massive tourist presence of the other islands and remains relatively untouched. The locals still rely on fishing and the town quay is regularly spread with sardines drying in the sun. The roads in La Sociedad, the main settlement, are sand, and in town there is not a lot to buy in the grocery shops. This is the Canaries as it used to be, so savour it before you head on to Lanzarote, Gran Canaria and Tenerife.

The Canaries are largely volcanic tufa bereft of water and vegetation.
This is Graciosa where barely a blade of grass grows

The route down to the Canaries and the Cape Verdes was well trammelled from the 16th century on. Columbus paved the way in 1492 stopping at the Canaries to provision for the Atlantic leg. It's possible the Phoenicians sailed down to the Canaries from the Mediterranean as they certainly sailed through the Pillars of Hercules and along the Atlantic coast of Europe under the Phoenician navigator Himilco. You would think that with the Portuguese trades blowing from the northeast that the Phoenician ships might have taken the easy option of coasting downwind from the Strait of Gibraltar rather than heading upwind along the European Atlantic coast. In Roman times the records tell of the expedition mounted by Juba II, the Romanised king of present day Mauritania, in 46BC. In fact it is Juba who most likely gave the island its name when he described Gran Canaria as taking its name from the dogs that inhabited it, though he may have been referring to the large monk seal population around the shores of the island.

While the islands were known, there was little regular traffic until the end of the Middle Ages when the Spanish and Portuguese likely visited the islands. Getting back to Europe and the Mediterranean must have been a nightmare for these early voyagers. With the prevailing winds blowing down from the northeast these unhandy boats would have had to beat to weather on the return trip and it's a passage that is a hard one even for modern yachts that can sail close to the wind. It's often said that the easiest way to get back to Europe from the Canaries is to cross to the Caribbean and then return along more northerly latitudes where there are westerlies to help you on the way.

Drying sardines on Graciosa

Ashore in the Canaries

Provisions

The large numbers of tourists who flock to the larger islands in the winter mean that facilities are well developed in terms of provisioning and last minute preparations for the passage across to the Caribbean. Most of the staples, fruit and vegetables, fresh meat and produce are shipped in from Spain. In fact there is very little that is not brought in from the outside. The large numbers of Europeans that visit the islands means that you can find foodstuffs from all over the EU in the larger supermarkets as well as Spanish products. Yachts tend to get ready in Lanzarote, Gran Canaria or Tenerife. There are large supermarkets near all the marinas, though you may need a hire car to transport all the provisions you will be buying. In some places, such as Puerto Calero and Marina Rubicon on Lanzarote the supermarkets are some distance from the marina. And don't forget to stock up on alcohol, whatever your tipple is, as it is relatively cheap in the Canaries.

Check over the list at the beginning where I mention what to look out for when provisioning in Spain. You will find all the same hams, chorizo, tinned stuffs and cheeses in the larger supermarkets in the Canaries and you might as well stock up here as there. Prices are around the same as on the mainland.

Eating out

You will struggle to find much in the way of Canarian or even Spanish food amongst all the 'international' style restaurants, British or other themed pubs, pizzerias, fast-food joints, alleged Mexican, Italian, French or just vaguely anonymous 'food' restaurants in the tourist centres. So much of the space on the islands is taken up with tourism and the associated hotels that they have submerged the native culture and its Spanish elements as well.

If you want to find more local food wander away from the waterfront and if you sniff around you can find smaller local establishments that feature strongly on Spanish food with tapas, various meat stews, and grilled meat and fish. There are a few Canarian specialities but don't expect them to titillate your taste buds that much. Much is made of mojo sauce, either a green or red spicy variety, and because you are here its probably worth buying a bottle or two to add to the boats stores. Oddly it is made with peppers that Columbus and others brought back from the New World so it dates from well after Columbus' voyages. Some restaurants will serve fish or meat with a mojo sauce, but on the whole it's better to look around for restaurants serving Spanish food and not worry too much about its provenance.

This is only part of the provisioning for a transatlantic

Leaving the Canaries and the easy-living in Porto Calero is difficult. It's tempting to settle into life here, as not a few who have been here for years have done, and just indulge in the good life in an equable climate. There are boats here on the Bluewater Rally (now defunct) setting out for Antigua, the ARC boats setting off from Gran Canaria for St Lucia, boats setting off on their own for the Caribbean and a few of us heading down to the Cape Verdes. After a bit of internet weather browsing it looks like there is a good window down to the Cape Verdes coming up. This is not always the case as the islands are sometimes beset with southwesterlies when a depression passes close north. Even worse you can occasionally get a tropical storm as we experienced leaving from Gran Canaria in early December 2003. The little irony of it all was that we were headed for Antigua to get married and the tropical storm was named Peter, Lu's father's name and my future father-in-law.

As it turned out the passage down to the Cape Verdes was a relaxed, even slow affair, in the trades. They blew at a good rate, but for some reason we were dawdling on *Skylax*, keeping everything very conservative and consequently our daily runs were not always the fastest at 133, 144, 149, 158, 166 and 164. From the figures you can detect the trades getting stronger towards the Cape Verdes or perhaps it was that the crew of *Skylax* were getting more confident.

Mindelo had been on our radar for months. We had planned to meet Andy and Ulla on *Balaena* here. While we sailed out of the rapidly cooling Mediterranean, Andy sailed south from an even colder Sweden. Andy and I wrote *Ocean Passages and Landfalls* and, though we have met on terra firma, this was the first time our paths had intersected on the water. *Balaena* is a 42ft gaff cutter that Andy built, a modern gaff cutter as Andy is always quick to emphasise, and he has certainly clocked some healthy daily runs in her.

Around 20 miles off Mindelo I saw a flash of tan sail on the horizon and we hove-to to wait for Andy. *Balaena* came flying across the swell, all sails up including the gaff topsail, a wonderful sight, and as they went past we took photos of *Balaena*. Then we opened up the genny and flashed across their stern while they took photos of *Skylax*. Weird and wonderful to meet up at sea, literally, and then sail in company down to Mindelo. Meeting up there called for a celebration.

The Cape Verde islands seem like something of a contradiction, a bit of Africa that has become detached and drifted off into the Atlantic. They were known to early Roman explorers, Pliny the Elder mentions them, and later Bartolomeiu Dias and Vasco da Gama rediscovered the islands while exploring new trade routes to the spice islands. The islands were colonised by the Portuguese in the 15th century and soon became an important stepping stone for the slave trade. Slaves were shipped from western Africa to the Cape Verdes and then onto the Americas. The present population are all descendants of slaves or Creole, principally of Portuguese and African extraction, which lends itself to colour, vibrancy, and a certain peppery flavour to the food. And to the music as well.

Day 1

22nd Nov 1000. Puerto Calero Lanzarote. Alongside fuel berth filled 125 litres diesel. Water tanks full.

22nd Nov 1500. Wind NE4. Speed 4.5 knots. We are trying out a downwind rig of poled out genoa and poled out staysail. No mainsail.

Day 2

23rd Nov 1200. Wind NNE5. Speed 6.2 knots. Daily run 133M. Lots of dolphins (20?) all around the boat.

Day 3

24th Nov 0625. Wind NE5. Speed 6.4 knots. Wind on the quarter. Big moon and shooting stars. Yacht abeam to starboard.

Day 4

25th Nov 1200. Wind NE5. Speed 6.6 knots. Large pod of Atlantic spotted dolphins (24?).

Day 5

26th Nov 1500. Wind ENE 5−6. Speed 7.1 knots. Yacht disappearing astern (called but no reply). Square rigger off port quarter!

Day 6

27th Nov 0600. Wind ENE5. Speed 7.2 knots. Rolly night with a few squalls. Cloudy - halo around the moon.

27th Nov 2045. Wind ENE 4−5. Speed 6.4 knots. Dark evening without moon. Still skipping along nicely.

Day 7

28th Nov 0900. Wind ENE 5. Speed 7.6 knots. Sunrise called up. Rudder is knocking badly and she is taking on water through rudder bearing. Bill can keep pace with the bilge pumps but we will keep monitoring his progress to Mindelo.

28th Nov 1830. Arrived Mindelo. Finally anchored 1915. 968 miles in six days six hours.

The Portuguese shipped slaves through here to Brazil to work on the sugar plantations. Sugar was a luxury item in the 16th century and by the 17th century Europe had acquired a taste for it. By the 18th century the plantations were booming, sugar production rocketed and West Africa was depopulated in the scramble to get slaves to work on the plantations. Up until 1560 the islands had a monopoly on slaves from western Africa and the other slaving nations, principally the English and the Spanish, would collect their slaves in the Cape Verdes before shipping them off to the Americas and the Caribbean.

After 1560 the Portuguese lost their sole concession to slaves from West Africa and the islands declined. When Vasco da Gama stopped here before voyaging around Africa to India, he pronounced the islands little use for victualling. In January 1832 Captain Robert Fitzroy on the *Beagle* stopped here en route to Patagonia and eventually to the Galapagos. On board was Charles Darwin whose research would ultimately lead to his remarkable theory of evolution. Darwin didn't think much of the Cape Verdes and pronounced the island of Santiago a bleak and unprepossessing place.

'The island would generally be considered as very uninteresting, but to anyone accustomed only to an English landscape, the novel aspect of an utterly sterile land possesses a grandeur which more vegetation might spoil. A single green leaf can scarcely be discovered over wide tracts of the lava plains; yet flocks of goats, together with a few cows, contrive to exist. It rains very seldom, but during a short portion of the year heavy torrents fall, and immediately afterwards a light vegetation springs out of every crevice. This soon withers; and upon such naturally formed hay the animals live.' Charles Darwin *The Voyage of the Beagle 1839*

Sailing ships continued to call here and one thing that could be found on these bleak islands was crew. Cape Verdeans became renowned as sailors and American whaling ships would frequently call here to take on crew. As whaling declined the Cape Verdeans themselves acquired the old sailing ships and used them for whaling and trading. Of these the *Ernestina* was probably the most famous. Built in 1894 she was acquired by a Cape Verdean living in Massachusetts and criss-crossed the Atlantic some 50 times before the Second World War and continued to do so after the war. She was then used to trade between the islands before she was eventually sailed back to New Bedford in 1982 under sail and without an engine.

Most yachts head for Mindelo on the island of São Vicente in the Cape Verde archipelago. It is a dry dusty island much as Darwin described with hardly a blade of vegetation anywhere. What little topsoil is left gets blown off in the trades and all over your boat in the anchorage as well. To call the islands '*verde*' (green in Portuguese) seems incongruous when you look at the barren hindquarters of the islands. The terrain looks like a mountainous desert. When the Portuguese first arrived here the islands were green, covered in trees and undergrowth, but the arrival of the Portuguese on these previously uninhabited islands upset the delicate ecology with the introduction of goats that ate anything and everything. The settlers cleared the land so the topsoil blew away in the trades and the little rain that falls swept away the rest of the topsoil. The impact of the settlers started an ecological disaster and droughts in the late 20th century finished the job.

The frequent occurrences of El Niño events in recent years that have caused drought conditions over Africa have exacerbated the damage done to the ecology and the locals will tell you that what little useful agricultural land that remained is now gone. There are patches of green on some of the islands including a valley on Santo Antão a short distance across the water. Here a high valley orientated east to west traps moisture picked up by the trades off the ocean and the moisture laden

Ashore in the Cape Verdes

Provisioning

In Mindelo there are a couple of small supermarkets ashore, a good fruit and vegetable market up the high street, and a rowdy fish market along the waterfront. You can get the basics here, but really you will have needed to stock up in the Canaries.

The markets are the best place to be. When the fishing boats are in there is good-sized tuna, mackerel, squid and smaller fish of indeterminate, at least to me, types. Most of the fish stalls are run by women who are pretty fierce individuals and handy with big sharp cleavers to cut the fish up. The fruit and vegetable market is a wonderful riot of mostly ladies selling their wares and entreating you to buy from them, 'not the other one' nearby. The stalls are alive with colour, surprising verdant greens and red peppers and tomatoes, in contrast to the barren dusty slopes around Mindelo. The women are wrapped up in colourful outfits, and the atmosphere is like an easy African market. You can also get jars of pickles and sauces, most of them pretty hot. Apparently a lot of the fruit and vegetables come from the island of Santo Antão across from Mindelo where there is a valley up in the mountains with that rare commodity in the Cape Verdes, water.

Simple but good. A local restaurant in the backstreet of Mindelo

Eating out

Ashore there is the Club Nautico, but on the street behind is a place called The Yacht Club on a first floor terrace with good food, cold drinks, and Wi-Fi. The Yacht Club will often have live bands on the weekends and Cape Verdes music is stunning, the best I have heard in local bars/cafés since Cuba. A lot of the restaurants around here will have live music with a five or six piece band crammed into the corner of the restaurant.

They are accomplished musicians renowned for their music all over Africa and Senegalese and Nigerian bands will often have musicians from the Cape Verdes in the line-up. The music is stunning and often sad, lamenting exile and struggle on the island or celebrating life, love and making love. Cesaria Evoia was born here and the Cape Verdes version of fado, morna, is wonderfully evocative even when you can't understand the lyrics. Don't miss it.

Music, good music, runs through the veins of Cape Verdeans and many of the restaurants will have a live band at weekends

air condenses in the higher altitudes of the valley and drops a precious misty rain across the high slopes to give rise to the miracle of patchwork market gardens which dot the sides of the valley. Much of the produce finds it way to the market in Mindelo, a strange and wondrous bounty on an island that looks like a moonscape parked in the ocean.

The desertification of the islands means there is little meat except for what is imported. Ironically the islands were used by the Portuguese to graze cattle to stock up sailing ships passing by and this destroyed much of the ground cover so that little now grows to graze cattle on. What the Cape Verdes do have is bounteous waters all around and lots of fish. The fish market in Mindelo has albacore and yellowfin tuna, wahoo, shark, even the occasional marlin as well as bream, squid and lots of inshore species. Down at the fish market we asked the lady chopping up a huge tuna for a couple of thick steaks, more than enough to

The tuna ladies in the fish market in Mindelo

feed four. Most of the vendors in the market are women with worn old aprons or a plastic garbage sack tied on as an apron. They are tough old cookies, no messing, no arguing, just ask for your fish and get what they give you, though the price is very reasonable.

Mindelo market with enough fresh fruit and vegetables around for the transatlantic coming up

The trades have been heaving through Mindelo at 25–30 knots and few of us have left. Each morning heads peer out of hatches sniffing the air and the red dust off Africa before going down for breakfast to report that, 'yep', the trades are still blowing hard. Much as we would like to stay in the Cape Verdes time is running out to get to Antigua for Christmas and so we do last minute shopping, haggle with the chicken lady in the market, and buy some unnecessary sauces and pickles in the main market along with some fruit and vegetables.

For many of the voyagers from Europe the Cape Verdes were the last chance for provisioning, however meagre, before continuing on to the Cape of Good Hope or across to Brazil and down around Cape Horn. On his third voyage in 1498 Columbus detoured to the Cape Verdes where he hoped to get some cattle for fresh meat. He was unsuccessful. Not surprisingly Columbus lost a high proportion of his crew to scurvy and other diseases. Not so Captain Cook who stopped by the Cape Verdes on his second voyage in 1772 to get fruit and vegetables. Cook was not popular amongst his crew for the regime he insisted was carried out on board. All crew had to wash and eat fresh fruit and vegetables to ward off scurvy. Those who didn't adhere to the regime were punished. As Richard Hough observes in his biography of Cook, this didn't go down well with the crew.

Fresh fruit, vegetables, meat and fish were nearly always welcome, but many of the antiscorbutics, like sauerkraut, were loathed. Cook was unmoved by the tastes of his men. He simply imposed these foods on them under the threat of punishment. After leaving Madeira, loaded with fresh water, having taken on board a large supply of wine, fruit and other necessities' along with fresh beef and 1000 bunches of onions, 'a custom I observed last voyage and had reason to think that (his men) received great benefit therefrom', he called at two of the Cape Verde islands, scarcely more than a week later, for more fresh fruit and water in order to avoid rationing.'

Captain James Cook: a biography Richard Hough 1994

Despite the unpopularity of this regime amongst the crew, Cook's insistence on antiscorbutics and cleanliness paid off. On his three voyages he reputedly did not lose a man to scurvy. By comparison Vasco de Gama on his voyage to the Indian Ocean in 1499 lost 65% of his crew to scurvy and likewise Magellan lost some 80% of his crew to scurvy in the Pacific Ocean.

Scurvy is commonly attributed to a lack of Vitamin C, though a lack of Vitamin B also contributes to the condition. Descriptions of scurvy sound like a mixture of decaying flesh along with a decaying mind akin to being on psychotropic drugs.

Scurvy seems to have disarmed the sensory inhibitors that keep taste, smell and hearing under control and stop us from feeling too much. When sufferers got hold of the fruit they had been craving they swallowed it (said Walter) 'with emotions of the most voluptuous luxury'. The sound of a gunshot was enough to kill a man in the last stages of scurvy, while the smell of blossoms from the shore could cause him to cry out in agony. This susceptibility of the senses was accompanied by a disposition to cry at the slightest disappointment, and to yearn hopelessly and passionately for home.

Captain Cook and Scurvy BBC

ATLANTIC

Day 1

7th Dec 1225. Wind ENE 4—5. Speed 5·5 knots. Cleared Mindelo. Three reefs in main just to cope with gusts.

7th Dec 1730. Wind E 2. Speed 5·5 knots. Motorsailing in the wind shadow of Santo Antao.

Day 2

8th Dec 0300. Wind E 6. Speed 6·9 knots. Lots of LBCs (little black clouds) with squalls. Reef genny a bit.

Day 3

9th Dec 0900. Wind E 5—6. Speed 6·7 knots. Light rain shower. All on board getting into the rhythm.

Day 4

10th Dec 2100. Wind ENE 5. Speed 6·4 knots. Lots of LBCs. Yacht Canica (140ft) passed en route to St Martin.

Day 5

Dec 11th 1500. Wind E 4. Speed 6·1 knots. Penyllan (friends who left Las Palmas three days ago) on radio. Broken lower shrouds. Motoring back 400 miles to the Canaries. All OK.

Day 6

Dec 12th 0300. Wind E 5—6. Speed 7·0 knots. BBC (big black cloud) brings gusts of 35 knots. Genny furled in until it has passed.

Day 7

Dec 13th 1200. Wind E 5—6. Speed 6·7 knots. Sunny and warm. Lure out.

Day 8

Dec 14th 1700. Wind ENE 5. Speed 6·4 knots. Wet and squally afternoon. Rains red dust on the boat. Past halfway point.

Day 9

Dec 15th 2100. Wind ESE 5. Speed 6.5 knots. Dolphins. Lumpy X-swell.

Day 10

Dec 16th 0900. Wind E 5—6. Speed 7·5 knots. Wind direction all over the place 260°—285°. Southern Cross visible at night.

Day 11

Dec 17th 0300. Wind E/ESE 5—6. Speed 7·4 knots. Bit squally but no rain. Yacht Walrus IV passed astern on opposite tack.

Day 12

Dec 18th 1800. Wind ESE 5. Speed 6·9 knots. Beers to celebrate under 350 miles to Antigua.

Day 13

Dec 19th 1030. Wind ESE 6—7. Speed 6·8 knots. Put third reef in main 0930. Bit of genny out. Showers in cockpit today.

Day 14

Dec 20th 0300. Wind ESE 5. Speed 6·9 knots. Wind a bit variable, but not far off course. Big moon, clear skies and lots of stars.

Day 15

Dec 21st 0255. Anchor down in Freemans Bay on Antigua. Several bottles of wine despite late hour.

On *Skylax* we leave after an early lunch with three reefs in the main and a bit of genny out. Between the high slopes of São Vicente and Santo Antão the wind whistles through the channel. As soon as you get just west of Santo Antão the high slopes stop the wind so a bit of motor-sailing was called for as we lurched about in the swell. It took a couple of hours motoring to get out of the wind shadow and then we were off with the wind on the quarter and pointed directly for Antigua.

In Mindelo we had picked up a refugee off an ARC boat, *Kaiso*, that had limped in with keel problems amongst others. Everything came out of the boat as most of the hatches and ports had been leaking and three of the crew opted to jump ship. Arabella walked the pontoon looking for a ride and although we were quite happy with just the two of us for the crossing, we decided to give 'Rab' a lift to Antigua where she was to join another boat. The only rule is that like everyone else on board, she has to cook.

The days ticked by with daily runs over 160M and up to 171M with everything on under-drive to keep it easy on us and on 'Mole' the autopilot. Most of the time we had two reefs in the main with wind E–ENE at 18–25 knots. We could have carried more sail but the girl was happy and 'Mole' in charge without any strain, so we left it at that. There were a few BBCs and LBCs ('big black clouds' and 'little black clouds') around, but fewer than on a previous crossing further north and with less weight of wind in them. There was not a lot of rain in the squalls either compared to the previous more northerly route and we carried a fair amount of the red dust that blows over Mindelo all the way to Antigua.

Often we didn't bother to reef the genny in as we were a little under-canvassed anyway. Most of the time we carried a reefed main and the genny poled out and when we were making too much northing and not enough westing, we simply gybed the main over and headed west for a bit. I still have a theory that the wind goes more towards the NE in the day and back towards east at night, though we are not talking major shifts here.

We ate well, too well, and when it looked like we were going to get to Antigua well before Christmas the mince pies were consumed, and then the Christmas cake, though we didn't get around to the Christmas pudding and brandy butter until

after we had arrived. Lu baked bread, we lost several fish and lures, and generally slept, read, ate and navigated to Antigua.

Landfall is much anticipated on any sailing boat. For days all our thoughts have been on what we will do when the anchor is down. A craving for certain food and drink dominates these thoughts. I don't normally eat a lot of hamburgers except those I make, but for some bizarre reason they are writ large on my neurons at the end of a passage. Ideally this is a homemade

You have no idea how good that smells and tastes in mid-Atlantic patty with sesame seed buns and a good wedge of lettuce, tomato and a few dill pickles. There is no food logic to this, after all we eat well on passage, and it must have something to do with my dopamine levels and a folk memory of a delicious hamburger somewhere in my past. Lu craves a steak, rare, with French fries, again for no good reason.

For early navigators arriving on these shores the promise of fresh uncontaminated water, of fresh fruit and vegetables, perchance fresh meat and fish, was an imperative that overcame fears about the hostility of any inhabitants. Columbus is sometimes mocked for his geography and his belief that he had arrived in the Spice Islands. What is forgotten is that for his calculated distance to the Spice Islands of around 3,000 miles, a calculation that was out by 9,000 miles with the true distance being something over 12,000 miles, no ship of the time could carry enough food or water for that distance and the general consensus was that everyone on such a voyage would die of thirst and starvation. It's no surprise then that Columbus and others who followed after him had to contend with mutinous crew and commanders who believed they were sailing to a certain death.

Luckily for Columbus the first voyage took just 34 days before he sighted land, an island he called San Salvador, probably in the Bahamas or the Turks and Caicos, the location of the island still something of a mystery. The sight of land was vindication for Columbus that he had reached the East Indies as recorded in the log.

Friday October 12
The vessels were hove to, waiting for daylight; and on Friday they arrived at a small island of the Lucayos, called, in the language of the Indians, Guanahani. Presently they saw naked people. The Admiral went on shore in the armed boat, and Martin Alonso Pinzon, and Vicente Yanez, his brother, who was captain of the Niña.
Having landed, they saw trees very green, and much water, and fruits of diverse kinds. The Admiral called to the two captains, and to the others who leaped on shore, and to Rodrigo Escovedo, secretary of the whole fleet, and to Rodrigo Sanchez of Segovia, and said that they should bear faithful testimony that he, in presence of all, had taken, as he now took, possession of the said island for the King and for the Queen his Lords, making the declarations that are required, as is now largely set forth in the testimonies which were then made in writing. *Christopher Columbus' Log 1492*

It's hard to imagine what the discovery of the West Indies meant for the European powers. It sparked the European age of discovery that set Vasco da Gama, Magellan, and Raleigh off on voyages of discovery. It generated huge fortunes and expanded the geographical vision and world view of Europeans. And it cost thousands of lives as sailors died on these voyages, not from hostile natives or piracy, but largely from disease resulting from the poor diet on board these ships.

It surprises me to find modern day voyagers setting out for the Caribbean with inadequate supplies of food and water. In the Canaries there are supermarkets full to bursting with everything you might need to provision up. Yet it happens. On a transatlantic in 2003 there were pleas from a yacht that had run out of water and was running low on food. It appeared that the delivery skipper had largely provisioned the boat with pizzas and these were running low, so he put out a call to any nearby boats for food and water. There are other documented examples, but I'll refrain from names here. What puzzles me is that monitoring your water consumption and getting adequate provisions on board for at least 30–40 days is not rocket science. On *Skylax* we have provisions for at least 60 days, probably more, just in case something goes wrong, the mast breaks or the rudder falls off, gods forbid, and we need to be at sea for longer than anticipated. And also because

Watch Keeping

Crew on *Skylax* is normally just the two of us. On a few occasions we have picked up additional crew, more out of charity than need, though the watch system stays pretty much the same except that we all get a lot more sleep. Well usually.

When we have crew for a crossing I generally send out odd emails on things to think about in preparation for the crossing. It is not meant to be a rigid list, more things to think about. The real preparation is when shipmates are on board and I show them where things are, how all the sailing stuff is rigged on passage, and the few rules we have. Things like no one goes forward of the cockpit at night without a safety harness. Everyone, but everyone on board cooks. The cook doesn't wash up. The person coming off watch at night makes the new watch a cup of tea or coffee. When we arrive the skipper (me) is responsible for a slap-up meal with lots of alcohol.

We run a three hours on, three hours off watch system whether there is the two of us or more. I've tried four hours and that's too long for one person to stay awake and happy. Two hours is too short for the person off-watch to get a decent kip. We run just one person on watch, although should there be problems, then the other person is roused out of bed. The watches only run at night from:

2100 to 2400

2400 to 0300

0300 to 0600

0600 to 0900

With just me and Lu on board I take the first and third watches, really only because we have fallen into that routine. In the day we operate a loose cover so that if one of us feels a bit tired then off they go for a kip. It all works well because we are both fair about time off in the day.

With three crew we run the same watch system, but instead of that meagre three hours sleep, you get a wonderful six hours and every third day one of us gets a miraculous nine hours off-watch should we need it. With the loose cover during the day we have only ever had one person who took more than his fair share of time off in

the day. Neither of us mentioned it. From small beginnings a minor criticism can rumble about and become a major problem and you don't need that in the middle of the ocean. Besides me and Lu were both pretty happy getting at least six hours sleep a night.

Recently a friend was bringing a boat back for me with two other friends. All of them had life-long friendships. Before they left I thought I ought to at least mention the fact that while they were good friends who had known each other for a long time, they had never spent three weeks together cooped up on a small boat without an escape route. 'No problem', I was assured, 'we are all really good mates and we look after each other ... no probs at all'. Still I persevered and again they all gave that look which said '...don't patronise us/we know what we are doing.' I figured I had tried and left it at that. Well they didn't kill each other or inflict horrible injuries on one another. None of them went bonkers and jumped over the side. But there were definite tensions on board and some muttering about offloading crew, never talking to one or other again, and mean-minded and mean-spirited behaviour. It happens and keeping crew happy on board can mean the difference between a memorable passage and one you never want to do again.

Night watch goody bag

On watch at night you need goodies to munch on to get you through the watch. In lots of places you can buy mini chocolate and other bars like Mars bars, Yorkies, Twix and sesame seed and honey bars. Apart from the chocolate/sugar rush our favourite is a nut and raisin/currant dried fruit mix usually referred to as 'Trail Mix' or something similar. You can also put in some Ritz or similar little cheese biscuits and other biscuits like cookies, digestives and the like.

And if you are a crisps fanatic you will probably need a small packet of those in there.

we like a varied diet and with a good stock of provisions you can choose, within the confines of the stores, a varied cuisine depending on weather and personal whim.

We entered Freeman's Bay at 0300 on the 21st, probably a silly thing to do, but we did so very slowly and I have been in there a few times before. After the anchor was down we popped the cork on a couple of bottles, though we were by now pretty dog-tired so the last bottle didn't get finished before we all slept.

It was hard to believe we were there with so little fuss after previous crossings and encounters with Tropical Storm Peter in 2003. Still, a dip in the morning into the warm soupy water of Freeman's Bay soon convinced us we were in the Tropics and a trip ashore and a celebratory bottle of Carib beer sealed the matter the next day. And, I did get my hamburger.

At last, that hamburger in the Mad Mongoose in Antigua

CARIBBEAN

Around the Windward and Leeward Islands

Land was created to provide a place for boats to visit. *Brooks Atkinson*

The Caribbean is one of those places that resides in the dreams of sailors in northern Europe setting off on bluewater adventures. It's the idea of all those sandy beaches, of palm trees swaying in the trade winds, of swimming in waters like warm soup, of an easy life sailing up and down the chain of islands in steady trade winds. Ashore the easy life of 'island time' where you need to 'cool your heart mun' and have another rum while watching for the elusive 'green flash' is so removed from the European and American 'busy life' it makes you wonder why on earth you didn't get here sooner. It's a beguiling picture and one that draws and captures the cruising sailor so that many end up staying here for years. And who can blame them.

We left *Skylax* in Jolly Harbour while we returned to the UK to work and then miraculously in March it was time to return. This is not our first time in the Caribbean and I'm always aware that

Christmas in English Harbour on Antigua.
Dress code: barefoot casual

Ashore in the Windward and Leeward Islands

Provisions

Heading for Panama it's worth remembering that the provisioning in Colon and Balboa is excellent with large American-style supermarkets and a good selection of everything including quaffable cheap Argentinean and Chilean wine. If you are heading back across the Atlantic to Europe then you will need to provision adequately in the Caribbean. Some islands are better than others for provisioning and the following list gives some indication of places to stock up though it is in no way definitive. It's worth remembering that in the Caribbean most things are imported, usually from the USA with the exception of the French islands where many of the things you would expect to find in a French supermarket will be found.

Road Town BVI Supermarket on the outskirts of town and speciality provisioning in the Moorings marina. Mostly imported from the USA.

Sint Maarten One of the best places to provision up. Duty free with large well stocked supermarkets. French supermarkets on the French side and Dutch on the Dutch side. You will really need a hire car to go to the largest supermarkets (there is one before you get to Philipsburg from the Lagoon). There is also a good fresh fruit and vegetable market in Marigot on the French side. Also the best stocked chandlers (Budget Marine and Island Waterworld) in the Caribbean and a whole range of yacht services from rigging to hauling. The only caution here is that there are a lot of muggings and some murders here. It's wise not to take unlicensed cabs where a scam often operates and you may well be mugged or worse. Just be careful out there.

Antigua Epicurean supermarket in Jolly Harbour is well stocked and convenient. There is a reasonable market in St Johns in the mornings. Also chandlers and hauling.

Martinique Le Marin. Good French supermarkets a dinghy ride away from the anchorage. Chandlers and yard.

Guadeloupe Good French supermarket a short distance from the marina in Pointe à Pitre though you really need a hire car.

Fruit and vegetable delivery in Dominica

In all of the islands you can find a reasonable selection of the basics in small supermarkets and local shops. There are also some local markets with fresh produce, though the quality and selection can be meagre in places.

Heading for Panama it's useful to stock up on French or European specialities: good salami, ham, good cheeses like Brie, Camembert, and goat cheeses, tinned paté, fine liquor, all of the goodies that French supermarkets have. When you get to Panama there are well-stocked big supermarkets where you can do the big shop for the Pacific.

Ashore in the Windward and Leeward Islands

Eating out

Eating ashore in the Windward and Leeward Islands is a lottery. In places the food is bland international cuisine and often expensive. You can eat very good food in up-market restaurants on most of the islands, but that will be expensive. And you can eat in some local restaurants where the food can be excellent or at worst interesting and different to steak and frites or chicken in a basket. You can also get some good street food, though you need to look around or take some local advice.

Around the islands there is good seafood to be had, though not everywhere. You need to work at finding restaurants and for the most part avoiding those that offer huge servings with little in the way of imagination. It can be a struggle unless you shell out often substantial amounts of money, but amongst others try Trappa's around Falmouth and Harmony Hall (expensive but worth it) in Nonsuch Bay in Antigua; Guadeloupe where there is more of an Afro-French mix than the other French islands; Dominica where there are some good local eateries and good seafood; Martinique around Saint Pierre and Le Marin; and the True Blue restaurant in Grenada. In the end you will often be sitting in a pretty spectacular location on the seafront with the waves lapping on the shore and you can forgive a lot when it's like this.

Local food is generally good and cheap. When it's good it's very, very good, when it's bad, it's average. There are good local snacky meals to be had in the Caribbean. Mostly they open in the daytime, but you get quite a few that open in the evening as well. The list below covers the sort of street food you will likely encounter.

Roti Most of the islands will have a roti shop in even quite small centres. A roti in the Caribbean is the traditional unleavened Indian roti, a slightly thicker cousin of the chapati, which is wrapped around a curry mixture, usually chicken, vegetable, beef and occasionally goat curry. You will more often than not find the roti shop has good fruit juice as well. Probably my favourite roti shop is King Roti in St Johns Antigua, but there are other good ones in St Georges in Grenada and in Portsmouth on Dominica. Really in most places, the roti satisfies.

Jerk chicken Chicken is the most common jerk food you will come across, but you also get pork, fish and vegetables as well. Originally a Jamaican dish, it can be found all over the Caribbean these days. Jerk chicken is often on offer in everything from quite swanky restaurants to snack shacks or even just a barbecue set up on the side of the road. The jerk mixture coating the chicken is a spicy affair with a fair amount of chilli as well as allspice and other spices mixed in. In fact you can buy jerk spice to make your own in the grocery shops. Once the chicken is coated in the jerk mixture it's barbecued and you might get some rice or bread with it.

Patties These are a sort of shortcrust pastry pie or small pasty with a filling of curried chicken, goat or pork. You can often find them in bakeries or some of the snack shacks.

Kid curry A curry, often quite hot, of young goat or 'kid'. This can be excellent and is well

Roti and fruit juice for lunch

worth tracking down. It sometimes goes by the name 'kid colombo' on some islands, don't ask me why. It usually comes with rice or bread.

Flying fish sandwich Usually fried fish, often shark, served up in a hamburger bun or bread with salad. I'm pretty sure I've never had one with actual flying fish which are small and bony.

Des Haies on Guadeloupe. Wonderful baguettes from a wood-fired oven, good coffee and good fish on the waterfront

Take a punt. It can be good, sometimes very good, rarely worse than average

The lure of the Caribbean, all palms blowing in the trades over turquoise water

Antigua is not the Caribbean, that the Leeward and Windward Islands are not the whole picture. It's often forgotten that the Leeward and Windward islands in the Lesser Antilles are just the outer Atlantic rim of the Caribbean Sea. To the north lie the Greater Antilles with Cuba nearly butting up to Mexico and the slender isthmus of the Americas bridging the bulkier North and South Americas. Around the southern rim of the sea is the top of South America completing the circle where Venezuela nearly meets Trinidad. We were headed for the tiny sliver of a gap through Panama into the Pacific.

In Antigua we take on a few provisions at the Epicurean supermarket in Jolly Harbour, but most of our provisioning will be in Sint Maarten, the holy grail of provisioning in the Leeward Islands with big French and Dutch supermarkets, and even better it's duty free on the Dutch side.

From Antigua we cruise fairly quickly up to Sint Maarten with the wonderful interlude of a young humpback whale accompanying us for over an hour. I say a young humpback, but 'Humphrey' was as long as *Skylax* and kept winding us up by charging up from astern at full speed and then diving under the boat at the last minute. Even after an hour we still held on tight while he dived and only let go when he popped out at the side or in front.

Rum

The Caribbean is the epicentre of rum production and possibly consumption as well. Outside of the Caribbean I don't drink much, but in the Caribbean some strange mien comes upon me and rum is my tipple. Rum types and tastes and costs vary up and down the island chain and while much of it is good, some of it is very, very rough.

In the 18th century the large sugar cane plantations on the islands encouraged rum production. The Mount Gay distillery in Barbados was established in 1663 and is still producing the amber liquor. All of the islands in the Lesser and Greater Antilles have their own district rums and some of the French islands produce rums claimed to be as good as a fine cognac. They certainly tasted fine to me.

Rum is either white or dark depending on how it is distilled and stored. White rum produced from sugar syrup in column stills has little natural taste, a bit like vodka. Dark rums produced from molasses in pot stills has natural contaminants from the distillation process and is frequently aged in oak barrels where it acquires an 'oaky' taste. Most rum is a blend of different rums in much the same way whiskey is blended from different types to meet the tasters requirements. Like whisky rum is often aged for long periods and my favourite, though not an everyday drink, is an Appletons made in Jamaica and allegedly matured for 15 years.

White rum is usually used as a mixer. The most famous white rum in the Caribbean is Havana Club made in Cuba. Bacardi was originally made in Cuba, it may have been the world's first white rum, but after Fidel Castro nationalised all industry without compensation the Bacardi family members moved production and all trademark rights out of Cuba. Many of the other islands produce white rum which can vary quite a lot, though to some extent that doesn't matter by the time you get to the third mojito or daquiri. It's only in the morning that you will know.

Dark rums are a different beast again with considerable variation in smoothness and flavour. Aficionados of rum in the Lesser Antilles recommend Domaine de Bellevue and Rhum Bielle on Marie Galante, the Macoucherie Distillery on Dominica and Chateau Depaz Distillery from St Pierre on Martinique. There are lots of others and these, recommended by a friend who lives out there, are more akin to fine blended whiskeys in taste although slightly cheaper. Apart from the Appletons mentioned above I'm also quite partial to Pussers Rum made in the BVI. This is the original Royal Navy rum doled out as the grog ration, half a pint two times a day for each sailor until the practice was discontinued in 1970. For everyday consumption I'd just experiment or pick up a bottle of the local rum on whichever island you are on.

Somehow that island time encourages a rum punch or a mojito around sundown

Sint Maarten to Panama

Day 1

10th Apr 0830. Anchor up in lagoon and waiting for 0900 bridge opening into Simpson Bay.

10th Apr 2050. Wind ENE5. Speed 6·5. Wind up a bit so second reef in main. Easy cassoulet supper. Yacht passing heading west on port side.
Small moon.

Day 2

11th Apr 0900. Wind ENE5. Speed 7·0. Gybed main onto starboard tack. Big rain squall with a bit of wind in it.

Day 3

12th Apr 1200. Wind ESE4. Speed 6·4. Daily run 161M. Gently rolling along. Lu asleep.

Day 4

13th Apr 0910. Wind ESE5. Speed 6·6. Had email from Penyllan to say there is long waiting list for canal transit. Change course for Colon.

Day 5

14th Apr 2105. Wind ENE4. Speed 6·2.
Speed over ground 8·8 so at least 2½ knots of current with us thanks to Herb's [Herb Hilgenberg Southbound II] routeing.

Day 6

15th Apr 1200. Wind ENE4–5. Speed 6·9. Still ½ knot current with us. Daily run 177M with current. Showers in cockpit.

Day 7

16th Apr 0600. Wind NE6. Speed 7·1. Grey old morning, some rain and blowy. Time to gybe for Colon.

Day 8

17th Apr 0600. Wind NNE5. Speed 6·8. Over a knot of current against us. Grey and rain.

17th Apr 1745. Anchor down in the Flats anchorage at Colon. 1,178 miles in 7½ days easy sailing.
Average speed 6·5 knots.

Sint Maarten is not quintessential Caribbean, in fact it is so built over it's difficult to find a wild place on the island, but with a good selection of supermarkets and a selection of yachting services, it's a good place to aim for before heading east or west. We have a shopping list for the chandlers, there are two of the largest chandlers in the Caribbean on Sint Maarten, and it's duty free so these are the best prices you will get in the region. Heading west there won't be another chandlers of this size until New Zealand or Australia.

We leave in moderate trades and are soon wing and wing en route to Panama. Our plan is to sail to the San Blas Islands and then trundle down to Colon to do the paperwork to transit the Panama Canal. Days go by and though the trades are a little boisterous and there is the occasional squall, we are soon settled down to navigating and keeping watch and thinking about what to cook for dinner. Apart

Marigot market on the French side of Sint Maarten

from the first passage meal, we don't really plan what we are going to eat and really just choose from the range of ingredients we have on board. And there is also the chance we might catch a fish and then dinner is settled for the next few days at least.

Our reverie is soon shattered by an email from Pete on *Penyllan* who is already in Colon when he tells us that yachts are backed up because of a go-slow by the canal pilots and it would be as well for us to head directly for Colon to get our names on the list. The waiting period is already two months. We adjust our course to head for Colon and figure we can head off for the San Blas islands once we have completed the paperwork to get on the list. After all we will have two months to fill given the backlog of yachts waiting to go through.

We left St Maarten on the 10th April and arrived in Colon seven days later, a nice easy comfortable trip covering 1,180 miles in seven days and eight hours. We didn't really get into 160 mile plus days until a few days had gone by and we were boat-fit again... and our body clocks had adapted to the three on three hours off routine through the night. We ate too much and finally caught a fish, the first return on Lu investing a small fortune on a Penn reel, new 200lb nylon and enough lures to stock a small shop. On our approaches to Colon the fishing line screams out and after a 15-minute tussle we haul a fat yellowfin tuna on board. Tonight will be tuna straight, maybe with a little pickled ginger and wasabi sauce as well. After that tuna in satay sauce for a mate who isn't keen on fish straight onto the plate and then ...

Good yellowfin and we landed it!

fish for a few nights.

Ciguatera

Ciguatera is a type of fish poisoning which can leave you very ill for weeks with some of the symptoms persisting for a year or more. You get ciguatera from eating finned fish in tropical and some sub-tropical areas which have been infected with a dinoflagellate (a type of algae) associated with coral reefs. The toxin in the fish which infects humans does not seem to affect the fish itself, so a perfectly normal healthy looking fish can infect you. The toxin is usually found in fish higher up the food chain that have eaten smaller infected fish and concentrated the toxin. Pelagic fish are not normally infected with ciguatera.

The following should help you and if in doubt, leave it out. I for one do not eat barracuda in tropical waters and try to stick to mahi mahi (dorado), tuna, wahoo and other pelagic species.

Ciguatera areas

Cases of ciguatera have been reported between 35°N and 35°S. It is more usually concentrated around coral reef areas and one theory is that the toxic algae grow on damaged coral. Areas where it is prevalent are the Caribbean basin, the Pacific islands in the tropics and especially in islands from French Polynesia through Tonga, Fiji and Vanuatu, the tropical coast of Australia, and some of the islands in the tropics in the Indian Ocean. Strangely there seem to be few cases in the Red Sea.

Worryingly, in the last four years there have been several cases reported in the Canary Islands; well outside the normal geographic limits, linked to eating large amberjacks.

Symptoms

The initial symptoms are similar to any food poisoning with vomiting, diarrhoea, and stomach cramps. Symptoms normally appear within six hours. The neurological symptoms, which are the lasting ones, are numbness and tingling in the extremities, intense headache, vertigo and muscular weakness. There is one other bizarre neurological symptom, useful in identifying ciguatera, where temperature reversal makes cold things feel hot and hot things cold. There can also be cardiovascular symptoms with arrhythmia, tachycardia, and reduced blood pressure.

Treatment

There is no cure for ciguatera. There is also no definitive way of checking fish for ciguatera although ciguatera detection kits can be bought. Care of the patient is consequently palliative and involves making them comfortable, warm, preventing dehydration and getting medical help for any cardiovascular problems. In the early stages an emetic may be useful to empty the stomach of any remaining fish. The mortality rate for ciguatera poisoning is very low with children most at risk.

Suspect fish

All the fish associated with ciguatera are reef fish. Pelagic species appear not to be implicated. The type of fish to be avoided varies with the geographical area, but the following fish have commonly been associated with ciguatera.

• *Barracuda* A definite suspect in many cases. I avoid it.

BARRACUDA

• *Groupers* Various members of the grouper family including black grouper, yellowfin or yellow grouper, coral grouper, goliath grouper, tiger grouper, potato grouper. In fact just about any of the groupers found around coral. Groupers from non-coral areas such as the Mediterranean and New Zealand appear not to be infected.

GROUPER

• *Snapper* Various species of tropical snapper including yellowtail snapper, dog snapper, and red snapper.

• *Moray eels*

MORAY EEL

• *Mackerel* Some types of mackerel including king mackerel. Pelagic mackerel such as horse mackerel, Atlantic mackerel, and other pelagic species are unaffected. Even mackerel in the Red Sea appear to be unaffected.

• *Parrotfish* Though commonly eaten in the Red Sea.

• *Amberjack* Only the greater amberjack appears to be implicated.

• *Wrasse* Hogfish has been implicated.

• *Sharks* Some small species of shark have been implicated.

There are a lot of other species implicated, possibly up to 400 species, and in any area the incidence of ciguatera is sporadic. One year some species may harbour ciguatera and in the next the species may be free of the toxin.

A common bit of advice is to ask local fishermen in the area. Given the high incidence of ciguatera amongst local populations I doubt this is a reliable method of ascertaining whether ciguatera is present or not. In some cases whole villages have been poisoned.

Probably the best thing you can do is check with a local sub-aqua club. I've done this in the past and members of a club seem to have a pretty good handle on the incidence of ciguatera in a particular area.

The toxin appears to be most concentrated in the head and internal organs of suspect fish so at least avoid eating these in areas where ciguatera occurs. The ciguatera test kits which are advertised are not considered entirely reliable. They take at least an hour for results and the procedure must be followed to the letter. Research is ongoing to find a reliable and relatively cheap test kit for island populations in remote areas.

Panama

So here we are sitting in the Flats anchorage in Colon with 50–60 other boats and that's not counting the boats in the Panama Canal Yacht Club (PCYC), Shelter Bay Marina over the other side and boats cruising the San Blas while waiting their turn. It seems the canal authorities make a lot more money out of big ships going through (and Pana-Max, the biggest ship that a lock can take, it fits exactly into a lock, is very big) and so only a dozen or so yachts are being let through every week. But there are rumours around that more will be let through soon, so we are hopeful, though it's still looking like June or at best the end of May ... we live on the ripe smell of every bit of cruiser gossip that goes around.

For me Panama was going to be all hot chilli, tortillas, empanadas and spicy stews. In fact it turns out that much of the cuisine around the Panama Canal is heavily influenced by third and fourth generation Chinese whose forebears were originally brought in as cheap labour to build the canal. In fact many of the restaurants around are Chinese with a few concessions to Panamanian cuisine. Not that we go to many restaurants in Colon as it's pretty much a no-go area on foot with muggings and some pretty brutal murders going on all the time. While we were there three yachties were mugged with one of them, a South African delivery skipper and hard as old boots, being lucky to survive a knife attack which punctured his lung. Everyone takes a taxi around Colon, to the bus station, to the supermarkets, to anywhere, which is not too hard a penance as the rides only cost between $2–5.

Panama City is redolent of American cities complete with large shopping malls

Colon to the San Blas Islands

Once we had sorted the paperwork for the canal, the admeasurer had measured, and we had completed some boat jobs, we hauled up the anchor and set sail for Portobello. This is the bay where Drake based himself while sacking Spanish cities up and down the coast and he is reputedly buried at sea off a small islet at the entrance still called Isla Drake. The scourge of the Spanish Main, sacker of cities and privateer for Queen Elizabeth terrorised this coast and for centuries mothers would keep the kids in order by telling them El Terrible Drake is coming to get you. The Spanish fortified the bay, although that didn't stop Henry Morgan from sacking it nearly a century later. We anchored under San Fernando fort where the jungle comes right down to the water's edge and howler monkeys can occasionally be heard at dusk. The town across the way has basic shopping and, inevitably, several Chinese restaurants.

The coast up to the San Blas has anchorages aplenty in small bays on the mainland coast and behind islands. You clear into the San Blas at Porvenir where the Kunas charge a small tourist fee. These are more cays than islands with fringing coral protecting the anchorages. As long as the sun is reasonably high in the sky you can see the reefs and passages through them. It is no place to rely on electronic charts. As soon as you arrive at Porvenir the *mola* ladies in their *ulus*, dugout canoes, arrive to sell molas. They are pretty insistent and you will often have two or three canoes holding on to the boat and mola ladies imploring you to buy their molas. After that it's bon-bon and caramello request time for the kids in the canoes.

As we sat in the cockpit watching the *ulus* paddling and sailing around and waving our *molas* at approaching *mola*-saleswomen to show we already had some, my thoughts turned to dinner. We had plenty on board to cook, but I had heard stories of abundant crayfish around the San Blas. Sure enough an *ulu* rocked up with the bottom covered in crayfish. There had to be 10 or 12 of the little beauties in there.

'How much for two?' I asked in my best bargaining voice.

The little nut-brown fisherman waved his hand and said 'Ten dollars'.

'Ten dollars!!! Too much. Five dollars each... but big ones mind' I countered.

The *mola* ladies pounce in the San Blas

How Columbus changed the cuisine of Europe

When Columbus reached what he thought was the fabled East Indies described by Marco Polo, he was not a little mystified that he couldn't find the treasure trove of spices he was after. Sailing from the Bahamas he sighted Cuba and believed it to be an island off China. Coasting along Cuba he failed to find either gold or spices. He continued on to Hispaniola and lost the Santa Maria off what is now Cap Haitien. He built a fort ashore from the remains as a temporary settlement. On Hispaniola he found some gold to appease his Spanish masters and he also took on an assortment of fruit and vegetables that was to radically change the cuisine of Europe.

The following fruit and vegetables were brought back to Europe by Columbus and other Spaniards on various voyages to the New World. Not all of them would grow in Europe and some were so damaged on the voyages that it needed several attempts to import them and get them growing.

• *Chilli pepper* Columbus wanted to find the valuable peppercorn in the Indies. He did not find it, but he did collect the chillies the Indians used to flavour their food, a spice he declared in a bit of wishful thinking that was 'the pepper which the local Indians used as spice is more abundant and more valuable than either black or melegueta pepper'. The chilli pepper was growing in Spain soon after and then was spread throughout the Mediterranean and with the Portuguese to India and the Far East.

• *Capsicum (peppers)* The bell pepper arrived in Spain along with the chilli pepper and was soon grown there and used in local dishes. Later it spread to the Mediterranean countries where it became a mainstay of local dishes. In Hungary it was dried to produce paprika, the essential ingredient in Hungarian goulash.

• *Tomatoes* The tomato may have been brought back by Columbus on one of his voyages or may have been introduced later, probably in the early 16th century. At first it was treated suspiciously, it is a member of the deadly nightshade family, and took a while to be accepted into Europe. The name comes from the Indian *tomatl*, but it went by a number of names including 'golden apple' and 'love apple', the latter because it supposedly had aphrodisiac qualities. By the 17th century it was cultivated and used in Spain and Italy and gradually spread throughout the Mediterranean to become a mainstay of the cuisine. Pasta with a tomato sauce, something we imagine to be intrinsically Italian, was made in the 18th century and tomato ketchup was first bottled in the USA in the mid-19th century.

• *Maize (corn)* Columbus brought maize back and it spread rapidly through the old world and down through Africa, India and to China. The Portuguese took it to Africa to provide foodstuffs for provisioning their ships and also as dried mealy to feed the slaves on the passages across to Brazil. Magellan took maize with him on his circumnavigation and soon after corn was grown in the Philippines and Near East. The significance of this foodstuff in our world is difficult to overestimate.

• *Beans* Many of the varieties of beans we use were brought back from the New World. Again many of them like kidney, black, pinto, haricot and lima beans were from the Americas and an important item in the local cuisine.

• *Cocoa (chocolate)* Columbus brought back cacao beans, but it is unlikely he knew about the drink made from them. Soon after other voyagers discovered the drink the local Indians made from the beans and it started to spread outwards from Spain. It soon commanded astronomical prices and was believed to have a wide range of medicinal properties including as an aphrodisiac. The chocolate bar, emulsified chocolate and sugar, was first made by John Cadbury, the very same as on the wrapper of modern chocolate bars, in the mid 19th century.

Difficult to imagine that more than half the fruit and vegetables in European markets didn't exist until Columbus

- *Potatoes and sweet potatoes* Potatoes were mostly cultivated in Peru and Chile and it is likely that the Spanish first brought them back to Europe in the 1550s after the conquest of the Incas. It took some time to spread through Europe, though Sir Francis Drake may have brought the potato in his ships stores to England at the end of the 16th century. The Spanish and the Portuguese were taking them on board for stores in the same period as they last quite well at sea. Not until the 19th century do we find potatoes in Ireland and England. It's difficult to think of how we ever did without them.

- *Avocados* The Spanish noted that the local Indians ate the avocado in the early 16th century, but no one seemed too keen on it and it wasn't cultivated in Europe until the late 19th century. 18th-century English sailors knew of it and called it 'midmanships butter' and used it to spread on ships biscuit in an attempt to make them more palatable.

- *Pineapple* Columbus encountered the fruit on Guadeloupe and was instantly impressed. So were the Spanish and by the 1520s were growing it in Spain. The Portuguese carried pineapples back to Europe on the homeward voyage from Brazil bringing with them its common European name of ananas from the Guarani language spoken in Southwest Brazil. It means 'excellent fruit' in Guarani.

There were other foods brought back; groundnuts or peanuts, manioc which was used to make bread in the Caribbean and brought back to Europe and introduced to Africa, squash and gourds, the latter used by the Indians as storage vessels after they had been dried, sunflowers which were used to make oil, and the turkey which was soon cultivated in Europe for food.

The process was not one way. Columbus and fellow voyagers introduced cows, onions, carrots, beets, peas and wheat to the Americas where it was grown to provision their ships for the return voyage to Europe. The Portuguese introduced sugar cane from Asia to Brazil and after they had decimated the local populations for slave labour on the plantations began importing slaves from Africa. Soon many of the islands in the Caribbean were burnt off to provide land for sugar plantations and everyone from the Spanish to the French and English were importing slaves on the west-about route and returning with sugar on the east-about route.

'OK'. He looked puzzled and put two crayfish in a bag, and then another two. 'No no… just two'. And then I got it. He meant ten dollars for all the crayfish in the canoe. I smiled and gave him five dollars for the four. Two crayfish each was good. We met him again before we left and with a big smile he said 'Two crayfish – five dollars yes'. I had just introduced rampant inflation into the San Blas Islands.

We sailed around the Lemon Cays, back to Porvenir and the other cays nearby and over to Chichime Cays. I've got to be honest here. There are only so many white coral sand beaches fringed by coconut palms that I can take. Three to four days is good for me before heading back to places that have a little more human activity going on and are in their own way just as beautiful. Besides we need to get organised for the Panama Canal.

Four crayfish for $5. Can't be bad

The first date we got for a canal transit was 23rd June. In the end the authorities decided to speed things up and larger numbers were soon being transited through the canal. Transit times tumbled and soon we were scheduled for 22nd May. Most boats are stocking up keenly in Colon where a couple of large American-style supermarkets stock just about everything you need. Taxis were stuffed full of bags of goodies for the return trip to the boat.

One of the important preparations needed for the transit is what the evening meal on the first night will be and what to prepare for lunches. Apart from the pilot from the canal authorities, all boats have to have four line handlers on board and these are usually other yachties who help out and get helped out by others in return. We had three line handlers including a back-packer who wanted to transit the canal and two other yachties. On hindsight yachties are to be preferred only because they understand the loads on ropes and the mechanical advantage of winches and sweating a line onto a cleat. Landlubbers don't and can be hurt when the tension comes on a line with an 18-ton boat on the other end.

So we put thought into what sort of meal the line-handlers and the pilot will like. The line handlers will be sleeping on board on the first night so will need dinner and breakfast and lunch and a few snacks in between on the subsequent day. You need something already cooked that you can heat up when you get through the first set of locks so I go for my old fallback passage meal of a good ragu and pasta with a salad. Lu does bacon sandwiches for breakfast and lunch on Lake Gatun is cold chicken from the Rotisserie in Colon, a couscous salad and a potato salad.

Balboa on the Pacific side of the Panama Canal is altogether a more prosperous and safer place than its sad cousin at the Caribbean end. Even the environs seem greener, cleaner and somehow healthier, though that may just be a splinter of joy on arriving in the great Pacific.

Descending down the last lock and so into the Pacific
Peter Metherall

Ashore in Panama

Colon

There are not many opportunities for dining ashore in Colon, principally because the city is just too dangerous. We mostly dined at the Chinese oriented Panama Canal Yacht Club restaurant and with its sad demise most people will now be eating ashore in the Shelter Bay Marina restaurant. It serves an 'international' cuisine.

Provisioning in Colon is excellent. Basically you take a taxi to one of the two big supermarkets on the outskirts of Colon and these are secure guarded areas. In the supermarkets you can buy most staples, most of them American in origin, and fresh fruit and vegetables and even good cheeses and fresh meat and poultry. You can also get very cheap beer and good Chilean and Argentinian wine.

Balboa

Eating out in Balboa varies between chain 'American-style' restaurants like TGI Friday and Plumpjack to some very good local restaurants on the end of the spit near Flamenco Marina. Going into town to local restaurants is probably not a good option here. If you like ample portions of BBQ spare ribs, hamburgers, steaks and fried chicken then you will find restaurants producing this sort of stuff around the waterfront at Balboa and in town.

If you want food with a more local flavour then in the evenings stalls set up near Flamenco Marina and you can get very reasonably priced street food in the balmy evenings. There are all sorts of things like roast pork, Chinese, pizza, fried chicken, most of it served with rice and beans and maybe a bit of salad.

Provisioning can be done at large supermarkets in Panama City, but the closest and most convenient is in the large bus station and the vast American style Allbrook Mall near Balboa. There is a large supermarket within the mall. Either take a cab or you can take a local bus. The Allbrook complex is secure and has lots of other shops as well.

Panama Canal Yacht Club

For decades the Panama Canal Yacht Club was at the centre of yachty life in Colon. Part of the reason was that it was one of the few secure places in Colon. Beyond the perimeter the wild streets of Colon were dangerous and every year a few hapless yachties who ignored advice not to wander around outside the club compound would come to grief.

There was nothing flashy about the yacht club. A few rickety buildings with corrugated iron roofs. Ceiling fans that struggled to move the humid air. A restaurant that did reasonable Chinese food and passable English breakfasts. The beer at a dollar a bottle was always a hit. It had Wi-Fi and a lean-to laundry and a small yard where you could haul ashore. Out the front were some rickety catwalks with maybe 40 yacht berths.

Nothing flashy but a place where yachties gathered, had a beer or three and told tales, swapped information and organised line handlers.

And now it's gone. Not long after we were sitting here drinking beer, planning the transit through the canal, gassing, getting taxis into town and the supermarkets, filling up the water cans… and now this club, loved by yachties over its 80 year history, is gone. That was in 2009.

The 'late' Panama Canal Yacht Club. It has now been bull-dozed by Hutchinson-Whampoa and after 80 years exists no more

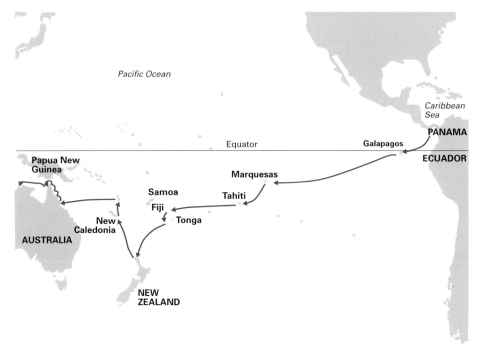

On Desert Island Discs when you are asked what book you would take with you how come no one ever asks for *How to Build a Boat*? *Douglas Graeme*

At anchor under Amador Island at the Pacific end of the Panama Canal we are doing some last minute provisioning in the Allbrook Mall at the main bus station. It's quite a lot like being in the USA here where the official currency is the US dollar and shopping is mostly in big malls like the Allbrook. You are only nine or so degrees north of the Equator here, but surprisingly it can feel cold at times, not least from the incessant rain and the squalls sweeping through the anchorage. This sort of weather doesn't encourage you to leave and nor did a MAYDAY call that came screaming through the morning radio net.

A trimaran heading up the coast and off Costa Rica was caught by an early season cyclone. The sails and rigging are damaged, the engine is under water and won't start, there is some panic in the skipper's voice. The old steam radio SSB net swings into action and the net controller keeps the frequency clear for the emergency. In under an hour a yacht at anchor in Costa Rica has alerted the coastguard ashore, another phones the US coastguard who get an aircraft up to overfly the yacht, a coastguard cutter is dispatched to the coordinates given and the skipper is advised on the operation in progress. It all ends happily and the trimaran is escorted by the cutter to a safe anchorage in Costa Rica by the next day.

Well I wasn't going to move him on. That's a really big beak

Not that we are heading for a cyclone area en route to the Galapagos, but nonetheless the grey weather and squally winds don't lend confidence to starting this trip. Still we look at the grib files, I cook up some Moroccan minted beef for a passage meal and we leave the next day.

Sailing from Panama to the Galapagos turned out to be a largely wet slog with lots of lightning flickering around the sky, a predominantly grey sky pocked with little black squall clouds for much of the time. This was almost entirely a windward leg and a rainy one as well. Although we were supposed to be well south of the ITCZ, the Intertropical Convergence Zone, nonetheless we mostly encountered entirely overcast days and rain. Lots of rain. For one period 20 hours of torrential rain. And wind shifts all over the place. It felt like the ITCZ to me.

We followed a plan to go east of Malpelo Island on starboard tack and then hopefully we could flop over onto port and make it close to the Galapagos on one tack. It was a fond dream hatched in Balboa, but like many passage plans it bears little resemblance to reality. In fact we tacked back onto starboard with any favourable wind shifts and headed for the equator and then back over to port when the wind switched to SSW–SW. On reflection it might have been better to head down to the equator past Malpelo Island earlier in the trip where the winds were more likely to be S or even SSE.

And Neptune did come on board. Crossing the Equator on passage to the Galapagos doesn't feel like a proper crossing experience at all. It's rainy and not that warm and so it's difficult to get a tropical mindset on the whole Neptune experience. Anyway we gave Neptune lots of fine Monkey Bay New Zealand Sauvignon Blanc and because he can't hold his liquor at 10 in the morning he became most amenable. Which is just as well given how rambunctious Neptune and his cohorts can become.

The origins of the tradition are not really known, though it's likely it developed sometime in the 17th century when European ships began crossing the Equator. Usually King Neptune arrives on board with his court, including Davy Jones, Amphitrite, a doctor and a barber. The ceremony involves the *Shellbacks* (those that have already crossed the Equator) making the *Pollywogs* (those who haven't) perform a number of disgusting acts. Once Neptune is satisfied a certificate is awarded to the newbie *Shellback*. Commonly the *Pollywog* is smeared with rotten fruit, oil, garbage, basically anything disgusting, and made to drink some evil alcoholic concoctions, the sort of thing designed as a penalty drink like ouzo and beer. And then the *Pollywog* has his hair shaved off. The ceremony was common in various navies, although today it is a more muted affair after some pretty awful sexual acts performed on the *Pollywogs* was leaked to the papers and the Royal Navy was instructed to ease up on the violence.

Neptune with all the apparatus for naming and shaming first-timers

Day 1

30th May 1030. Anchor up off Balboa.
Heading for fuel quay in Flamingo Marina and then towards the Galapagos.

30th May 1500 Wind SSE 3. Speed 5·3 knots.
Not quite heading in the right direction but sailing.

Day 2

31st May 1200 Wind WSW 3. Speed 6·3 knots.
Taiwanese/Korean fishing boats around.
Small squally bits. 136M daily run.

Day 3

1st June 0300 Wind WSW3—4. Speed 5·9 knots. Rain squall. Lots of lightning around.

1st June 1200 Wind SSW4. Speed 7 knots. Approaching Malpelo Island.
Daily run 135M.

Day 4

2nd June 1800 Wind SSW4. Speed 5·4 knots.
No need for sunglasses all day. Wind backing.

Day 5

3rd June 1500 Wind SSE 4. Speed 5·3 knots. Still hard on the wind.

Day 6

4th June 1200 Wind SSW 4. Speed 5·7 knots.
Stormy petrel. Young booby. Big fishing boat.

Day 7

5th June 0300. Wind SSW 4—5. Speed 6·6 knots. 1 knot of current against us. Sea of the long black cloud, lone stars and unfavourable currents.
Fishing boat passed to S.

Day 8

6th June 1200 Wind SSW 4. Speed 5·4 knots. Long lines around, kilometres long with flags. Big fishing boat a few miles away and dory with fishermen. Photos and waves. Seem to have wended our way through them. Phew.

Day 9

7th June 1010 Wind SSE 4. Speed 6·3 knots. Crossed Equator. Seems surprisingly cold for the Tropics, guess it is the cold Humboldt current flowing up from S.

Day 10

8th June 0330 Wind SSE 4. Hove-to waiting for daylight.
Misty visibility.

June 8th 1000. Anchored in Puerto Ayora.

Tuna and the sushi dilemma

Anyone sailing to the Galapagos will come across them. Kilometres of long-lines, and I mean kilometres, joined by marker buoys in a spider's web over large swathes of the sea you are sailing through. Ecuadorian and Columbian fishing boats spend weeks out here catching tuna and like others we got caught up in the lines.

Early one morning out of the corner of my eye I saw something following behind us. When I looked there was nothing there except some odd swirling water. Then as I watched a blue barrel buoy popped up a couple of hundred metres astern doing the same speed as us. When I walked up the side deck I could see the iridescent flash of nylon line in the water. The line was around the keel so I called Lu up and we came head to wind to slow the boat down so I could catch the line with the boat hook. We hauled in loads of line before it became evident that this could go on for kilometres, so with apologies to the fishermen somewhere over the horizon I cut the line and we resumed sailing.

There will usually be a mother boat and one or two long dories, often around 40ft, with a big outboard on the back. If you get caught up and they see you, they will attempt to guide you around the end of the long-lines. If there is no one around you will have to try and get the long-line off the best way you can and this often means cutting it.

It's common knowledge that fish stocks around the world are diminishing at an alarming rate. Depending on your source, tuna stocks in the Pacific are endangered and will be exhausted in anything from 5–15 years. It depends on which tuna you are talking about. A recent paper in Science authored by NOAA scientists puts Bluefin tuna, the Japanese sushi favourite, on the critically endangered list. Bigeye tuna is endangered. Marlin is vulnerable. In this huge expanse of water fish stocks are less diminished than in the Atlantic where Bluefin tuna stocks are severely depleted.

Tuna long-lining skiff encountered en route to Galapagos. These guys seemed to have problems identifying where all the long-lines were and how to get around them

In the Mediterranean Bluefin tuna are given a scant three years before extinction in a recent WWF study.

Fishermen always deny that numbers of fish are declining and though I'm no fisherman, I've found fewer and smaller fish on my trolling line over the years. In times past I've had to declare no fish days because we were sick of tuna. Not any more and a catch on the line is a treasured bonus. Now I love sushi, but you have to worry a little bit when as I write a Bluefin tuna was just auctioned off in Japan for $1.7 million (US). And the price is only set to go higher, an indication of diminishing supplies.

Much of the overfishing is not from the long-liners like the Ecuadorian and Columbian boats en route to Galapagos, but from giant purse seine netters that use spotter planes to seek out the schools of tuna and then lay their giant nets around them. This is fishing on an industrial scale and in other parts of the world I have seen these small ships come in and offload hundreds of tons of tuna. It's no wonder that small fishing communities living on isolated islands around the oceans of the world have watched catches dwindle and have become angry at large corporations scooping up their everyday food.

Long-lining mother ship off the coast of Ecuador

We slowed down towards the end and then hove-to so we could make the final approach in daylight. Just as well as visibility was around two miles and the approach has surf crashing on the shores all around it. All in all 8½ days was not bad considering it was windward work all the way except for the last day when we had to slow down anyway.

The Galapagos was discovered accidentally when a ship en route to Peru drifted into the vicinity of the islands. In 1535, Tomás de Berlanga, the Bishop of Panama was en route to Peru. His ship was drifting without wind and was carried by the currents to the Galapagos. In a letter to the King of Spain the bishop described the islands by saying:

'I do not think there is a place where one might sow a bushel of corn because most of it is full of very big stones and the earth is much like dross, worthless, because it has not the power of raising a little grass.'

The bishop and the crew, like many early visitors, arrived in the islands thirsty and were less than impressed by the lack of water. He didn't even bother to give the islands a name. It wasn't until 1574 that the name 'Islands of Galapagos' (Island of Tortoises) first appeared on a map and has remained the Galapagos Islands ever since. It was at the end of the 18th and early 19th century that the islands became a useful stopover for whalers and a few roving Buccaneers who stocked up on fresh water and tortoises for food. The water was found inland and higher up and the tortoises were everywhere. They were prized food because they could be kept alive for months before being killed for fresh meat.

If there is any one name associated with the Galapagos it is Charles Darwin. He arrived on the *Beagle* in 1835. Captain Fitzroy of the *Beagle* had gone to the Galapagos to survey the islands and, like the whalers, pick up fresh water and tortoises for fresh meat. Darwin's main preoccupation on the voyage was not just for the zoology and botany of different countries, but also for the geology of the different geographical regions. Of the Galapagos he said,

'I look forward to the Galapagos with more interest than any other part of the voyage. They abound with active volcanoes, and, I should hope, contain Tertiary strata.'

For Darwin this fortuitous visit sharpened his nascent theory of evolution with his examination of the particular development of species on the islands. He noticed that different species of the same family were differently adapted on the different islands. In five short weeks around the islands while Fitzroy completed his surveys, incidentally surveys still reproduced by the Admiralty and used until recently, Darwin amassed the collection that would later form a significant part of the 'light bulb' moment leading to his theory of evolution that changed how we see the world.

The anchorage at Puerto Ayora in the Galapagos. Uncomfortable and rolly, but worth the discomfort for everything ashore

Puerto Ayora has to be one of the most uncomfortable anchorages around with a swell up to a metre curving around into the anchorage. Yachts put a kedge off the starboard quarter to hold them into the swell. Sitting on board the marine life is prolific: frigate birds, pelicans, red and blue footed boobies, wedge tail petrels, gulls and of course a few of Darwin's fabled finches are all around. A pelican adopted us early on and the pulpit was definitely his

Ashore in the Galapagos

Puerto Ayora is the hub of the Galapagos Islands, though it is not a huge place and you can easily walk to the perimeter of the town. It has most of the things you need, a laundry, internet cafés, small grocery shops and wonderful cafés and restaurants. Although lots of processed food comes in the coaster from Ecuador, it's surprising how much the islands produce given earlier descriptions. If you look around the bare basalt shores it's difficult to see how anything would grow. That is until you go into the lower slopes where the misty haze that hides the islands condenses and gradually scrub and then stubby trees and grasslands appear. For Puerto Ayora water is produced by a reverse osmosis plant and water is nearly as expensive as petrol. Well it seems like it at US$40 per hundred gallons.

What's really odd here, just a few degrees south of the equator, is how untropical it all feels. The cold upwelling currents around the Galapagos mean temperatures are, well, temperate. At night you need a sweatshirt to keep warm. There is not the sweaty, muggy heat of the Caribbean.

Provisions

Basic provisions can be found in the grocery shops, at least enough to top up basics until Tahiti. In any case most yachts will be well stocked from the big supermarkets in Panama.

The fresh fruit and vegetable market in Ayora on Tuesdays and Saturdays has most of what you need. It seems everything is a dollar a bag (they supply the bags) so whether you put six limes or a dozen in, it is still a dollar. Potatoes, onions, limes, passion fruit, tomatoes, peppers, and lots of other things are fresh and keep well. Something of a blessing when it is over 3,000 miles to the next bit of land. Buy a bit more than you need. Lu accidentally bought two big bags of passion fruit. The passion fruit lasted the whole way so for breakfast we had muesli and yoghurt with fresh passion fruit dribbled over the top all the way to the Marquesas.

The one place you should visit is the small fish market on the waterfront. Even if you don't want to buy any fish, just go to watch the local customers. There is usually a

couple of sea lions, a pelican or two, and some boobies. They are not shy about wandering in and nudging the vendors there to give them a morsel or two. And if your luck was not in on passage here you can buy excellent fresh fish at very reasonable prices.

Most other things are shipped into the Galapagos and then brought ashore on small lighters. Consequently anything shipped in, which is nearly everything except for some fruit and vegetables and a bit of beef or goat, is expensive. Often there will be shortages of items until the supply ship arrives.

Eating out

Eating out in the local restaurants is excellent and good value. The restaurants are along the waterfront and somewhere like 'The Rock' has excellent food at good prices and not surprisingly the fish is fresh and always on the menu. The seared tuna here is nearly as good as the seared tuna on board *Skylax*. There are also some local Ecuadorian dishes with seafood mixed in with coconut and plantain and the like. Alcohol is imported so a little more expensive.

In uptown Puerto Ayora, away from the waterfront, there is a local restaurant street where at lunchtime small restaurants, some not much more than a stall, have set lunchtime menus for very little, often only US$4–5. This is where the locals eat and the food is good basic Ecuadorian fare. It usually included excellent soup, with chicken and corn and thickened with pounded yucca or something similar. Main courses are often fried chicken with rice, salad, crispy plantains and sometimes barbecued corn on the cob. And occasionally there is a dessert. Restaurant street is the place to be with the locals going about their business, stopping by to get a quick bite or just passing the time of day.

The cafés around the waterfront are a reminder that Ecuadorian coffee is very good indeed. Coffee is grown in the highlands of the islands and you can buy bags of beans or ground coffee in the town. The locals are proud of their coffee and rightly so, it is good.

Customers queueing up at the fish market in Puerto Ayora

new home. Have you seen how big a pelican's beak is when you try to tell him to shove off? Marine iguanas are everywhere and sally lightfoot crabs are like orange polka dots on the bare black basalt. A sea lion used *Skylax* as a backrest while it tenderised a 10 inch sea worm and then popped it down whole.

You get ashore with water taxis which weave in and out of all the craft anchored in Purto Ayora. There are tripper boars, charter yachts, workboats and barges for unloading the coaster when it comes in and anchors in the outer anchorage. And a few cruising yachts. Ashore the small town hums with tourists though it never feels overcrowded and the locals are on the opposite side of frenetic.

You get around Puerto Ayora in the local taxis where, like the fruit market, every local trip costs a dollar. The taxis are all 4-wheel drive pick-ups, mostly Toyota Hi-Lux's, which might seem a bit excessive around the little town, but are needed for some of the rutted tracks outside town. You can hire a cab and guide at very reasonable rates for a trip into the highlands. Here you can see the giant land tortoises that were very nearly wiped out by whalers and others hunting them for fresh meat.

Hunting is hardly a term you can use for capturing the lumbering beasts. They are not very fast and when they see you give a bit of a hiss and then retreat into their shell. A bit like a ready packaged meal really. The tortoises can live for months without food so were a good deal more useful than other livestock onboard. A fully-grown tortoise can weigh anything from 200–250kgs (400–500lbs). I'd guess that at least half of that weight must be useable flesh, so these slow moving beasts were ideal prey for fresh meat on board.

On the outskirts of Puerto Ayora the Darwin Institute has a research and breeding programme for the Galapagos turtles. In one enclosure there is poor old 'Lonesome George', the last of his sub-species on Pinta and when his time comes, he will die and that will be the end of his kind. Sadly he died while I was writing this on the 24th June 2012 aged around 100 years. Fortunately species from other islands have been breeding and their numbers expanding so all is not lost, but you had to feel sorry for 'Lonesome George' looking forlornly out of his enclosure.

Galapagos giant tortoise. A big chunk of meat that came ready packaged for sailing ships of yore

PACIFIC

Galapagos to the Marquesas

Galapagos to the Marquesas is the longest passage most tradewind sailors will do. It's something over 3,000 miles to the Marquesas so if you only made 100 miles a day then the passage could take over a month. Along this stretch of the South Pacific the route arcs gently west just under the equator to the Marquesas. This is about as far from land, as far from civilization and emergency services, from food and help, as you can get. This patch of sea is out of the range of emergency services and far from the regular shipping routes.

Skylax left the Galapagos fully loaded with food and water on a fairly direct rhumb line route to Hiva Oa. Like all first days at sea it took a while for us to settle into the rhythm of wind and sea and the regular roll of the boat in the trades. We tend to be a bit conservative at the beginning of a passage and probably don't do our best speed with the wind we have, but after a few days we shook a reef out of the main and *Skylax* started to pick off the miles to the Marquesas. At times like this you sometimes feel you are a bit incidental to the boat, alert passengers who reef and let out more sail, write up the log, and ponder what lunch and dinner are going to be. It's the boat that does the work, ploughing on day and night to our plotted destination without too much effort from the crew. We listen to old familiar noises and listen for any new noises that might tell us that something is chafing badly or needs to be tweaked for the sea and wind that we have.

For sailors of yore life at sea was a more intense and tense time. The seas were not well charted and there were plenty of islands and reefs not marked at all. Life on the whaling boats was hard and there was no help at hand if things went wrong. So it was for the whaling ship *Essex* that was sunk by a sperm whale in November 1820. Owen Chase the mate on board reported that

'... The surf flew in all directions about him with the continual violent thrashing of his tail. His head about half out of the water, and in that way he came upon us, and again struck the ship.' *Owen Chase*

The crew took to three of the whaleboats and reached Henderson Island in the Pitcairn group. Finding little to sustain themselves they set off again for the coast of South America and it was on this voyage that the horrors of survival at sea

overran the norms of human life. They soon ran out of food again and as men began to die the others began to eat them. On one of the lifeboats, the one with the captain on board, there were just four left when it was decided that one of them would be killed for food. Lots were drawn and a young crewman drew the losing

Dusk falls and another night of three hours on and three hours off begins

PACIFIC

Day 1

14th June 0850. Anchors up in Puerto Ayora. Main bower anchor is stubbornly in the black sand bottom.
14th June 1945 Wind S3 Speed 6·1. Chicken stew for dinner. Tight hauled but heading in the right direction.

Day 2

15th June 1200. Wind SE 5. Speed 7·5. Scorching along now. 157M day. Still chilly.

Day 3

16th June 1800. Wind ESE 4. Speed 7·1. Shook out second reef in main and going sweetly now with most of genny out. Muffins for tea.

Day 4

17th June 1800. Wind SE 5. Speed 7·7. Dolphins briefly. Definitely getting warmer as no socks needed for night watch now.

Day 5

18th June 0500. Wind SE 4. Speed 7.5. 100% cloud cover. Rain. Wind all over the place.

Day 6

19th June 1200. Wind SE 4—5. Speed 7·5.Overcast. Fishing line out. Daily run 187M.

Day 7

20th June 1200. Wind ESE 4—5. Speed 8·5. Whale blows 300m off port quarter. Dolphins all around. Daily run 187M again.

Day 8

21st June 1200. Wind ESE 4. Speed 7. Genny now poled out on port side. Daily run 185M

Day 9

22nd June 0900. Wind ENE 4—5. Speed 7·1. Favourable current. Gybe main onto starboard.

Day 10

23rd June 1500. Wind ESE 5 Speed 7·6. Big lumpy confused seas. Clouding over in the E. Time for a reef?

Day 11

24th June 1500. Wind E 5. Speed 7·3. Lovely sunny afternoon. Just a bit rolly wing and wing.

Day 12

25th June 1500. Wind SE 4. Speed 6·9. Replaced cable tie repair to top two slides on mainsail. Third from top slide broken off.

Day 13

26th June 0900. Wind SE 3. Speed 5·6. Wind fitful ENE, E, ESE, S. Put in second reef.

Day 14

27th June 1500. Wind E 4. Speed 5·9. Shook out reef to full main. Gentle sailing, a bit rolly.

Day 15

28th June 2000. Wind 5. Speed 8·5. Squally rain clouds passing. Put 1 reef in main. Dry so far.

Day 16

29th June 1800. Wind E 4. Speed 6·4. Sunny afternoon. No BEEB.

Day 17

30th June 0900. Wind E/ESE 5. Speed 6·8. System coming up from SE. Rain and wind to 30 knots.

Day 18

1st July 1200. Wind E 4. Speed 6·5. One reef in main. Daily run 154M.

Day 19

2nd July 1800. Wind E 4. Speed 5·6. Slowing down in approaches to Hiva Oa. Talking to Ramprasad on VHF.

Day 20

3rd July 0700. Anchored fore and aft in Atuona after heaving-to for part of the night. Came in accompanied by Ramprasad.

lot. He was shot and his body consumed. His executioner died a few days later and he too was consumed. The captain and the other crewman were rescued a few days later by another whaling ship.

One of the sad ironies of this tale is that the decision had been made not to head for the Marquesas, downwind of where the *Essex* sank, because of fears of cannibalism on the islands. The whaling ships were often away for two to three years, drifting about this vast ocean in search of whales and only occasionally putting into anchorages like the Galapagos for water and victuals. Communication was sporadic and information on anchorages and the inhabitants in them, whether they were friendly or not, was sparse. On *Skylax* we clock into the SSB radio net every evening, we hear about other yachts in the vicinity, communicate our position and what weather we have, hear about the facilities to be found in the next landfall.

The days fall into a wonderful rhythm of a few sail changes, a wander around the deck in the morning checking for chafe and collecting the flying fish that have miscalculated their trajectory in the night and stranded themselves outside of their watery medium. The nights are full of stars and the Milky Way is like a huge cloud of light. Strange things happen on night watch. I see a huge eye in a black body emerge off the quarter of the boat and then submerge again. I see what I can only imagine is space debris burning up for 30 seconds or more on the far horizon. Lu doesn't believe any of this and puts it down to my febrile imagination.

What if?

A week out of the Galapagos an old and apparently innocuous lump on Lu's neck became infected. In the middle of this lonely patch of the Pacific any medical emergency is a big worry. There really isn't anyone around to help. I had a similar subcutaneous cyst on my arm some years ago which became infected and subsequently led to blood poisoning with my whole arm twice its normal size, so I was worried. I put Lu on a wide spectrum antibiotic (Amoxycillin) and this seemed to contain the infection, but not to stop it.

The passage to Hiva Oa in the Marquesas was fortunately fairly fast and we arrived after 18½ days. That meant Lu had been on antibiotics for nearly two weeks and by the time we anchored and set off for the tiny hospital on the island the cyst was very painful and obviously badly infected. Here the only doctor on the island prescribed some more antibiotics and that Lu go straight to the larger hospital on Nuka Hiva to have it operated on. We duly booked a flight for the morrow and off Lu went. After treatment Lu flew back the next day and for a week we went to the hospital at Atuona to have the wound cleaned and re-dressed. In the meantime Lu developed a rash, most likely a contra-indication to all the antibiotics she had been taking, but that soon cleared up when they stopped the medication.

I have say a big thank you to Dr Chassefaire and Dr Hoff and the staff in both hospitals and the locals on the islands. They were great and the French health system that funds these services for the relatively small population in the Marquesas works well. So it's worth carrying some wide spectrum antibiotics on board for any passage at sea far from an A&E. Try to persuade a friendly GP to give you some or buy them over the counter where you can (the Galapagos is one such place). They may save someone's life.

Finally, a good sized wahoo after all the other fish that got off

By the second week *Skylax* is bustling along, clocking up 180–190 mile runs over 24 hours and we are looking good for a fast passage to Atuona. The temperatures are warming up as we head west and we no longer need to have several layers on at night to keep warm. There are squalls about, some with a bit of rain, but generally no more than 20–25 knots for 10 minutes or so. A couple had 30 knots plus, but that was an exception causing us to pull a reef in with a bit more alacrity than normal.

We catch six fish and landed just the one. We get two mahi-mahi up to the transom before they get off. Two fish screamed line off the reel before they got off, one of them biting the lure in half so we probably didn't want to know what it was. Other yachts had more luck though most had the best fishing in the first week and then less luck further on.

And then we catch a nice wahoo. The flesh of wahoo or mahi mahi is excellent and they are some of the best pelagic fish for eating in the ocean. The fish is a wonderful shimmery blue and silver but fades as it lies in the cockpit while Lu gives it the coup de gras Japanese-style with a spike. It's sad to watch the rainbow colours fade to grey on death and this vibrant living beast is reduced to grey flesh. One useful hint to relieve the suffering is to squirt a bit of alcohol, ethyl or methyl, into the gills, sending the beast to whatever fishy nirvana they go to in a reverie of alcohol induced happiness. Well maybe not happiness, but some sort of dulled state anyway.

As we rocket along we have been talking to Sam on *Ramprasad*. Sam is single-handing and left Panama at the same time as us. He was struggling to get to the Galapagos and in the end when he found the trades way, way south of the Galapagos he decided to just carry on for the Marquesas. Getting close to Hiva Oa and the harbour of Atuona we are catching Sam who by now has been at sea for more than 40 days. Forty days of managing the boat, reefing and unreefing, cooking, keeping watch, talking to yourself except for the daily sched on the radio. As we close Atuona in the dusk we see Sam's navigation lights and despite the temptation of navigating into the anchorage at night, we both decide to heave-to and wait for dawn.

The sky in these parts is an inky black peppered with stars and a waning moon and I can just make out the silhouette of land. I can smell the land, a rich moist smell of black soil and tropical forest overlaid with hints of wood smoke. There are a few lights around the shore, but nothing that is going to make a significant contribution to light pollution in this part of the world.

In the early morning light we stowed sails and motored into the harbour. It is tucked around a high point and you can't see it until you are close in. With the tradewind swell heaping up on the shore this is all a bit scary until you get inside the breakwater where it is relatively still, though you need to anchor fore and aft in here to keep the bows into the residual swell that enters and also because there is just not room enough to swing to an anchor. It's a busy time, not so much to do with anchoring and stowing the boat as to do with fielding all the 'hellos', the 'how are yous', the 'welcomes' from friends in other boats in the anchorage and strangers too. These hellos are a tacit acknowledgement of safe arrival after a long passage.

I still have to keep checking back to the log to work out that we did average 168 miles a day, an average speed of 7 knots from Galapagos and that's in locked down passage-making mode. I put it down to the boat with Lu and me just hanging on and keeping ourselves fed and watered while the girl picked up her skirts and scampered across the Pacific.

These islands are savage places, a bit like mountains placed in the sea without much in the way of coastal flats and plains. Settlements are perched precariously around the edges of slopes climbing out of the sea and cut by razor back ridges and sheered off to leave high cliffs. Waterfalls tumble down hundreds of feet to the sea. And the whole lot is covered by thick jungle. What looks like a short climb up to a ridge is disguised by the sheer height of the peaks and turns out to be a hot and exhausting climb.

Add to this tropical paradise sensuality and sex, an easy almost lazy life enjoyed by the locals, a place where you plucked fish out of the sea and fruit off the trees, a place where Rousseau's noble savage existed on South Sea islands, then you can understand why early visitors saw the Marquesas as paradise. Like any Garden of Eden there is a snake, and in the Marquesas and other islands that was cannibalism. Herman Melville, he of *Moby Dick* fame, described his sojourn on the islands in *Typee*, his first book, and introduced the world to bare breasted wahines, brotherhood in the valley of the *Typee*, and cannibalism. He was also critical of the missionaries who came here with their western ideas of what the natives

A fully recovered Lu gathering coconuts. All the fruit trees are owned in the Marquesas so ask permission before you help yourself

Landfall in Atuona after 3,000 miles of ocean

Ashore in the Marquesas

On the islands there is little in the way of public transport. The odd Toyota Hi-Lux double cab taxi, but little else. What happens when you are wandering along the road is that the locals will stop and offer you a lift. If you need anything they will try to help. I've been squeezed into cars with big mama's cradling infants in ample bosoms, a trio of kids hanging out the window and larking around, and some very big tattooed Marquesan males.

If one thing is sure the local population will look after you. Polynesians live communal lives and visitors are often incorporated into the extended family. When Lu had to fly to Hiva Oa for her operation I calmed her fears saying the locals would look after her, make sure she got to where she was going, take care of her. And so they did and Lu was sold on Polynesia.

Provisions

Nearly everything in the Marquesas arrives on the supply ship every couple of weeks or so. Everything bar some fruit and vegetables and fresh fish. Flour for the bakery, eggs, meat, dry goods and tins, all of this arrives by sea from Papeete. If the supply ship is late for any reason then the shops start running out of things. In Nuka Hiva the ship was late and there were no eggs to be had and the bakery only had enough flour for a few more days before the baguettes ran out.

In the townships like Atuona, Taiohae and Hakahau on Ua Pou, you can hardly call them towns, the basics can be found. The bakers produce beautiful French baguettes, but only if you get there early. There are a few small grocery shops where you can get the basics. In Taiohae there is a truck that has fresh fruit and vegetables from a small market garden if you get there early. By 0900 it was often sold out. Not until you get to Papeete can you think about reprovisioning properly.

One of the things that puzzles newcomers to the islands is the fact you can't buy fruit in the markets. The reason for this has an elegant Polynesian simplicity to it. Everyone here has fruit trees or has family that own them so no one needs to buy fruit. The fruit trees all 'belong' to someone, even the laden mango tree on an isolated mountainside and you should always ask before helping yourself. You will almost always be offered more than you can carry and return laden down with more mangoes, bananas, coconuts and pamplemousse than you know what to do with. Now it's your turn to find some small gift on the boat to reciprocate with. It's the Polynesian way.

Eating out

Eating out is also a bit hit and miss in the Marquesas. On the more populated islands there will be a small hotel of some description which will have a restaurant. In Atuona there are a couple of cafés but little else. In Taiohae likewise there are a couple of cafés and a pizzeria. Around the bay is a hotel with a restaurant. Wonderfully in the village of Hatiheu on the north side of Nuka Hiva there is Chez Yvonne. If you sail around to Anaho Bay and climb up to the ridge you can descend down into the village of Haiheu. The scale of the Marquesas, these mountains jutting out of the sea, mean it's quite difficult to judge how high that ridge is. It seemed very high to our little band of adventurers who all puffed and panted to the top before gambolling downhill to the village. Chez Yvonne survives by repute, there are very few tourists around, and serves good local food with a French flair to it. And cold beer which you need quite a lot of after the hike to get here. Our party elected to return by local speed boat and despite the eye-watering cost, there were no volunteers for the hike back to Anaho Bay.

CAUTION

You are prohibited from bringing in more than 2 litres of spirits and 2 litres of wine per person into French Polynesia. If Customs searches your boat and discovers more it will be confiscated and you will have to pay a fine of anywhere between €200–500. We are not talking 'cruiser myth' here as I have been in the same anchorage as a boat that was searched, 80 litres of wine confiscated and a fine levied. On *Skylax* we were boarded by Customs but explained that we had drunk most of our wine stock on board (nearly true). You are also limited to 200 cigarettes and 250g of tobacco.

These islands are like mountains, very steep-to mountains, plonked into the ocean

should wear, who they should worship, and how life imbued with the western work ethic should be.

After Melville it is Gauguin and his canvasses that shape our ideas of the Marquesas. He lived in Atuona for years, in the embrace of this or that wahine, and produced the paintings whose colour and brush-strokes bleed sunlight and sensuality. Life on the islands is still simple and achieved without too much effort. There are fish there to be caught. A patch of land is cultivated for vegetables. Fruit trees scattered around the island are owned by families who take what they need. A few pigs are kept and sometimes a few cows. And if the supply ship doesn't come in no one is going to starve.

Open air fish market on Taiohae in the Marquesas. You need to be quick when the fish arrives as it all disappears pretty quickly

We left the Marquesas from Anaho Bay on the NE corner of Nuka Hiva with a 35 knot squall and rain pushing us west with just two reefs in the main and nothing else up. Eventually the huge squall system passed and we put out some more sail to bucket on towards Rangiroa in the Tuamotus. By the next day the wind was a lot lighter and we put up more sail. From the weather forecast we knew the wind was going to go light, but we reckoned we could still maintain a reasonable speed and get to the Tiputa Pass into Rangiroa by early morning on the fifth day. The wind gods decided otherwise and overnight the wind died down and we slowed to a stop.

The sea by now was magically calm and so we relaxed, read a lot, cooked some good food, had a glass of wine or two (in wine glasses – it was that calm), and revised our arrival date to Saturday morning instead of Friday. It's what being at sea is about, none of those desperate journeys to arrive at some scheduled time, just drifting along like sailing ships of yore used to.

Slow light wind day in the Pacific

We are heading towards the Dangerous Archipelago, the graveyard of sailing ships in days past and a lot of yachts in days not long past. The currents around the atolls of the Tuamotus are variable and strong. The atolls and reefs are not well charted even to this day. And the low-lying atolls themselves are difficult to see. No high mountains like the Marquesas and the main islands around Tahiti, just coral with a few motus, where sand has built up upon the coral to just a few feet above sea level.

One of the mysteries of navigation in this area is how the remaining three ships under Magellan missed all of these reefs and islands. He had finally made it into the Pacific from the bottom of South America through the maze of channels now named after him. After leaving the coast of South America the boats found the winds so steady and the weather so temperate Magellan called the ocean Pacifico. They found two islands, St Paul's which was too deep to anchor off and Shark Island, which had neither water nor vegetation. As they proceeded northwest to about where we supped on fine food and wine, the crew on the three remaining boats were near to starving. Antonio Pigafetta who kept a record of the passage describes what it was like.

'We ate biscuit, but in truth it was biscuit no longer, but a powder full of worms, for the worms had devoured it's whole substance, and in addition it was stinking with the urine of rats. So great was the want of food that we were forced to eat the hides with which the main yard was covered to prevent the chafing against the rigging. These hides, exposed to the sun and rain and wind, had become so hard, that we were obliged first to soften them by putting them overboard for four or five days, after which we put them on the embers

Marquesas to the Tuamotos

Day 1

21st June Anchor up in Anaho Bay.

21st June 2000. Wind ENE5-6 Speed 7 knots. Starry, starry night. Seas lumpy with the occasional sploosh into the cockpit.

Day 2

22nd June 1800. Wind ENE 4 Speed 6 knots. Clear night and wind eased. Chicken salad for supper.

Day 3

23rd June 1200. Wind NNE3-4 Speed 4 knots. Sails slatting a bit downwind in the swell. But progress. Daily run 138M.

Day 4

24th June 0830. Wind NNE 3-4 Speed 3·8 knots. Beautiful calm morning.

Day 5

25th June 1930. Wind SSW 1. Main down and stowed. Genny rolled up. Sea is unnaturally calm so dinner with wine... in wine glasses!

Day 6

26th June 1000. Through the main pass at Rangiroa and anchored off in the lagoon inside.

And then the wind died away in the middle of the Pacific so out came a bottle of wine to go with the salmon and cream pasta

and ate them thus. We had also to make use of sawdust for food, and rats became such a delicacy that we paid half a ducat apiece for them.'
Antonio Pigafetta

For Captain Cook on his first voyage into the Pacific the perils of navigation are vividly recorded in his detailed diaries. Often the ships would sail up and down a reef at night listening to the roar of the breakers on the reef and sounding with the lead where possible. They would sail in through unknown passes reliant on the pilot forward calling depths and sighting dangers. The presence of uncharted land or reefs was deduced from birds flying out to the boat, from logs of wood or other organic detritus in the water, from cumulus cloud over the atolls which is indeed the first sign telling you that you are approaching an atoll. Like us Cook didn't seem to have much luck fishing, recording that off the Tuamotus 'Here we caught a King Fish, being the first fish we have got in these Seas.'

I've been doing lots of reading on Magellan, Cook, Darwin and Fitzroy, the ExEx under Wilkes, so I'm in awe of these navigators and their sailing and pilotage skills around a largely unknown ocean. For us we have charts, though they are acknowledged not to be accurate for the Tuamotu archipelago, satellite navigation,

Happy spear-fishing local in Rangiroa. And that was just snorkelling around the dock

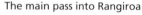

The main pass into Rangiroa

Ashore in the Tuamotus

The atolls, even the most developed like Rangiroa, have little in the way of provisions or restaurants. The more remote atolls have literally nothing except maybe the odd pearl farmer and some are uninhabited. On Rangiroa you have a couple of hotels that have restaurants and a snack bar on the edge of the water on the pass into the atoll. The fish here are fed from the snack bar and I saw more fish here eating lunch than I did snorkelling in the pass.

Lunch stop a dinghy ride away

a French pilot book for the archipelago, radar, and some good polarised sun glasses to cut down the glare over the reefs. We are off the Tikepuka Pass into Rangiroa lagoon in the early morning and motor through the flat water between the breaking surf on either side to get into the lagoon.

The short passage down to Tahiti is a hop-step-and-jump at 175 miles, bringing us into the fleshpots of Papeete and wonderfully civilized shopping for provisions. This is the capital of French Polynesia, and along with Moorea and a handful of motus, forms the 'Windward' part of the Society Islands. Cook, Bligh, Bougainville and countless whaling and trading ships visited here on their voyages around and through the Pacific and many of our images of the place are shaped by the experiences of these early sailors. This was paradise, Fiddlers Green where the women were beautiful and free with their virtue, a seaman's heaven, where there was water, water enough to wash away the grime of the voyage, where there was meat and game, fresh fruit and vegetables, and where the comely wahines would accommodate the priapic sailors. No wonder many of them wanted to stay, deserted ship and went bush with a local lady, hated the captain and officers who forced them to leave, fomented mutiny which in the case of Bligh, did happen later.

Bligh was Cook's navigator on his troubled third voyage to the Pacific and in 1787 was appointed commander of the *Bounty*. The ship was to sail to the Pacific

PACIFIC

Ashore in Tahiti

'It's a bit built up isn't it.' 'Hate it, not a real place'. 'We're moving on to somewhere more real'. Well that was a few of the comments but you need to balance those against others. 'Love it, love Carrefour, love the restaurants, love the buzz'. 'Love the anchorage with good swimming off the reef and a bar ashore'. 'Love the shopping'.

I'm not sure why some cruisers expected to find a few native huts and a pristine beach in what is the biggest city on the leg from Panama to New Zealand until you get to Auckland. It's actually not all that big, but it has a wonderful range of services; everything from marinas, fuel docks, gas, huge French supermarkets like Carrefour, and lots of bars and restaurants of all persuasions. I'm firmly in the latter camp, especially as we ran out of gas at five in the morning in the approaches to Papeete so no hot drinks until I zoomed off down to the nearby Mobil garage and swapped my empty cylinder for a full one and bought some baguettes at the same time. It's good to get back to a busy city, even a small one, and indulge in all those things you have run short of.

We are anchored off Marina Taina, there is Wi-Fi in the anchorage, the Carrefour supermarket is a 10 minute walk away, Papeete central is accessible on le truck, the small trucks with wooden seats and a ply top that run back and forth to Papeete, the fuel dock is nearby, there are restaurants and bars, and yes it isn't cheap given that everything, or a lot of everything is shipped in, but even so it's great to indulge. There are plenty of smaller more intimate places in the Marquesas and Tuamotus, but for the time being I'm a pig in a muddy place and happy.

Provisions

There are a number of supermarkets in Papeete and these are supermarkets with aisles and trolleys, where you can get just about anything. At least anything manufactured in France along with a few items from New Zealand and Australia. It comes at a bit of a price, but then when you are low on pesto or salami or brie, it seems worth it. There are also smaller grocery shops, but by and large it's worth making a trip to the supermarket.

Apart from the supermarkets there is a fresh fruit and vegetable market in downtown Tahiti with the best selection of fruit and vegetables you will get until New Zealand or Australia. There is everything here from the basic potatoes and onions to frisée lettuce, cabbage, red cabbage, spring onions, parsley and coriander, all sorts of vegetables you won't have seen for ages. And a good selection of fruit including wonderful mangoes, papaya and bananas. You can also try taro, breadfruit and plantains, though apart from plantains, I'm not a fan of taro or breadfruit. Stalls also sell jars of sauces, pastes of uncertain use and bottled fruit and vegetables. Upstairs in the market are some local restaurants worthy of lunch serving everything from Chinese to Indian and French-style food.

You can also get gas bottles filled and it's worth remembering that until you get to the more populated islands like Rarotonga in the Cook Islands or Neiafu in Tonga that this will be your last chance to get cooking gas.

Eating out

Eating out varies from street stalls to expensive and very up-market French restaurants. In Marina Taina the Dinghy Bar is the haunt of yachties passing through and next door is Casa Bianca serving good pizzas. On the waterfront boardwalk are a couple of more upmarket restaurants including Les Quai des Iles, excellent French food with a Polynesian twist, though at a bit of a price. For a more local experience there are the food stalls that set up around the docks in Papeete with everything from Polynesian, Chinese, and French-ish snack meals. It's well worth the visit or is just outside the cockpit if you are on the yacht pontoon in the town basin.

Marina Taina looking out to the anchorage under the reef. A little bit of civilization in the middle of the Pacific

Papeete market with one of the best selections of fruit and vegetables until you get to New Zealand or Australia

Les Roulottes

These are the food trucks that set up on the waterfront docks in downtown Papeete, but can be found parked up in other places like a petrol station or some patch of ground near a beach where there are people about. The waterfront docks are the best place where les Roulottes set up around dusk. The food is varied and cheap. There is Chinese with chow mein and other noodle dishes and Peking duck. Pizza trucks are popular. Crepes with different fillings savoury or sweet. Salads and sometimes *poisson cru*. And ice cream vans.

The whole place buzzes with families wandering around keeping the kids occupied and teenagers trying to look cool while dribbling ice cream on their mobile phones. Everyone is out and about in the cool of the evening just chilling out and it's a good place to people watch while eating some good street food.

to load breadfruit plants and take them to the West Indies to cultivate for food for the slave population there. Anyone who has tasted a breadfruit would need to be hungry, really hungry. It is used as a vegetable and tastes something like boiled cardboard or mushy glue. While Bligh delayed leaving Tahiti his crew were delighting in the wahines ashore and eating well. That means a lot to these sailors of yore and not surprisingly they didn't want to leave. Even Bligh wrote that

'The women are handsome … and have sufficient delicacy to make them admired and beloved – The chiefs have taken such a liking to our people that they have rather encouraged their stay among them than otherwise, and even made promises of large possessions … to fix themselves in the midst of plenty in the finest island in the world where they need not labour, and where the allurements of dissipation are more than equal to anything that can be conceived.'

The mutiny on the *Bounty* was almost a foregone conclusion with Fletcher and the crew living in a sailor's paradise and then being forced by Bligh to leave it all behind.

You can see Moorea a short distance across the water from Papeete. Moorea and the Iles Sous le Vent, or Leeward Islands, lie scattered to the west of Tahiti. These are often the islands that shape ideas of what a South Sea island looks like. The peaks rear up out of the water. A barrier reef encloses blue water off the coast. The slopes are covered in tropical rain forest and the beaches are all white sand. Even the names are evocative: Huahine, Raiatea, Tahaa, and Bora Bora.

Moorea was the setting for *South Pacific*, the movie that is, and the steep peaks in fantastic shapes jutting up into the tradewind clouds are a fantasy landscape. It

Anchorage in Opunohu Bay on Moorea. Just swimming, eating and the occasional walk ashore

Ashore in the Iles Sous le Vent

Surprisingly there are good supermarkets in Fare on Huahine, Uturoa on Raitea and on Bora Bora where you can do some final provisioning before setting off to points further west.

Dotted around the islands are some fine restaurants like the Maitai at Haamene, Taravana Yacht Club on the southwest corner of Tahaa with convenient moorings, Chez Louise on a motu off the west coast of Tahaa, the marina restaurant on Raitea, the Mauari in Fare on Huahine, making the islands a bit of a gastronome's paradise. All through French Polynesia, in fact all through the South Pacific, you will find Chinese restaurants and snack bars set up by Chinese merchants who have filtered down through the islands over the last couple of centuries.

View from the very fine restaurant at Taravana YC on Tahaa

is the place where Bali Hai existed and Bloody Mary presided over, a Hollywood fantasy you can almost believe existed in this setting.

Cruising around the Society Islands turns up some interesting culinary delights. They seem to attract eccentric locals and odd French folk who have decided to sell up and set up a restaurant or a cafe in some out of the way places. In Haamene on Tahaa we were storm bound for five days and got to visit the restaurant ashore a few times. Haamene is a hamlet with just a small grocery shop, a post office and the Maitai restaurant. Bruno François in the restaurant-cum-café trained as a chef in France and came out to Papeete to work in a restaurant. He fell in love with the islands and bought this restaurant on Tahaa. That's how you get fine French dining, *soup de poisson*, *blanquette de veau*, *cassoulet*, *salad au chevre chauds*, and excellent coffee, in a hamlet on a little known island in the Pacific. How long Bruno lasts is anyone's guess, but I hope he is there next time I visit.

Sometimes the received idea of the Tropics is all sun and white sandy beaches and coconut palms. There are plenty of beaches and coconuts, but it rains more often in the Tropics than most people think and at times can be grey and squally for days. So it was when we left Raitea for Palmerston Atoll and Neiafu on Tonga. Palmerston Atoll was to be no more than a two-day breather for us en route, though as it turned out it was not to be.

For nearly two days it rained, there was more son et lumiere than anyone needs, so much so that we turned off all the radios and put the handheld GPS in the oven which is a makeshift Faraday Cage in the event of a lightning strike. And then things fell apart. Lu was off-watch after lunch when the wind started to increase. I called her up and we started to reef. As the wind rapidly increased to 50 knots we struggled to get all sail off and then steered directly downwind doing over 7 knots under bare poles. At times the wind was hitting 60 knots and the seas rapidly heaped up and dumped themselves into the cockpit. At times like these you go into lock-down mode, all the hatches are closed, we are in full wet weather gear with safety harnesses clipped on. I'm steering downwind through the waves with the cockpit cushions floating around me as waves dump into the cockpit at odd times and the gods have decided that a big fat hot sun will come out and shine down on us in this windy maelstrom.

It's a funny feeling when you feel relieved when the wind has dropped to 40 knots. We put out a scrap of genny to keep us moving so the collapsing waves don't catch up to the boat and plop into the cockpit. During the entire circumnavigation this was the strongest sustained winds we had over the open ocean. After three hours the wind was back down under 30 knots and we hoisted the main again and let the tension drain out of us. We had a cup of tea and special chocolate cookies, reserved for times like this, when you need to spoil yourself a bit.

Lu and I didn't say anything until the wind was into the 30s, but both of us were thinking of our encounter with Tropical Storm Peter in the Atlantic in December 2003 and of what to do next. I kept edging us north towards the safety of equatorial latitudes with both of us wondering if this was the start of a very early season cyclone in the South Pacific. Glad to say it wasn't.

In the early morning of the sixth day we nosed into the exposed anchorage off Palmerston Atoll. Really this is just a bight on the leeward side of the atoll with several moorings. These are already taken by other yachts and the anchorage close to the reef is in 20m with the reef just behind should the wind go around to the north and northwest. Sadly we decide that the prudent option is to carry on for Neiafu on Tonga.

Palmerston Atoll has a population of just 50 or so people and gets one supply ship a year. Any visiting yachts bring in emergency supplies and get people off the island and onwards to Tonga where they can get flights to other places. The atoll is in many ways self-sufficient with a lot of fish in the lagoon and a lot of coconuts. Vegetables are grown and chicken and pigs roam the motus. Not that we got to see any of this as we sailed the remaining 620 miles to Tonga.

Raitea to Tonga

Day 1

10th Sept. Anchor up at Raitea and headed out through Passe Rautoanui.

10th Sept 1500. Wind ESE 6 Speed 6·8 Third reef in main and gybed genny over. Big old swell up to 3m.

Day 2

11th Sept 0400. Wind ESE 6 Speed 6·2. Son et lumiere with lots of lightning. Rain.

1200. Wind SE 5 Speed 6·5. And still it rains. Everything very soggy. Daily run 155M.

1400. Barometer drops 8mb in 2 hours. Huge squall system with max wind 60 knots. Wind at 45–50 knots for several hours. Run under bare poles. Boat battened down and waves in the cockpit at odd times.

Day 3

12th Sept 1500. Wind ESE 6 Speed 6·6. Sorted out the main ready to re-hoist. Took down French Polynesia courtesy flags. Drying out.

Day 4

13th Sept 2000. Wind E 4–5 Speed 6·5. Skylax scorching along. Comfortable under autopilot. Big fat moon.

Day 5

14th Sept 1200. Wind ENE 5. Speed 6·9. Good sailing and sunny. Daily run 159M.

Day 6

15th Sept 0900. Off the anchorage at Palmerston Atoll. No moorings free and anchorage suspect so decide to carry on to Tonga.

Day 7

16th Sept 0900. Wind NE 4 Speed 6·0. Very salty deck and cockpit. Gentle sailing.

Day 8

17th Sept 0900. Wind ENE 2–3 Speed 5·0. Bread in the oven. Caught good-sized tuna. Showers in the cockpit. Main with one reef.

Day 9

18th Sept 1800. Wind E 4 Speed 6·0. Changed pole to port side and gybed genny over. Cloud building in the SE.

Day 10

19th Sept 1200. Wind NE 4 Speed 4·4. Slowing down for approach to waypoint off Neiafu. 53M to go. Daily run a pathetic 115M in light winds.

2000. Wind S 3. Speed 3·6. Rain, rain, and more rain! Lu's coconut fish for dinner.

Day 11

20th Sept 0930. On a mooring at Neiafu. Day changes to 21st as we have crossed the International Date Line on passage.

Small amusements

There are things that take on a quite disproportionate sense of importance on passage.

One is the goody bag on night watches where we keep a selection of biscuits, chocolate and other munchies. I'm not a chocolate person generally (except maybe for fine dark chocolate truffles made by some renowned Belgian chocolatier), but on passage I'm as rabid as anyone else for a Mars Bar or a Twix. Once on my own and hove-to in a gale in the southeastern Mediterranean (on passage from Port Said to Turkey), I managed to consume a whole catering box of some Egyptian coconut flavoured chocolate bars that I would normally never touch.

The midday 24 hour run entry in the log is another important time of day. Apart from the fact that you want to know what the daily run is, we also run a competition with an outstanding prize. At midday everyone submits their estimate of the next 24 hour run which goes into the unofficial log book. Next midday whoever is closest gets (with three crew on board) three points, the next closest two points, and the last one point. With two or four crew then the points awarded are calculated proportionately. The competition is intense as the prize for the winner is a meal and wine in the restaurant of choice when we arrive. The losers pay! I've had to pay for some outstanding meals which I get to participate in and likewise, I've been rewarded with the same meals.

It rained off and on, mostly on and mostly heavy, most of the way to Neiafu. Consolation prize was a very nice tuna landed on the way so we had fish all the way to Tonga. We arrived early Sunday morning and because Tongans take Sunday seriously, the Catholic church above the anchorage was transmitting island gospel most of the day, and I mean live not recorded, we picked up a mooring and cleaned up and dried out the boat a bit. We were early to bed.

Neiafu lives and breathes cruising yachts. They make up the largest number of visitors by far and restaurants and bars around the bay have sprung up to cater for the visitors. On Fridays the bars are full as the Moorings charter company organises an informal race around the bay. Simple rules: boats over 30ft do the long course (about four miles) while boats under 30ft do the short course (about three miles). First to finish wins: no handicap, no disputes. It's free to enter and everyone gets a prize donated by a local business.

The cruising around these sheltered waters is idyllic. It's all turquoise water over the reefs, palm trees ashore and the odd bar or restaurant built in an out of the way spot with a sunset view that astounds. As you sail around the islands and reefs humpback whales swim serenely by. They come to these islands to calve and spend a bit of time looking after the new calves before heading off to colder climes. As we left the Vava'u group in the north for the Ha'apai group in the middle, a mother and calf swam beside us for a while, no stress or strain, just the occasional undulation of the tail to stay at cruising speed.

As you sail down the chain of islands to the main Tongan island of Nuku'alofa it's salient to remember that you are sailing down a giant crack in the sea bottom, the Tongan trench, where volcanoes suddenly appear out of the water and the chart is peppered with warnings of volcanic activity reported on such a such a date. One of

Nice tuna on the way to Tonga

Ashore in Tonga

Like a lot of the islands Tonga gets most of its supplies from New Zealand. Much of the meat, basic stores like flour and sugar, tinned goods, all of these come from New Zealand.

Provisions

In Neiafu most things can be found with a little persistence. The butcher (Pete the meat) is up a back street. You can get groceries at Pua's general store, bread at the Austrian bakery up the hill or in town, fruit and vegetables from the market on the wharf.

In Nuku'alofa shopping is easier with a big covered market with an excellent selection of fruit and vegetables. There are big supermarkets and smaller grocery shops and stocking up for the onward passage to New Zealand is a doddle. Except you do not want to stock up on anything, from fresh meat to fruit and vegetables, eggs, all sorts of food items, that will be confiscated by the MAF (Ministry of Agriculture and Fisheries) officers when you clear in.

Eating out

All sorts of ex-pats have landed up on Tonga and stayed. The restaurants and bars around the waterfront on Neiafu serve a range of food with a good pan-Pacific take on Tongan ingredients. You get Italian-Tongan, English-Tongan, Australian-Tongan and at the Ovava you get wood-fired pizzas. On Tapana Island around the other side of Neiafu you can have a truly surreal but wonderful dining experience at Maria and Eduardo's place. Anchor off the reef near the floating gallery and then cross to the island where

Fruit and vegetable market in Neiafu

you get authentic, well with a bit of a Tongan take, Spanish tapas and main courses and likely some flamenco as well.

Down the island chain the theme goes on. In one horse Pangai there is the Mariners Café with an ex-yachty tending to the menu.

In Nuku'alofa most yachts anchor off Big Mama's, a motu around 1½ miles from Nuku'alofu port. Big Mama has more typically Tongan food as well as Tongan hospitality. While we were there Big Mama's husband had his 60th birthday and everyone in the anchorage was invited to the birthday feast. Roast pork, *poisson cru*, salads, sautéed potatoes, food of all sorts was carried out by the bucketful and everyone toasted the patron and Big Mama and we all wanted to stay there forever.

The general store in Neiafu

Swimming pigs

You hear stories about swimming pigs around Tonga and like a lot of stories you take it with a grain of salt. Except the pigs here, or some of them, really do swim in order to eat shellfish at low tide. They don't swim that far, just across a bit of deeper water to get to the shallower water where they can graze, if that's the proper word, on the shellfish And they aren't the most elegant swimmers, but somehow over the centuries they have adapted their behaviour to include eating shellfish when the tide is out.

My one regret is that I didn't get to taste roast pork from the piggy who dined on shellfish.

the worries for a small sailing yacht is that undersea eruptions produce vast numbers of gaseous bubbles in the water and this reduces the density of the water. Less density means that your boat has less buoyancy and could conceivably become negatively buoyant and sink. That's the theory and it doesn't half concentrate your senses looking for bubbles rising up to the sea's surface.

Pangai in the Ha'apai group is more or less halfway down the island chain from Neiafu in the Vava'u group. Pangai is a gem far away from the comparative metropolis of Neiafu. You anchor off the sleepy village and can get a few supplies and good food at the Mariners Café run by a yachty who has stopped for a while longer than she thought she would in Pangai. Not far from here Fletcher Christian set Bligh adrift with eighteen other crewman in a 23ft launch.

The mutiny on the *Bounty* occurred off this coast on the 28th April 1789. If you watched any of the movies on the mutiny on the *Bounty* you might think that it occurred in Tahiti or nearby. In fact it occurred in the sea area off Tofua, a volcanic island halfway along the Tongan Trench. The island is still there puffing smoke and ash out of the summit. When Bligh was cast adrift with 18 of the crew he first headed for Tofua to look for food and water to augment the meagre supplies they had been given by Fletcher Christian. On landing they were attacked by natives and one of the crew was killed. All they managed to get were a few coconuts.

Putting to sea again in the launch Bligh decided to sail for the East Indies. When they took stock of their food supplies it came to precious little for the remaining

Around Neiafu there are 'proper' tropical anchorages galore

Umu

Various companies can organise a typical Tongan feast, which is similar to the Maori hangi. The general term in the Pacific for the method used is umu, effectively a pit barbecue that is covered over so that food is baked and steamed at the same time. The Maori term from New Zealand, a hangi, is frequently used.

Essentially a pit is dug in the earth and wood piled in the bottom and allowed to burn down to hot embers. Rocks are placed in the earth pit with banana leaves or more often these days wet hessian sacks over them. Baskets of food, typically pork,

plantains, sweet potato, taro and fish, are placed on top, more banana leaves or wet hessian sacks are placed on top of the baskets and then earth is piled on top. The food is sort of half steamed and half baked.

I've eaten my fair share of this sort of food at Maori hangis and I should confess it's not my favourite mode of cooking. For me the flavours are too mixed and the meat is often fatty without the crispness you get from full-on roasting. The food also tends to get smoked as much as roasted in the process. Despite my reservations you should try it at least once to make up your own mind on umu cooking.

18 men on board. Just 50lbs of bread, 20lbs of pork, 28 gallons of water, three bottles of wine and five quarts of rum. Bligh had no charts and just a quadrant and his pocket watch to navigate with. And his steely will.

Although they sailed through islands on the way, through the Fijian archipelago and through the Torres Strait between Australia and New Guinea, they did not land for fear of attack by the natives. Bligh kept a diary on his epic voyage and the temptation to land on one of the islands to look for food and water must have been enormous. At the very beginning of the voyage Bligh rationed the food they had.

In his journal Bligh wrote …

… I adopted one [a musket ball weighing an ounce] as the proportion of weight that each person should receive of bread, and a quarter of a pint of water, at eight in the morning, at noon, and at sun-set. Today I gave about half an ounce of pork for dinner, which, though any moderate person would have considered only a mouthful, was divided into three or four.

As the launch sailed eastwards conditions on board got worse. The food was rationed to smaller amounts and they eliminated the midday rations and only ate in the morning and at night, if eating it can be called. Bligh records that,

Spam and mutton flaps

If you wander ashore in Tonga and lots of other islands you can't fail to notice there are a lot of fat people around. Obesity is a real problem in the Pacific islands with the World Health Organisation identifying eight of the world's ten most obese nations as being in the Pacific. Cases of Type 2 Diabetes have rocketed and strokes and heart disease are now endemic.

If you go into the smallest shop in the Pacific islands you are bound to find tins of spam and corned beef. In many of the islands cheap cuts of meat like mutton flaps, the fatty flesh around the stomach of a sheep, are exported to the islands from New Zealand and Australia. Where once the locals fished and farmed small-holdings and had a healthy diet revolving around

seafood and fruit and vegetables, you now find a diet revolving around imported processed food like spam and corned beef. In fact it's cheaper to buy mutton flaps in Tonga than it is to buy local fresh fish in the market.

In Tonga the last king, Taufa'ahau Tupou IV who died in 2006, held the record for being the world's heaviest monarch. He weighed in at 440lbs, over 31 stone or nearly 200kgs. Where once a king was a warrior, presumably honed and fit for battle, now he is massively obese. Likewise the locals who once walked or rode horses to get from A to B now drive. And all that spam, corned beef and the mutton flaps, high in saturated fat, have distorted the diet to produce an obesity time bomb in the Pacific.

I generally broke mine [bread] into small pieces, and eat it in my allowance of water, out of a coconut shell, with a spoon: economically avoiding to take too large a piece at a time, so that I was as long at dinner as if it had been a much more plentiful meal.

Bligh reached Kupang on East Timor after 48 days. Apart from the death of a crewman on Tofua, all of those in the boat survived. Fletcher Christian sailed back to Tahiti to collect sweethearts and others and then sailed to Pitcairn where the *Bounty* was burnt to prevent anyone leaving. It turned out not to be the tropical Arcadia imagined by the mutineers.

Nuku'alofa sits at the southern end of the island chain, the capital of Tonga and the logical jumping off point for New Zealand. Before we set off for Nuku'alofa there were mixed reports about the place. Mostly the place was damned as dull, difficult and not a patch on Neiafu. A fair number of yachts decided it wasn't worth visiting Nuku'alofa and were leaving direct from Neiafu for New Zealand. We decided we would take a look at the place and that turned out to be a good option. Sometimes you need to take cruiser rumour with a goodly pinch of salt.

Most yachts arriving in Nuku'alofa anchor off Big Mama's Yacht Club. Big Mama and Earl run a very friendly club here on a motu over a mile from the harbour at Nuku'alofa itself. You can swim, snorkel over the reef, eat and drink ashore, and the club runs a regular boat across and back from Nuku'alofa.

Good times at Big Mamas before the passage south

Passage out of the Tropics and down to the southern latitudes of New Zealand

The passage from Tonga to New Zealand is the great lemming leap from the Tropics and settled Trade Wind weather into the sub-Tropics and unsettled spring weather. Hours, days, weeks are spent analysing weather, signing up for weather routing, downloading masses of GRIB files and generally just worrying about it.

There was a time when you left on passage with just a 24 hour synoptic forecast from a newspaper. Then along came stand-alone weatherfaxes and phoning the local Met office. And then came the internet, GRIB files, and lots of bad advice in forums and other cobbled together web sites. The internet and weather routing services has spawned a group of cruisers who somehow believe that you can pull down a seven day set of GRIB files telling you what the wind and wave heights will be for the next week and set off anticipating a smooth trip with little disruption from naughty lows, fronts, ridges and any other meteorological phenomenon that might blight your trip. Well it doesn't work that way: weather is weather and as Bob McDavit, the New Zealand weather guru who helps route yachts down to New Zealand will tell you, forecasting is just trying to make a pattern out of chaos. We aren't anywhere close to understanding the complex interactions of pressure systems and making sub-Tropic passages is not like hopping on a train or plane to get from A to B.

As it turned out our weather window wasn't all that settled. We left Tonga heading for Minerva Reef, but 150 miles out it looked OK, though not that great, to head on a rhumb line course for Opua. So we did. We had a front pass over with gusts to around 35 knots though with the wind in the east it just bustled us along towards New Zealand. Afterwards came the SW winds and we tightened *Skylax* up and though getting nudged just to the east of our rhumb line, we were secure in the knowledge we would have a couple of days of motoring through the calm winds of the high pressure and then in all probability easterlies for the final part of the passage.

Motoring through the high was slow with an awkward sea and dirty bottom, but then the promised easterlies slowly kicked in rising to 30 plus knots at times and then even went to the ENE making for a fast final part of the passage. We slowed up on the last night out so we would have a daylight approach to the Bay of Islands and sailed right down to the buoyed channel leading to Opua.

One other thing that cruisers in the Tropics encounter here is that it is cold after tropical days and nights. All the woollies come out of the locker where they have been consigned for nearly a year and wet weather gear keeps the wind chill out. It's only spring in New Zealand and sitting here in Opua it's definitely a lot more chilly than up north in the Tropics.

PACIFIC

Tonga to New Zealand

Day 1

2nd Nov 0930. Anchor up at Pangaimotu. Heading through the reefs en route to Minerva Reef.
1100 Wind ESE 3-4 Speed 5·3 knots. Cross Tropic of Capricorn. Officially out of the Tropics.

Day 2

3rd Nov 1200. Wind ESE 4 Speed 6·5 knots. Changed course for direct run to Opua. Daily run 163M.

Day 3

4th Nov 1500. Wind SSW 2 Speed 4·8 knots. Wind light so motor-sailing. Overflown by RNZAF plane who ask for our details on VHF.

Day 4

5th Nov 0500. Wind NNE 4 Speed 4·9 knots. Sailing through primordial soup with squid everywhere showing up as phosphorescent flashes in the water.

Day 5

6th Nov 1500. Wind S 3 Speed 4·0. Sailing slowly.
500 miles to waypoint off New Zealand. Halfway?

Day 6

7th Nov 0800. Wind NE 2. Speed 4·2. Motor-sailing.
Caught 3kg tuna. Came aboard easily. Wind veering to NE.

Day 7

8th Nov 1500. Wind ENE 4 Speed 6·3. Wind increasing steadily. Sunny but still chilly.

Day 8

9th Nov 1200. Wind ENE 6 Speed 7·3. Zooming.
Fast, wet, and sun! Daily run 164M.

Day 9

10th Nov 1100. Alongside quarantine dock in Opua Marina.

Australasia The term encompasses New Zealand, Australia and the Pacific islands south of Asia in that region. It is a bit of a mish-mash term in the absence of any others and is derived from Australis meaning 'southern' so we get 'the lands south of Asia'.

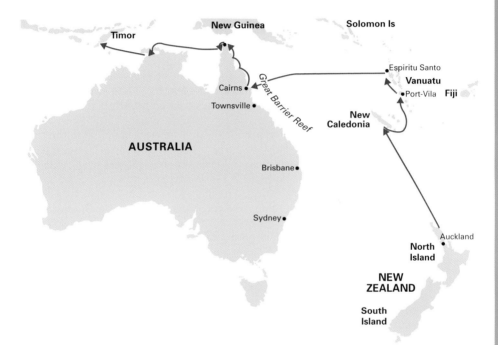

Crossing an ocean in a small yacht is a bit like living your life backwards.
At the beginning you die, then you get fitter and younger, and then when
you arrive you have an orgasmic celebration and the idea that life is just beginning.
Douglas Graeme

New Zealand

After a relatively easy passage of dodging fronts and motoring through a high, *Skylax* arrived safely in Opua. All yachts arriving in New Zealand must be cleared not just by Customs and Immigration, but also by the Ministry of Agriculture and Fisheries officials (MAF). The import of foodstuffs, plants and animals is strictly controlled in New Zealand, much to the consternation of some. At Opua you go alongside a detached pontoon and wait for the officials to come on board to check the boat over. Visitors sometimes complain about this strict control over the importation of food and plant matter, which can include tourist items made from

Opua Marina, a popular place to clear in and out of New Zealand

wood and bark, seeds, some herbs and spices, any meat including cured meat like bacon or ham, anything that might carry diseases that could affect the flora and fauna in the country.

Animal and plant immigrants have been arriving in these islands since the time of the Maori and the first Europeans. The first great migration to New Zealand was not the Maori but the Moriori, possibly Melanesian explorers who settled in New Zealand around 500AD. Around 1000–1100AD what is now called the 'Great Fleet', probably 10 or 12 catamarans, sailed from an area around the Cook Islands to New Zealand. These early explorers navigated using the direction and height of the waves, cloud types, by identifying stars and the moon, by observing seabirds and their direction of flight. Later navigators may even have had primitive stick and shell maps.

I can only guess that these early voyagers survived largely on fish they caught, on rainwater from squalls and on a few provisions like coconuts, yams, taro, and sweet potatoes (*kumara*) they bought with them. The Maoris brought these vegetables with them to plant in New Zealand, though only the sweet potato really thrived in the climate. They also arrived at some time with dogs and rats. Dogs and rats were the first mammalian quadrapeds in a country where many of the birds had lost the power of flight because there were no natural quadraped predators. Dogs were a source of food for the Polynesians and rats were also hunted for food.

When Captain Cook arrived he found it difficult to get adequate provisions ashore. The Maoris brought a few sweet potatoes and a few 'stinking fish'. What Cook was pleased to find was that fish were abundant. In the Marlborough Sounds on the top of the South Island he wrote in his Journal that

... Having the Sean [seine net] with us we made a few hauls and caught 300 pounds weight of different sorts of fish, which were equally distributed to the Ship's Company.

He also found good water in the streams and ample supplies of wood to make repairs to the Endeavour. What he didn't find was a good supply of fresh meat and vegetables.

On his second voyage in 1773 Cook had embarked sheep, goats and pigs to release in New Zealand to provide food for the crew. The Maoris ate the goats and sheep and only the pigs survived.

White pig

Maoris call white European settlers 'pakeha'. The origins of the word are a little obscure, but growing up in a small Maori settlement in New Zealand the local boys always used to say the Pakeha was 'white pig' because we tasted like white pig as opposed to wild pig, boar, where the flesh is more red and it has a gamey taste.

Cannibalism in the South Pacific and as far up as Hawaii was practised by the Polynesians, though various reasons are given for the practice. It was something more than just hunger that drove the practice though from Captain Cook's observations, it appeared to be an everyday and quite casual practice.

> Soon after we landed we meet with 2 or 3 of the Natives who not long before must have been regaling themselves upon human flesh, for I got from one of them the bone of the Fore arm of a Man or Woman which was quite fresh, and the flesh had been but lately picked off, which they told us they had eat; they gave us to understand that but a few days before they had taken, Kill'd, and Eat a Boats Crew of their Enemies or strangers, for I believe they look upon all strangers as Enemies. From what we could learn the woman we had seen floating upon the Water was in this Boat and had been drowned in the fray. There was not one of us that had the least doubt but that these people were cannibals; but the finding this bone with part of the sinews fresh upon it was a stronger proof than any we had yet met with, and, in order to be fully satisfied of the truth of what they had told us, we told one of them that it was not the bone of a man, but that of a dog; but he, with great fervency, took hold of his Fore Arm, and told us again that it was that bone: and to convince us that they had eat the flesh he took hold of the flesh of his own Arm with his teeth and made Signs of Eating. A.M., Careen'd, Scrub'd, and pay'd the Starboard side of the Ship; while this was doing some of the Natives came alongside seemingly only to look at us. There was a woman among them who had her Arms, thighs, and Legs cut in several place's; this was done by way of Mourning for her Husband who had very lately been Kill'd and Eat by some of their Enemies as they told us and pointed towards' the place where it was done, which lay somewhere to the Eastward. Mr. Banks got from one of them a Bone of the fore Arm, much in the same state as the one before mentioned; and to show us that they eat the flesh, they bit and Naw'd the bone and draw'd it through their Mouths, and this in such a manner as plainly Shew'd that the flesh to them was a Dainty Bit.
> *Captain Cook's Journal from the first voyage.*

Sadly as we know, Cook was captured and eaten in Hawaii on his third voyage. Eventually parts of his dismembered body were returned, though some of it had already been eaten. A common theory on cannibalism was that the spirit, the *mana* of the dead person, was ingested along with his flesh. It appears now that this interpretation was a later legitimisation of the practice and it is more likely that the destruction of a person's *mana* was the intent. By eating the person you destroyed their *mana*, their standing in the wider tribal community, and profited from their absence.

In all likelihood we will never find out why cannibalism existed amongst the Maori and other Polynesian and Melanesian peoples. Still it shouldn't ever be forgotten that Europeans have practiced cannibalism when *in extremis* such as amongst the survivors of the whaling ship *Essex* or the survivors of the plane crash in the Andes. And as to what human flesh tastes like … white pig I suppose.

With the arrival of Europeans the introduction of foreign species continued apace. Whalers and sealers released goats which eventually prospered. The first small groups of settlers brought sheep and rabbits. Later deer and odd species like the Australian possum were introduced. As Cook had observed earlier, New Zealand was one vast forest, an ideal habitat compared to the vast swathes of desert in Australia. By the early 19th century pigs, possums, deer and rabbits were serious pests and efforts began to cull the animals which were destroying the native flora and fauna. The Maoris had hunted the moa, a huge flightless bird, which is bigger

Ashore in Opua

Opua, a small township, in Europe you would call it a small village, is a logical and easy first stop in New Zealand and the tiny place fills up with yachts arriving from Tonga and Fiji in October and November at the beginning of the southern summer.

Provisions

There is only a small general store in Opua, enough to get a few basics, but not a place to do a proper shop. For that you need to get into nearby Pahia and conveniently a mini-bus does a regular daily run in the summer. Or you can use Geoff's fish and chip oil taxi, Nissan mini-vans that run on old vegetable oil from fish and chip shops and the like. In Pahia there is a Four Square supermarket and a Woolworths as well as bakers and a butchers.

Eating out

Everyone arriving in Opua eventually gets to the Opua Cruising Club, usually on the same day they arrive. The ever convivial Opua Cruising Club serves good food (nothing flash) and drink and everyone gathers on the outside deck overlooking the water to watch the Wednesday night racing You get to go three times for free before they ask you to join for a very reasonable fee. Down near the ferry dock is a more up-market restaurant and a fish and chip shop. New Zealand has arguably the best fish and chips in the world, English claims to that accolade not withstanding. In the marina there is also a café serving good food as well.

What Opua lacks in provisions it more than makes up for in yacht service facilities. There are several yards where there are all the skills to rebuild your yacht or just make a few mods.

Opua Marina

than an emu, to extinction before the arrival of Europeans. In the 19th century other bird species were declining or had become extinct. Even the iconic kiwi was becoming rare.

In 1886 an act was passed to prevent the further introduction of animals into the country and the origins of MAF and the strict control on the importation of animal and plant matter originate from this act. Yachts arriving from outside New Zealand are required to clear with MAF and frequently the boat will be searched for banned material. These regulations are all clearly laid out on the internet along with a list and description of banned goods, so on *Skylax* we got a big bin bag together of the vegetables and and other stuff that would be confiscated. We also put together a bag of 'maybe' goods. These requirements change your attitude to cooking as you come down the New Zealand coast and early that morning we had huge smoothies from leftover bananas, oranges, kiwi fruit and yoghurt. Off Opua we were desperately engaged in a giant fry-up of bacon, eggs and tomatoes, all banned. By the time MAF arrived to the lingering smell of bacon and eggs, it was early in the morning and they hadn't had breakfast while we were full of girth and could hardly have eaten any more of the food we had on board.

When yachts arrive down from the Tropics Opua fairly hums with activity. There is a fair amount of partying around the place with all the boats arriving from Tonga and Fiji and a not insignificant number stay on a lot longer than originally planned.

New Zealand is a popular stopover to get out of the Pacific cyclone season and get the boat back into trim. Yachts often spend a few seasons here cruising up to the Barefoot Islands, Tonga, Fiji, New Caledonia and Vanuatu, in the southern winter and back down to New Zealand for the summer. From Opua we sailed down to Gulf Harbour just north of Auckland. Like others arriving here after 20

One way to bring in custom to your café

The sheep have right of way OK. And there are more than 40 million of them

thousand-odd miles *Skylax* needed some care that included some new rigging and a new sail.

It took months before *Skylax* was ready for sea again. Like lots of other cruisers we hired a car and set off to explore the country I grew up in. And then it was time to return to the UK for work. It was nearly five months before we were back to prepare *Skylax* for the next leg of her voyage. Once back on board the old fears set in. Can I still do this? Have I forgotten what life is like on a small ship? Can I still sail this beast? The first time out after time away is always a bit scary. And that's just to get out of the berth at Gulf Harbour. I gauge the wind direction, which lines to let off first, a nervous look around and a warm goodbye to Paul the dockmaster and we are off. It all goes pretty smoothly and we motor out of the channel and *Skylax* moves to the light swell. Main up, one reef in just for the nerves and we only have our tiny jib on until we get the bigger genoas back from the sailmaker.

Skylax leans slightly with the wind and we are truckling along at 5 and bit knots. Ahead there is black cloud and a bit more wind and soon we are hard on the wind, 20–24 knots apparent, hitting 8 knots. Smooth water and a clean bottom.

We follow the edge of the big ship channel around the edge of Rangitoto and there is Auckland, the harbour bridge (50 years old this year), the Sky Tower, the skycrapers and a few yachts ambling downwind. Then a fleet of Young 88's emerges from the bridge, spinnakers up trying to make some progress against the flood. It's cold, it's been raining, but the sky clears for us coming into Westhaven Marina. The good folks here have a couple of helpers at the berth as I get it more or less right going astern betwixt tide and wind into the narrow slot between the piles and the finger pontoon.

Auckland was an easy lazy time. Sure we had things to do, the most important of which was to get the new headsail from Evolution Sails and the old repaired genny as well. Still we dallied, filled up the bilges with all the good things from the New World supermarket nearby and sampled the restaurant life in Auckland. If you are in New Zealand get some of the Cabernet drizzle made there – a concentrated essence of Cabernet for salads. Just put a little drizzle over the salad and then a normal dressing.

Eventually we decided we had to stop stocking up in wonderful Kiwi supermarkets, take leave of leaving parties and too much Sauvignon Blanc, make the boat ready for sea and just … go. We left Westhaven Marina for Ponui Island and in light winds only managed to sail for a couple of hours. I've several friends who profess to like sailing around in the winter more than the summer. Well there aren't a lot of boats around and the skies are huge and the visibility almost shocking at 20 or 30 miles, but you do need a heater. We had so many layers on we gave Michelin Man a run for girth size.

AUSTRALASIA

Ashore in Auckland

Auckland is the yachting mecca of New Zealand. All things boaty can be found and fixed. There are supermarkets, markets, bakers and butchers. And of course there are more restaurants and cafés than you can shake a spinnaker pole at. Most yachts will wind up for a while in Westhaven Marina and here you are just a short walk from downtown Auckland.

Provisions

Auckland is such a sprawling city that you will need a car to get places. If you are just doing a quick shop and dinner and then continuing on you can get by. The nearest supermarket to Westhaven is New World at the bottom of College Hill about 15 minutes walk from Westhaven. It has everything you will need including imported items. You may have to substitute Vegemite for Marmite, but all else can be found. This country is a place where you can grow just about everything. It produces excellent cheeses, everything from good soft whites like Brie and Camembert to good cheddars. Good bacon, salamis, smoked meats and smoked fish. Around Auckland there are any number of good supermarkets, bijou bakeries, Chinese supermarkets, butchers and fruit and vegetable shops. In Freemans Bay there are also several good wet fish shops and stalls. Outside the cities and larger centres there will be less choice, so stock up in the big smoke.

Eating out

Along the outer breakwater at Westhaven there is the Ponsonby Cruising Club which has a bar and does light snacks. They run regular race days and are welcoming to visitors. The Royal Akarana Yacht Club sits nearby and also has a bar and café. At the root of the breakwater is the ever popular Sitting Duck Café doing good food and

Westhaven Marina in the heart of downtown Auckland and a short walk away from restaurants and shopping

drinks. One other yachty hangout is the HQ café in Freemans Bay which also does good food and drink.

On the Auckland waterfront close to the Maritime Museum are lots of good restaurants and several up-market and trendy restaurants like the Soul, Kermadec and Portofino where you will probably have to book in advance. Just up from Westhaven is Ponsonby with a lot of good restaurants and cafés which though popular are usually more reasonably priced than downtown. And the list could go on so just look around and take local advice to track down what's good and what it costs.

Friday night racing off the City of Sails

Great Barrier Island is another world seemingly a thousand miles from Auckland and not the actual 50 that separates it from Auckland. It's so quiet you tend to speak in hushed tones. The light is a watery white and the steep hills are densely covered in bush. We anchored in Fitzroy, had a quick glass of Sauvignon Blanc in the cockpit and then disappeared below to get warm. Luckily Lu had the foresight to buy a hot water bottle in Auckland and we went to bed early with it … just to keep warm.

We dally for a bit in Great Barrier and then dawdle up the coast to Opua. It's time, even a bit late, to set off for the Barefoot Islands and the Tropics again.

Fusion food

Fusion food is a term much used to describe new culinary tastes combining ingredients from different countries and cultures. This is nothing new as all cultures have combined ingredients that were not indigenous into their cuisine and over time it seems like this fusion cuisine was the normal cuisine that had existed for aeons. Think of chillies from Central America that are used in India and Southeast Asia. Think of tomatoes from South America that are used in national cuisines all over Europe. In New Zealand we have the kiwi fruit, a fruit that was known as a Chinese gooseberry when I grew up in New Zealand. We also used *feijoas* and tree-tomatoes (*tamarillos*) originally from South America that are little used elsewhere these days.

In New Zealand much of the fusion food revolves around Asian fusion. Spices, ingredients and the combination of ingredients are fused with New Zealand ingredients in novel ways that are not strictly New Zealand cuisine or Asian. Most of this is new. When I grew up most of the cuisine here was a bland combination of a lump of meat, which was plentiful, cooked to death and over-cooked watery vegetables. Steak houses were popular and there was always the ubiquitous Chinese and Indian restaurants.

There has also been New Zealand interpretations of Italian, French and other Mediterranean cuisines. New Zealand has even exported some notable chefs, amongst them Peter Gordon whose cookbook I have from his Sugar Club where he championed some particular New Zealand ingredients like *kumara* and tree-tomatoes in new and novel dishes. In the cities and in some more out of the way places fusion food has blossomed and although the steak houses are still there, there is also an abundance of good and interesting food.

There are a few survivors from the old school well worth sampling. Pies, the sort you buy in a corner shop, are very good. Hamburgers can also be good where the patties are homemade. A New Zealand burger also has that magic ingredient of beetroot – try it though you need to be careful of dribbling red beetroot juice down your front. And New Zealand fish and chips are probably, I can't think of anywhere else, the best in the world with good fresh catch, often shark though it's usually called 'lemon fish', and good home-made chips (usually).

Fitzroy on Great Barrier Island in the Hauraki Gulf.
It feels a lot further away than the actual miles suggest

AUSTRALASIA

THE TRADE WIND FOODIE 101

Sitting in Opua we watched a tropical low develop between New Caledonia and Vanuatu and predicted to move west towards Fiji. With a 1030 high sitting in the Tasman off the west coast of New Zealand this looked like a re-play of the June 1994 'bomb' scenario. The 'bomb' wreaked havoc amongst yachts on passage to the 'Barefoot Islands'.

In 1994 yachts set out at the end of May with a 1030 high over New Zealand. In the Tropics a low formed. Contrary to received opinion, lows do form in the Tropics outside cyclone season and can generate storm force winds. This is not a recipe for successful cruising. The low dropped dramatically to 978 millibars and this low squashed up against the 1030 high over New Zealand produced winds over 60 knots and seas of 10–14m. Over this period sixteen yachts set off EPIRBS and 21 people were rescued. Three people were lost and seven boats lost. The 'bomb' is embedded in the New Zealand yachting psyche much like the 1979 Fastnet in the UK and the 1999 Sydney-Hobart in Australia where boats were lost and people died. Understandably we analysed and re-analysed the weather data.

On Tuesday the 16th June we looked at the weather in the morning and the tropical low was shown as filling and eventually disappearing to virtually nothing. So we stowed the boat, bought some pies for lunch and set off at midday for Fiji. We poked our nose out of the sheltered waters of the Bay of Islands into a fresh southerly and moderate seas, but with a couple of reefs tucked in and the wind on the quarter we made good early progress. On the morning of Wednesday the 17th the tropical low was shown as deepening again and moving just south of Fiji right into the area we would be in. The high sitting in the Tasman had reached 1035. It looked like it would be a race between us and the low to reach Fiji first. This was all looking like a re-run of 'the bomb'. A bit of hurried looking at charts and weather to the west got us thinking about skirting this low by going west and so we put *Skylax's* nose over and shaped a course for New Caledonia.

Over the next few days we were settling back into routine. For a first offshore passage in over six months it was a bit more boisterous than we would have chosen, but we were heading in more or less the right direction and everything seemed to be in good order. The temperature started rising, petrels and the Black-browed albatross followed astern looking for fish in our wake, we ate well and most of all the weather was benign compared to the north near Fiji. We were a bit smug about our tactics with a few too many pats on the back as it turned out.

On Friday we looked at the weather again and while the forecast showed not much more than 20–25 knots from the east and southeast, the weatherfaxes showed a little indentation in the isobars over New Caledonia. This was not so good and it became a small low with a front over New Caledonia. The matter of trying to get order out of the chaos of weather patterns was about to breathe fire on us, well at least a lot of wind. One of the questions I always get is '… aren't you scared out there in bad weather'. There is always a tension about incoming bad weather and big seas. They can break boats and equipment and severely dent your spirits and a lot of the time it feels like just holding on and hoping the boat

Day 1

16th June 1145. Misty morning. Filled water tanks. Cleared customs.

Day 2

17th June 1200. Wind SSE 5—6 Speed 7·9 knots. Good speed but not quite in the right direction. Daily run 178M.

1800. Wind SE 4—5 Speed 6·5 knots. Change course for New Caledonia. Tropical low has reformed.

Day 3

18th June 1500. Wind S 6—7 Speed 7·6 knots. Grey whale with small dorsal fin dives under the bow! Squall system around. Third reef in.

Day 4

19th June 1800. Wind E 5 Speed 7·1 knots. Flying along. Took a bit of genny in for the night.

Day 5

20th June 0015. Reefing line breaks on roller reefing genoa. Remains of line taken around foredeck cleat and genny rolled to a pocket handkerchief. Bit of panic for a while!

1800. Wind E 8 Speed 7·2 knots. Lolloping along. Wind feels good when it drops under 30 knots.

Day 6

21st June 1520. Wind E 7 Speed 7·2. Some big BBCs [Big Black Clouds] passing. Otherwise sunny and warmish afternoon.

Day 7

22nd June 1200. Wind E 5 Speed 7·1. 11M to waypoint off Boulari Passe. Daily run 167M.

1730. Alongside in Port Moselle.

Off watch and secure in the knowledge that the other is keeping watch

will get you through it all. It's not surprising that we all build up a thorough-going anthropomorphic relationship with the boat where you pat it, urge it on, marvel at how it lifts its stern to the waves, slices along towards our mutual destination.

By Friday night we had 30–35 knots from the east to southeast and by Saturday we had 30–40 knots with gusts up to 45 knots from the east. To make things interesting the roller reefing line for the genny had chafed on the drum and exploded with a bang on Saturday night letting the whole genny out. The flapping genny shook everything violently in the wind threatening to tear the mast out, at least it felt like that. Flapping sails make an awful lot of noise and have a violence in them that is difficult to tame. We put harnesses on and crept up the deck to find the chafed end of the line and managed to get it in with just a pocket handkerchief of sail left. We tied off the reefing line to a foredeck cleat and as it turned out that was enough until we reached the pass through the reef and into the channel leading to Noumea.

Sunday was pretty much the same with 30–40 knots, but at least the front had moved off to the north of New Caledonia and the squash zone was lessened between the low and the 1035 high still sitting solidly over New Zealand. With three reefs in the main (and our third reef is a deep one) and the patch of jib *Skylax* flew towards Noumea doing 170M days in pretty difficult seas of around 3–4m with breaking crests. There was a lot of water over the deck and in the cockpit, but I opted for the policy of keeping the boat going fast in this weather and as long as we didn't nose-dive into too many seas this worked well. I think Moitessier was the first to adopt this sort of tactic in heavy weather in the 1968 race around the world. Instead of trailing warps to slow his heavy old steel boat *Joshua* down, he kept sail up and ran at speed with the weather.

We came through the Passe de Boulari, with its huge lighthouse guarding the entrance, in six days with a distance travelled of 986 miles. I won't say the entry through the pass with 35 knots and rain squalls reducing visibility to not a lot was a piece of cake, but we got through OK and then motor-sailed up the narrowish channel in the lagoon to Noumea. I have a little confession to make here. While we had charts for Fiji we had no detailed charts for New Caledonia. Bless the French who not only buoy the channels, but also maintain the buoys so well they almost look new.

It's not the sort of first passage you would choose, but *Skylax* looked after us a treat. As a friend Peter likes to say, 'You don't learn a whole lot out there about

Passe de Boulari lighthouse in the entrance into the lagoon off Grande Terre, New Caledonia

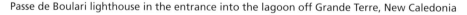

Isle des Pins. Those tall spindly pines are the very ones the island is named after

New Caledonia is on the edge of the Tropics but has all the bits, warm turquoise water, palms, white sandy beaches and temperatures in the 20s, associated with the Tropics

AUSTRALASIA

life, the meaning of life or anything remotely resembling that, but you do learn a whole lot about your boat'.

Once tied up at the marina, alongside several familiar yachts, the entry formalities were swiftly completed. We were tired and salty and needed a shower, but making a safe landfall after a passage like that gives you a big adrenaline boost. It was time for a bite and a drink, and to catch up and swap stories with friends.

New Caledonia, along with French Polynesia is a French Territoire d'Outre Mer in the Pacific. It is something of a question mark for many cruisers though not to Australian and New Zealand cruisers who regularly use it as a stepping stone around the southwest Pacific. Although in the Tropics it is some 20° south of the equator so has a slightly cooler climate than islands closer to the equator. Even so its seascape conforms to ideas of the Tropics: coral reefs, coconut palms and white sandy beaches with air temperatures in the low 20°s C.

After a week in Noumea we were more than topped up with provisions. Vanuatu was to be our next destination and by all accounts the shopping was not as good there. *Skylax* nosed out of Port Moselle and down into the lagoon south of New Caledonia. The lagoon is often described as the biggest in the world, though I suspect that may be a bit of local PR given the area encompassed by the Barrier Reef off the east coast of Australia and some of the large lagoons in the Tuamotus.

Iles des Pins was to be our jumping off point for Vanuatu, though the fine sandy beach and turquoise water delayed kick-off for a few days. The famous pines here are a weird spindly trees that dot the landscape all around the island. Sadly the famous restaurant ashore was not so great though the situation is stunning.

Ashore in Noumea

New Caledonia has a large resident population of yachts and the best yacht repair facilities outside of New Zealand and Australia in this part of the world. If you have problems around the islands or en route to them then New Caledonia is the place to head for. Add to this French patisseries and baguettes, some half decent restaurants and French supermarkets with a selection of French cheeses and other goodies and New Caledonia takes on a whole new perspective. You can also fill your gas bottles here. Like Tahiti and the French islands to the east it comes at a bit of a price, but still a good Brie is worth it to some of us.

Provisions

In Noumea there are two supermarkets on the waterfront near the marina. These have a reasonable selection of goods, but the big supermarket is around the bay in the industrial park at Logicoop. You can get there on a bus or take a taxi or a hire car. There are also small grocery shops and fruit and vegetable shops in Noumea itself. Close by the marina is the market with excellent fresh fish and prawns at a bargain price. It also has fresh fruit and vegetables and local sauces and condiments.

Eating out

There are restaurants scattered around town and around the beaches. Most of these have a French take on Pacific cuisine. The Zanzibar near the central park and La Chaumière near the market have good French food. Le Bout de Monde right in the marina is a popular watering hole for yachties and serves food as well. In the car park area near the marina mobile vans serve local food and snacks in the evening. There is also a McDonalds nearby, fast food tasting of polystyrene but with a good Wi-Fi connection.

Around some of the bays and islands like Ile des Pins are hotel restaurants which can be good.

Noumea market. Why do the French have such good markets?

Noumea fish market with excellent prawns at a good price

The southern islands of Vanuatu lie less than 200 miles off the west coast of New Caledonia and the capital Port Vila is just over 300 miles away. It's just a matter of timing so you arrive in daylight off Port Vila to make the transit through the reef into the inner anchorage. On *Skylax* we nosed into the bay after an uneventful passage of a day and a half and then motored through the narrow pass between the reefs to the anchorage just off the town and sheltered by Iririki Island.

The islands were only named Vanuatu this century. Before that they were called 'The Great Cyclades' (Bougainville in 1768) or 'The New Hebrides' (Cook in 1774) until independence was declared in 1980 and it became the Republic of Vanuatu. This chain of islands is something of a crossroads in the southwest Pacific with boats from New Zealand on the Barefoot Circuit coming across from Tonga and Fiji before curving down to New Caledonia and then back to New Zealand and boats en route to Australia and Southeast Asia leaving from here to cross to the Coral Coast in Australia or towards the Solomon Islands and New Guinea.

Vanuatu is one of those oddities of the Pacific where the English and French never quite got around to declaring sovereignty and in the end decided on joint rule rather than a sea battle to determine whose colony it was. So the respective colonial powers set up joint institutions: French and English governors, English and French schools that taught in English and French, English and French hospitals, two parallel administrations that would confuse anyone, let alone the native population.

The island chain has never been a homogeneous group and although basically Melanesian, different languages were spoken on different islands and even between different villages. Some sources reference 150 different languages in the chain. The islands had a reputation for cannibalism and savagery that troubled Bligh enough on his epic voyage to by-pass the islands even though he and his crew had precious little to eat. The reputation for cannibalism existed right up into the 20th century with one anthropologist recording the last act of cannibalism in 1989 on the island of Malekula. Fortunately the menu has changed and it is beef they are famous for now.

Port Vila anchorage once through the pass.
Ashore is the Waterfront Bar and Grill with those juicy Vanuatu steaks

Laplap

The traditional way of cooking in Vanuatu. The name actually applies to the green leaves used to wrap the food in though it has pretty much come to describe using an underground oven to cook the bundles of food. Usually meat is cooked with a mashed taro or yam mixed with ground coconut and wrapped in the leaf. There may be chicken or pork in the mixture as well. This is then cooked in a pit oven like the New Zealand hangi. It's OK, but although you need to try it once, it's not my favourite sort of food.

You can get laplap for lunch in Port Vila market.

Ashore in Port Vila

Provisions

Provisioning is more meagre than New Caledonia, but you can find most of the basics. There are several supermarkets of a sort and on the waterfront is the fruit and vegetable market. Islanders come here by ferry from outlying islands with their wares and the whole place is more than worth a wander around. It buzzes with life, with the vendors selling everything from mangoes and bananas to taro and cabbages. The different islanders have different styles of dress and frequently a different physiogamy. Some of the women have frizzy hair and some straight. Vanuatu is a made-up state embracing different tribes and different languages and you can see it all in the market.

They also do local food for lunch, usually laplap served up on a banana leaf.

The ladies take it easy in the market at Vila. We printed off photos of them which they found highly amusing

Eating out

Along the main street and around the waterfront are numerous restaurants of a French/Vanuatu persuasion and a few Chinese restaurants as well. In the lagoon the yachty hangout is the Waterfront Bar and Grill, just a dinghy ride away with excellent steaks (I came back for more) and good fish. Also popular is Chili on the waterfront in the bay with good steaks (actually nearly everywhere has good steaks) and good pizzas. La Pizzeria up the hill has pizzas and a lot else besides. It's remarkable how much good eating this little place has, possibly more than Noumea with a wider spread of styles. There is also an excellent patisserié/café, Le Café du Village, in the high street.

Putting together a laplap in Port Vila market

AUSTRALASIA

Port Vila was wonderful with more good eateries than I could have imagined. A lot of this is down to odd Australians, Kiwis, French, Italian and British souls who have arrived here and set up shop. We meandered up the island chain stopping at whim or at the whim of the weather.

Port Havannah, named after the British warship *Havannah*, is a huge natural harbour used in the Second World War by the American fleet. At one time it was the main settlement on Efate Island, but Port Vila soon eclipsed it and today is a sleepy hollow with a few villages around the edge of the natural harbour. In the small boat anchorage the locals come across every day in outrigger canoes to work in their market garden on the main island. One or other would come alongside to barter fruit and vegetables and I asked them why they didn't have a market garden on the same island as the village. 'No good land,' they said. 'No water.' 'Over here near the river there is good land.' The only problem, they said, was that they had to leave guards overnight so no one came and stole their produce. Every Thursday they went into the main market in Port Vila

to sell their produce. 'Why Thursday?' I asked. Apparently different villages and different islands have their own market day and Thursday was the day for Sounnai Island.

Chief Don and 'pikinini' on Malekula up the island chain in Vanuatu

Vanuatu beef

I'm not a huge steak eater when dining out. I often prefer some sort of combo-dish combining different ingredients and cultural influences. But in Vanuatu I had heard that the beef is so good that it only needs to be seared either side and served with a simple salad. So that was what I had first night out in Port Vila. It is that good. So good that the next night I had exactly the same thing just in case I had been kidding myself on the first go.

I'm not sure why the beef should be so exceptional. The cattle graze all year round on grass and are said to be disease free. No antibiotics are used and most of it qualifies as organic beef. It might seem a bit incongruous to see cattle grazing under coconut palms and nosing their way through the bush, but somehow it all works to produce wonderful lightly marbled beef.

Bislama

With the amalgamation of the islands a common language, Bislama, a variation on Pidgin English, united the villages and islands under a common thread that soothed over old feuds and disputes. It is also used in the Solomon Islands and Papua New Guinea. The language is quite easy to get a handle on once you hear it. Some of my favourite phrases are below.

Thank You	*Tankyu tumas*
Hello	*Alo*
Goodbye	*Tata*
Child	*Pikinini*
Food	*Kakae*
To hit	*Killem*
To hit and kill something	*Killem ded finis*
To ruin	*Baggerap*
Piano	*Wan bigfala bokis, I gat tith, sam I waet, sam I blak, taim yu killem I sing out.*
	(My favourite: One big box, he got teeth, some are white, some are black, if you hit it, he sings.)

NOTICE

PLIS NO USUM SHARP OBJECT LONG TABLE YA. MO NO SAKEM TOTI OLBAOT.
PLIS SAKEM TOTI LONG STRET PLES BLONG EM.

THANKYOU LONG UNDERSTANDING BLONG YOU.

Cruising up the islands of Vanuatu takes you back in time and the heavily wooded islands and outlying reefs are just stunning. Many of the villages are isolated places where the locals welcome any cruising yachts and will want to trade for fruit and vegetables and introduce you to the village. Not until you get to Luganville on Santo do you reach somewhere with shops and cars and a good restaurant to moor up outside.

Ashore in Luganville

This is a much smaller place than Port Vila and you shouldn't expect to find too much in the way of supplies. In any case many yachts will be heading to Australia from here and, like New Zealand, the Australian Quarantine Service is strict about bringing foreign foodstuffs in so you need to plan to have just enough fresh food on board for the passage. Luganville has the large island of Aore opposite it and off the intimate little resort and restaurant here there are yacht moorings. These are pretty handy as the depths in the channel are considerable and there aren't too many good places to anchor.

The resort has a bar and restaurant which serves steaks (again) and good local seafood. The mahi mahi is excellent. A ferry, really a big speed-boat, runs across to Luganville so you can hop on that and spend the day in Luganville. There are some provisions to be had, a bit of a market and several restaurant/cafés. The Natangora Café on the High Street was good for lunch and there is the ubiquitous Chinese restaurant as well. I did notice that all the shops had serious pull-down metal shutters so I'm not sure what Luganville would be like at night. It seemed a bit edgy compared to Port Vila.

Barter

Most yachts will head up the island chain and should stock up on everything before heading off. Until you get to Luganville on Santo there is very little available and what you can get will be through barter. Many of the places you go to here are self-sustaining or nearly so. On many of the islands there are no roads and no communication by sea. The populations here need all sorts of odd things.

Exercise books and pencils go down well. Balloons to entertain the kids, especially when you blow them up in front of them, surprise and delight. Old T-shirts, shoes and clothing. Fish hooks and line. Old oil (from an oil change) is used for chain-saw blades.

Balloons go down a treat with kids on the islands

Epoxy glue to patch up old dug-out canoes is like gold. Tins of anything, but especially corned beef, is prized. Old ropes you might still be carrying on board will find a welcome home here.

Fizzy drinks and sweets might sound like a good idea, but I was admonished by an Australian dentist for handing them out. He had set up a mini-surgery in the front of his boat and sailed around the islands providing free dental treatment for these far-flung villages that never went near a dentist, even if they could. Some of the chiefs you meet will greet you with a wide grin… and no teeth.

Bartering for vegetables in Havannah Bay

In the villages up the island chain you might get a few vegetables and some fruit depending on what is being grown and what's in season. Coconuts are always on offer. Really you should just think of the things you have as a gift to the locals who will often want to show you around the village, sit down for tea (you may have to bring sugar) and a chat. All the villages have a chief, even villages close to each other will have their own chiefs, and it will probably be the chief who paddles out in an outrigger canoe to welcome you to his patch. He is, of course, the one who should get the major share of the booty to distribute as he sees fit.

The Coral Sea crossing can be a windy and bumpy old affair. The trades often get reinforced by highs coming off Australia and the 15–20s become 30s and more. So it was.

We left Luganville in comparatively calm weather and had a light wind sail for the first couple of days. We even had to motor for six hours when the wind died away altogether. But we knew from the weather forecasts and especially from a nasty little bump in a nearby isobar on the weatherfaxes that there was a lot more to come.

For the passage to Cairns you need to get north a bit to avoid a whole jigsaw puzzle of reefs and then drop down to the Grafton Passage through the Barrier Reef and into Cairns. And you also have to give 96 hours warning of your arrival to Australian customs as well.

Surely enough the bump in the isobar produced a little more than the 25–28 knots on the gribs. By the end of day two we were down to third reef in the main and a patch of jib. It was enough to do 170 to 180 plus mile days for the rest of the trip and we arrived in Grafton Passage a week out from Luganville even after a slow start. Perversely the trades get deflected up the Australian coast to a more southerly direction and by the time you arrive at the Grafton Passage you are on a SW course that means you have to beat down the passage to get in.

It wasn't so much the wind as the seas that were bad in the Coral Sea, although we recorded a top wind speed of 46 knots. There was a wicked cross sea with up to 4m breaking crests, usually just where *Skylax* was, and we had more water in the cockpit than we have had for a long time. Nothing dangerous, but it's very wearing when you have large buckets of water raining down on you and sloshing around the cockpit before they drain out.

For some reason we had stowed the lifejacket/harnesses in one of the cave lockers in the cockpit and with one spectacular splosh of water the cave locker must have filled. It was enough water to set off the automatic immersion

mechanisms which meant I had two inflated lifejackets trying to get out of the cave locker like a couple of demented blow-up dolls. Well at least they worked and Lu fixed them that evening with the spare cylinders and immersion mechanisms we carry. Everything was salty and we changed clothes twice a day to keep the dreaded saltwater itch from driving us crazy.

Ferry from the resort across to Luganville

Vanuatu to Cairns

Day 1

28th July 0730. Slipped mooring off Aore Island Resort. Heading out of west channel.

Day 2

29th July 1500. Wind SE 4 Speed 6·8 knots. Sailing at last. Warm and sunny. Australia here we come.

Day 3

30th July 1200. Wind ESE 6-7 Speed 7·8 knots. Grey and overcast. Rattling along in lumpy sea now. Daily run 174M.

Day 4

31st July 1200. Wind ESE 6-7 Speed 7·7 knots. Still wet. Several big waves dump in cockpit. Daily run 176M.

Day 5

1st Aug 0900. Wind SE 7 Speed 7·4 knots. Heavy grey skies and huge waves. And rain. And a red-footed Booby as well.

Day 6

2nd Aug 1500. Wind ESE 6-7 Speed 7·1 knots. Heavy rain squalls one after another. Big lumpy cross-swell.

Day 7

3rd Aug 1200. Wind SE 5-6 Speed 7·3 knots. Squally and wet. Oh what a blasted sea but no madness yet. Daily run 186M.

Day 8

4th Aug 0900. Wind ESE 6 Speed 7·2. Blue sky and hesitant sun to accompany squalls this morning. Heading for Grafton Passage.

2220. Anchor down in Mission Bay. Hurrah.

We also had a persistent visitor. Every evening a big red-footed booby would circle the boat and unlike other boobies that have tried to land, this one was an aerial artiste. He had a wingspan of over a metre (can be up to 1.5m my bird book tells me) and still managed to duck and dive between sails and rigging without once getting it wrong. The first night he tucked up on the spinnaker pole. The second night he perched on the back of the bimini and wouldn't move. Have you seen the size of those beaks up close? I gave up trying to dislodge him... or her. The third night he decided the foredeck was home. Now I'm all for boobies, amazing birds, but large, fishy booby poop is just a pain and moreover seems to burn through canvas and discolour teak with whatever acid there is in their gastric system.

So it was a fast passage. Personally I like it a bit slower and more relaxed, but nothing broke and really we just held on while *Skylax* and Mole the autopilot did the business. With permission from Customs we anchored in Mission Bay off Cairns at 2200 at night and cooked up a huge fry-up and cracked a good bottle of New Zealand Cabernet Sauvignon. We might have had another bottle to celebrate, but the passage had bruised and battered us and in any case we had to get up early in the morning to get into Marlin Marina where customs and the quarantine gang were waiting for us.

Arriving in Cairns was a delight after the Coral Sea crossing. The guys from AQIS (quarantine) helped us berth in Marlin Marina with a cross-current and the wind shushing into the berth. Then they came on board, asked a few questions, filled in a few forms and then thoroughly searched the boat from stem to stern. They might be nice guys, but they don't mess around when it comes to doing their job. Customs arrived not long afterwards with all our records on the computer and the relevant papers all printed out. Sign here and here and you get the cruising permit.

Marlin Marina is a short walk from downtown Cairns and it has grown in recent years to become something of a tourist resort. At least a dozen big catamaran tripper boats (I'm talking a possible hundred people on board) leave each morning to go out to Green Island on dive tours. Another dozen smaller boats also leave including some yachts more or less converted to be small dive boats. Some of the boats are pure dive boats, but most of the larger boats have a mix of diving and sight-seeing. All the boats have their own allotted mooring at Green Island and, although the reef around it is pretty extensive, you can't help thinking it must be a bit like Green Island Junction out there.

Close to the marina there is a huge public infinity pool with grass around it and even a little beach on one side. I guess the proximity of crocs (and there are

Marlin Marina right in the middle of Cairns. Excellent restaurants of all types and supermarkets with everything you need in them

Ashore in Cairns

Downtown Cairns is a mix of cafés, restaurants, bars, backpacker hostels and shops. This is the place to do the big shop before Darwin and Indonesia. Between Cairns and Darwin there aren't too many shopping opportunities and not a lot of places for eating out or a cappuccino either.

Provisions

There is a Woolworths a few blocks back from the waterfront but within easy walking distance where you can get the basics. Further into town near the railway station is a mall with a huge supermarket and lots of other food shops as well. The supermarket, Coles, has everything you need and the butchers here can vacuum pack meat for you. There are good bakers shops in the mall and in town as well.

In this part of the world, Queensland and the Northern Territory, you cannot buy alcohol in supermarkets but must go to a 'Bottle Shop'. There are a number of these in Cairns and in one we found them selling off bin-ends of wine at less than half price. A bargain for good Australian wine.

Eating out

Within a short walking distance of the marina there are lots of good restaurants with everything from honest Australian tucker to some excellent pan-Pacific fusion food. You don't have to stray far from the marina as here the up-market Sail House restaurant serves good food in a wonderful setting next to the marina although it's a bit pricey. A bit further into town there are Italian, Spanish, French and pan-Pacific food. There are several excellent pizzerias as well. All of this reflects the diversity of migrants to the 'Lucky Country'. They have come from Britain, Italy, Greece, the old Yugoslavia, India, Southeast Asia, China, Turkey, the Middle East, it really is a wonderful hodge-podge of a country and the cuisine reflects this.

Close to the waterfront is a night market with stalls selling Asian and other food and all sorts of other knick-knacks. You can get Chinese, Vietnamese, Japanese, Indian and lots of other snack food. And don't forget the free barbecue facilities where you can pick up some steaks and snags and a bit of ready made salad from one of the delicatessens and DIY with a view out over the river. The only drawback is that you are not allowed to drink alcohol in public in Queensland.

saltwater crocs around the river in Cairns according to the local cruisers anchored out) means that the pool is a better bet than taking a dip in the sea. Around the waterfront there is a boardwalk and public barbecue shelters with gas-fired barbecues for public use. They even have a cleaner who arrives every morning to scrub the gunk off and polish the stainless. It's a great waterfront.

This is BIG country and if you take a car from Cairns you are soon winding up through high mountains covered in tropical rain forest to a fertile plateau around the Atherton area. There are lakes in old volcanic craters. Small townships. A deep ravine where two mountain ranges push up against one another with a waterfall that drops some 250ft to the bottom of the gorge. There is sugar cane everywhere and also huge plantations for coffee beans, tea, peanuts and bananas. There is also a narrow gauge railway which presumably used to take the sugar cane to the mills. Everywhere you get the feeling of space, of the immensity of this country, and of its abundance outside the central deserts that make up so much of Australia.

One of the amazing things you find is that even in small townships there can be a couple of cafés serving good local fare, homemade bread, excellent coffee made from the beans grown nearby. The quality of food out in the boondocks is surprisingly good. And there is always the great Australian pie, messy to eat, but tasting of real meat and proper pastry.

Alan Lucas in his *Cruising the Coral Coast* (a book everyone should have on board) says of the coast that it 'rivals some of the world's great tropical beauty spots such as the Marquesas of the Central Pacific and the Grenadines of the West

Company along the Coral Coast

Shrimper along the Coral Coast

Indies'. He is right. This coast is stunningly beautiful with mainland Australia on one side, a great long tract of coast virtually uninhabited once you are past Cooktown, and the reefs and sandy cays along the Barrier Reef on the seaward side providing protection from the trade wind swell and wonderful anchorages as well. It is one of the wildest places on earth I have cruised in.

Once you set off from Cairns you are pretty much on your own with the exception of Cooktown some 75 miles north of Cairns. You need to be self sufficient in food, water and fuel until you get to either Thursday Island in the Torres Strait or more usefully Gove or Darwin in the Northern Territory. Apart from any fish you catch along the way there are no shops or even a bar or restaurant except for Lizard Island, so you need to make your own fun. There are enough Aussie boats cruising the coast to make it convivial and they are a great lot. We were given fresh oysters and a sweetlips fish and managed to catch a nice blue tuna off the top of Australia.

With the southeast trades behind us and tucked behind the Barrier Reef we pottered up the coast anchoring behind islands and cays and in bays off the mainland coast. With virtually no sea this is champagne sailing. After some of the passages in the last few months we loved it and this is one of those coasts I'd cruise again.

You are not alone. There are a few shrimping boats around. And a bit of shipping in the main inshore ship channel running inside the reef, though in a yacht you are rarely in the shipping channel. And there are the Australian customs patrols. All up and down the coast customs aircraft or the Australian Air Force patrol the coast and call us up on the radio. After a while they get used to our leisurely progress and call us up by name, enquire whether we are OK, and wish us a safe journey onwards. It's all very friendly and after a while you start looking forward to the daily fly-by.

Around Cape York at the very northeast tip of Australia the tides run fiercely through Endeavour Passage. Once we had caught the tide and been whooshed through with up to 4 knots under us *Skylax* nosed in between the islands on the west side of Cape York and we dropped anchor in Simpson Bay for the night. Even here the tidal stream is quite strong and even with 20 odd knots of wind, the boat is lying to the tide.

The Gulf of Carpentaria is a huge gulf, something over 300 miles across, with nothing much around it except an ore loading port at Gove on the northwest corner and Karumba harbour in the southeast corner where the fishing fleet, mostly shrimpers, unload. The gulf is famous for banana shrimp that apparently come up to the surface at night to be scooped up by the shrimping boats.

On *Skylax* we had a gentle sail across and then on towards Van Diemens Gulf. The water is full of life and just about every day we encountered sea snakes, the black and yellow-banded variety. Some were swimming and some appeared to be asleep curled up into a coil on the surface. There were turtles, seabirds and the obliging tuna that we hooked. At night the water is alive with phosphorescence including, I guess, some banana shrimps. I'll make a point of trying them when we get to Darwin.

It's often assumed that Captain Cook on the *Endeavour* was the first to explore and chart much of this coast. That would be to forget the Dutch who controlled the East Indies and who ventured down this way. In Cairns we came across a working replica of a ship called the *Duyfken*, a Dutch ship which under Willem Janszoon explored much of the coast and drew the first charts of it in 1606. It's a wonder that Australia was never claimed as a Dutch possession given their strength in the East Indies and that they knew about it, even if not the full extent of the land mass. Not until 1770 did Captain Cook chart the east coast and raise the British flag.

Like an apparition in the desert Darwin appears over the horizon after some 1,200 or so miles around from Cairns. Skyscrapers (well a few), cars, ferries, sidewalks and cafés, cappuccino and pizza (*pide* actually in a little Turkish café), people and places. It's great and the city is small enough to be convivial but big enough so you can get most things. Darwin is a bit like a city on a micro-scale. You can walk around it in an afternoon

We anchored off Cullen Bay Marina behind a drying sandbank where the shelter is OK except when high tide coincides with a boisterous afternoon sea breeze. The tides here are huge, around 7m at springs, and the boat lies to the tidal stream and not the wind. You know about the tides here because at low tide a sandbank

Anchorage in the Flinders Islands along the Coral Coast. This is one of the wildest coasts I have cruised with no settlements ashore for hundreds of miles

Crocs and box jellyfish

This coast looks like paradise. It's all sand cays and palms under the Barrier Reef and dense bush on the mainland side. There are long silver beaches with silica so pure it is used in glass-making and high temperature ceramics. Off the coast the water is often turquoise over sand and coral. The problem is the crocs and box jellyfish.

There are crocs. Most Australians don't swim here and even off some of the little sand cays there have been sightings of crocs. Coming into Morris Cay we met up again with an Australian yacht who buzzed over in his dinghy after we had dropped anchor. I was ready for a swim in the clear water. 'Did you see the croc?' our friend asked. Australian humour I thought. I hadn't seen a croc. 'You nearly dropped your anchor on him' he said. 'Look, there he is.' He pointed to a spot 40-odd metres in front of the boat and sure enough, there was a long snout just above the water.

'Around a 10 footer' our friend said, '...no swimming here mate.'

The saltwater crocodile inhabits these waters, can grow up to 7m and weigh up to a ton, and is a stealthy and cunning hunter by all accounts. Personally it put me off swimming and even on a sand cay like Morris Island it means you sit on board and cool off with a beer.

And there are box jellyfish. These mostly descend down from the estuaries in the summer months, but there have been warnings of box jellyfish around in some winters. The neurotoxin that these tiny little beasts kill their prey with can kill a human being. Sometimes within minutes. A lot more people die from box jellyfish stings than do from saltwater crocs. The advice from the authorities is not to swim anywhere near the shore. Further out in the Barrier Reef there are unlikely to be box jellyfish.

Paradise?

Cape York to Darwin

Day 1

30th Aug 0700. Anchor up in Simpson Bay on the west side of Cape York. Strong tidal stream.

Day 2

31st Aug 1200. Wind E 4 Speed 6·1 knots. Got a fish on the line but it got off before it was landed. Wing and wing. Sunny and warm. Daily run 149M.

Day 3

1st Sept 1530. Wind E4 Speed 5·6 knots. Caught a 4—5kg tuna. Lu has gutted and filleted so tuna for dinner.

Day 4

2nd Sept 1500. Wind E 5 Speed 6·0 knots. 1·5m sea snake, yellow and black bands. Eastbound. Clocks back one hour.

Day 5

3rd Sept 0200. Wind E 5 Speed 6·2 knots. Beautiful clear night under 7/8th moon. Staying on port tack for now.

Day 6

4th Sept 0600. Anchored off on a shoal patch in the Van Diemen Gulf waiting for the tide to turn.

1500. Anchored off Cullen Bay Marina in Darwin.

Ashore in Darwin

Provisions

There is everything you need here. A big Woolworths and a Coles supermarket. To get there from Cullen Bay there is a regular bus running from the marina and the drivers seem quite accustomed to yachties clambering on board for the return journey clutching multiple bags of groceries and other stuff. Like Cairns you need to get alcohol from a 'bottle store' and there are several in downtown Darwin. Around Cullen Bay Marina there is a small general store, a laundry and a very nice little bookshop. It's worth remembering that until you get to Singapore and then Langkawi in Malaysia that there are not too many opportunities for stocking up on wine and that here in Australia you are in a country producing excellent wines. Make the most of it.

Eating out

In downtown there are plenty of restaurants and cafés. All the usual influences from Southeast Asia, the Mediterranean, Europe and India as well as home-grown influences are here. At Cullen Bay Marina there are also several restaurants and cafés in a fairly up-market setting.

In the dry season and for a bit of the wet season there is Mindli Beach market lying mid-way between Fannie Bay and Cullen Bay. You can get there on the bus or it's a bit of a walk around from Cullen Bay. There are food stalls galore with everything from Asian, Japanese, Indian, hog roasts, pizzas, burgers, well just about everything. There are also lots of stalls selling all sorts of other knick-knacks and the place fairly hums with the crowds.

Mindli Beach market in Darwin. You can get everything from barbecued suckling pig to Vietnamese fish cakes and more

When the tide goes out in Darwin the locals zoom out to the sand bar with barbies and pergolas. A few hours later the sandbar is submerged again

surfaces on the seaward edge of the anchorage like some colossal white whale. The sandbank is obviously the best beach in Darwin and at the weekends the locals are out in force erecting pagodas and beach umbrellas, getting the barbie fired up and sinking a few chilled tinnies. Then the tide comes in and off they go. Given the beach is submerged twice a day it's about as pristine as you get. The other beaches off Fannie Bay and elsewhere are all gooey black mud under the half-tide watermark so nowhere near as appealing as the sandbank.

Darwin is such a compact little city that once you are there you can walk around it in a couple of hours. It's a pleasant laid back place to wander around and there is enough pavement culture so you can stop off anywhere for a cappuccino and a snack. Like the rest of Australia it's also culturally diverse. The first café we stopped in was Turkish so you could get Turkish snacks with your coffee. The next café was Greek. Add to this a mixed population of Asians and Europeans not to mention the Aussies themselves and you get a fair old selection of influences on the different sorts of cuisine you can get here.

SOUTHEAST ASIA
Indonesia

All cruisers' plans are written in the sand at low tide. *Anonymous*

Sailing across to Southeast Asia is crossing the line between the Aussie version of westernised behaviour to the Orient and Asian values and culture. It is a leap of the imagination crossing from one culture to another and a surprise that such a short distance separates these two very different cultures. On one side is Darwin, all cappuccino and panini, fusion Asian food, supermarkets with shrink-wrapped everything. On the other side is Kupang full of noise and litter and little hole-in-the-wall grocery shops where loose beans and rice spill over the floor, the rag-tag night market where hygiene is not monitored by health and safety and the locals squeeze in next to you for chicken and rice eaten with your hands. And all of it separated by the short stretch of the Timor Sea.

The passage from Darwin to Indonesia is traditionally a light wind or no wind passage, so we needed to hone those light weather sailing skills. It was just as well that we had topped up the diesel tank in Darwin before we left. Some yachts have spent a number of extra days out here, low on diesel and drifting around, because they didn't believe you couldn't sail the whole way with a bit of patience. In fact we sailed for around 60% of the time, but some of that was very slow with a lot of slatting sails which can really get on your nerves. As Bob sailing on *Boomerang* said: 'I hate to turn that darned engine on but to get across here you need to burn up quite a few dinosaurs.'

As in the Gulf of Carpentaria we saw a lot of sea life. Sea snakes were everywhere, usually coiled up on the surface. When we passed near to them the snake sometimes raised its head to give us a hissy stare, but rarely swam away. There was a whale, maybe a humpback, tuna though we didn't catch any, turtles

Day 1

11th Sept 0830. Anchor up in Cullen Bay. Customs cleared the day before. Heading for Kupang.

1500. Wind ENE 3 Speed 5·7 knots. Motorsailing. Whale, maybe a humpback, heading slowly west.

Day 2

12th Sept. Wind NE 3 Speed 4·6 knots. Sailing slow and easy. Coast watch check-in. Daily run 133M.

Day 3

13th Sept 1500. Wind ENE 3 Speed 4·0 knots. Sailing slowly goose-winged. 36°C below. Slow progress.

Day 4

14th Sept 0200. Wind E 2–3 Speed 5·4 knots. Motorsailing. Three fishing boats nearby. Whale breath. One large moth. Lots of shooting stars.

1930. Anchor down in Kupang.

and sea birds working the water around the boat. Once you get close to Indonesia you start coming across local fishing boats bobbing around on the sea. The latest 'must have' for smaller Indonesian fishing boats are strobe lights (all colours including white, blue, green and red) arranged in no particular order on the boat. They have a range of less than half a mile and give you few clues about what the boat is doing.

We didn't pick up any wind over 10 knots until around 80 miles off Kupang when a southerly began to build, eventually getting up to 20 knots or so. It felt like half a gale after the preceding calms. We just managed to get into Kupang on the evening of the fourth day courtesy of a beautiful close reach up the southern hook that you round to head up to Kupang town. You wouldn't want to do it in the dark as there are badly lit fishing boats everywhere and fish farms extending some distance out from the coast.

We nosed into suitable depths for anchoring at dusk and had the customary bottle of wine to celebrate arriving, as it happened just off one of the mosques that had a sermon from the imam that lasted most of the evening – it was Ramadan. In the morning we called up the agent, Napa, on the VHF and he suggested moving a bit further along to 'his' beach. Our anchorage was where 'bad people' are... so we pottered a little further up and anchored off Napa's beach.

Once the dinghy was in the water it was off to see Napa who was waiting on the beach to clear us into Indonesia. Now I knew it was going to cost something extra for the Customs 'retirement fund', and I figured it would cost around $US100–150. So it was a bit of shock to find the cost was $US250, though the figure was confirmed by other boats and a couple of sympathetic locals I talked to. Anyway apart from handing over the money it was all pretty painless and our paperwork and passports were back the next day and we were cleared in ... 'all the way to Nongsa Point where you exit Indonesia', Napa said. 'You have any problems with Customs, you just ring this number', and he wrote down the phone number of the head of Customs in Kupang. It's corrupt, but efficient.

Night markets

Night markets exist all over Asia. In Bahasa they are called Pasar Malam, (*Malam* = night), which not surprisingly literally means a 'night market'. These markets open at night to avoid the heat of the day and also when the locals have knocked off work. There are stalls selling everything from clothes, shoes, toys, knick-knacks and importantly street food.

The food stalls have gas rings and charcoal grills with food of all sorts for sale. Most of the stalls have some rough wooden tables and benches where you can sit down with the locals and order up some food. Often the food is just excellent and even ordering it is easy. The food to be grilled or flash-fried in a wok will be on show, fish, kebabs, chicken and beef for the grill or stir-frys, the odd crustacean, and probably some bits you will not be too sure about. Most of the meat will have been marinaded in some sort of sauce, often quite spicy and occasionally eye-wateringly hot.

Choose your fish and get it charcoal grilled in the night market

Modern aids to get the charcoal going in the night market

As well as charcoal grilled and stir-fry there will often be pots of other food. There is always sticky rice and sometimes noodles. There will be all sorts of stews and curries. Just point out what you want and it will be ladled onto a plate, almost always with rice. Some of this food is just divine.

There is rarely alcohol available. Indonesia and Malaysia are Muslim countries and night markets do not cater for the odd beer or local hooch. What they often have, or you can get from a stall nearby, is real fruit juices, made on the spot and often more resembling a smoothy than straight juice. One of my favourites is a mango and starfruit juice, the acid of the starfruit taking the sweet edge off the mango.

In Indonesia and a few other places you won't often find cutlery to eat with. This is finger food though I've always found it difficult to eat with the right hand only, especially when you have an adept local sitting next to you. And of course these night markets are incredibly cheap places to eat.

Ashore in Kupang

Provisions

You can get the basics, but there is little in the way of imported goods and it can be a little difficult sorting through the labels to identify exactly what is what. Just along from the fishing harbour is the main market, the pasar, with fresh fruit and vegetables. It's a bit of a walk to get to though you can take a *bemo* (local minibus). Otherwise there are market stalls in town.

Eating out

There are a few vaguely western eateries in town, though I wouldn't recommend most of them. Near the fishing harbour is the Café Lavalon with eccentric service and a wonderful view. And Wi-Fi.

For eating out in the evening the night market is the place to go. At night the main street you come up to off the beach is barricaded off and becomes a night market with small stalls serving excellent food of all types. You can get seafood, grilled chicken, lamb, stews of various types, nearly all of it comes with sticky rice. If you are having fish it will be displayed for you to make your choice of which one you are having. Some of the stalls have gone up-market and have an electric fan to get the charcoal burning and give it a bit of a boost when it dies down.

Fruit and vegetables on the hoof

The bread van

Kupang is a ramshackle city littered with rubbish where the whiff of drains lingers in the street. It is also delightfully un-touristy, vital and has a brilliant night market. From the anchorage you land on the beach and one of Napa's 'boys' keeps an eye on the dinghy. If the afternoon sea breeze blows onshore it can be a bit wet landing or departing the beach, but there were always willing hands to drag the dinghy out onto the beach or help launch it.

Wandering around town you can find some things you need and lots you don't. The streets bustle with bemos (mini-buses) and motorbikes buzzing about. There are only a handful of tourists here and that makes you a target for the half a dozen touts selling ikkats, the traditional hand woven cloth usually worn as a scarf when getting dressed up or as ceremonial adornments, usually signifying rank. Different islands have different patterns and the yarn is dyed with vegetable dyes, well at least that's the story, and woven by hand on looms with stylised lizards, fish and birds and more abstract emblems. Lu bought a couple after three days of intermittent bargaining – they used to meet us on the beach when we came ashore.

The voyages of exploration in the great European age of exploration were spurred on by tales of gold and silver in the lands of the east, of the new lands themselves, and of the spices that came from the east and especially the fabled East Indies. This is where the mythopoeic kingdom of Prester John was said to be close to, a kingdom of Christians where voyagers would be made welcome amongst their own and who would share the fabulous wealth of the kingdom.

Columbus was the first to set off, sailing westward for the East Indies only to discover the West Indies and its own wealth, though not the fabulous spices of the East Indies. The Portuguese had long been attempting a route directly to the east around Africa and in 1498 Vasco da Gama made it to India. 'I come in search of Christians and spices'; Vasco da Gama said, but he quickly forgot about the Kingdom of Prester John and loaded up with spices. He returned to Portugal with a cargo of spices and the king lost no time in sending off subsequent expeditions. By 1501 the Portuguese were established in India and in Europe the price of pepper was used to set currency rates. It wasn't long before the Dutch were using the eastbound route and setting up rival trading bases through the Indian Ocean. Clashes between the Portuguese and Dutch were frequent with the Portuguese generally coming off worst. In 1519 Magellan set off on his voyage around the world to find a westbound route to the east. He died in the Philippines before he

Man-eating dragons

While Komodo is known as the place to go and see Komodo Dragons, Crocodile Creek on the small island of Rinca is often the favoured stop for cruising boats. According to our guide, and you have to take a guide, Rinca actually had more dragons on it than Komodo Island. Our young guide, a student from Labuan Bajo working here to get money to go to university, was full of facts on the fauna and flora of the island, though he bemoaned the fact he had been here for two months with 'no girls' and had another two months to go.

Although I had seen pictures of the giant lizards, I somehow expected them to be a bit like fat over-sized iguanas. But the size of these things is just frightening. Adults can grow up to 10ft long and they are bulky beasts with a prehistoric menace to them. Add to that the fact they can do 17km/hr for short bursts and I began to feel distinctly uneasy. Our guide had a forked stick to keep them away, but given that he was five foot nothing and slightly built, I reckoned the dragons would find him nothing more than a snack with us as the main course. Apparently they bring down their prey (Timor deer, water buffalo, young komodo dragons, monkeys, scrub fowl and the odd human) by biting them and tracking them as they die. The mouth of the Komodo Dragon is full of nasty bacteria and a poison and the prey dies from being infected and gradually weakened, rather than the physical injury itself. The dragons just wait until the prey is too weak to defend itself.

Young Komodo Dragons live in the trees for three years to avoid being eaten by their larger cousins. The only drawback to

That forked stick the guide carries is all that stands between us and a hungry dragon. Didn't fill me with confidence

this is that sea eagles like to pick them off in the trees. The female lays a clutch of eggs in a hole in the ground and then guards them for around three months. The eggs don't hatch until 8–9 months depending on the temperature and after that the young are fair game for the adults.

The Komodo Dragons are quite hard to see initially as they lie very still and their grey skin provides good camouflage in the dry landscape. 'So do they attack humans?' I asked. Our guide nodded nervously. 'How do you keep them away with that stick?' He told me that the Komodo's nose was very sensitive so he just poked the nose with it. I didn't feel very assured by this. 'So have any of the guides been attacked?' 'I have been attacked, just once, but last year a guide was attacked and killed' he said. 'And in March a fisherman was killed.' I just made sure I had a clear route of escape as we wandered around the park on what I can only assume the Komodo's thought was a dinner path. After all dozens of tourists walk around here every day on the same route and a lot of them looked like they couldn't run very fast.

Komodo Dragon. Eats water buffalo, goats, monkeys and the occasional human

set eyes on the fabled spice islands, but his pioneering route paved the way for the British and French to follow.

In the 1500s the East Indies were firmly in the hands of the Dutch and provided much of the wealth that modern Holland is built on. These islands produced spices in abundance, especially nutmeg, and the Dutch were determined to keep it that way. In many ways the European economy ran on the huge spice market and items like pepper and nutmeg acquired an unrealistic economic value. A pound of pepper could buy a cow. A pound of nutmeg could buy a house. And it was not just pepper and nutmeg, but cinnamon, ginger, mace, and cloves that were brought back in quantity.

In an age where food readily spoiled these spices were used to preserve food and disguise the taste of salted meat. It was only the rich who could afford to do this and not surprisingly you demonstrated affluence to others around your table by serving highly spiced sauces and puddings. Spices were also believed to have medicinal properties and there are all sorts of potions using spices for warding off bad humours, curing diseases, sweetening the breath and adding to general well-being. Ginger was believed to aid digestion, to calm flatulence, ward off colds and flu, to stimulate appetite and sexual appetite as well. Cloves were used to aid digestion, combat flatulence and as a local anaesthetic. Clove oil is still used today as a local anaesthetic for toothache – we carry it onboard. The rich also used spices to disguise their own rank odour in an age where washing yourself was thought to be dangerous and to give rise to bad humours and disease.

The Dutch were keen to keep their monopoly on the spice islands and even went as far as to uproot nutmeg and clove trees on some islands and re-plant them on other more easily defended islands. This all came to an end when in 1770 Pierre Poivre, a French botanist, smuggled nutmeg and clove trees and the pepper vine out of the East Indies and re-planted them in Mauritius, the Seychelles and other French colonies. By 1795 the English were growing clove and nutmeg trees in Penang off the coast of Malaysia. This broke the Dutch monopoly so that by the 19th century the spices were more widely available and prices dropped. I just love

Agar Agar

In lots of the bays in Indonesia you will come across marine farms with lots of buoys in rows or sometimes just clumps. There may or may not be a large buoy or a floating platform marking the extremity of the buoys. At first I thought they might be mussel farms, but you don't get too many mussels on the menu in Indonesia, then maybe they were for pearl cultivation. It was only in Telok Bari that I discovered from some curious teenagers who had paddled out to the boat that many of the marine farms were growing seaweed (and that took some time with the aid of a Bahasa – English phrasebook), agar agar to be precise.

Anyone who did biology at school will know that agar is used to prepare a sterile nutrient jelly that is used in petri dishes to grow cultures of bacteria and fungi. Agar, it appears, is used throughout Southeast Asia in desserts, to thicken soups, it is used by vegetarians as a gelatine substitute as well as for a sterile medium in microbiological work. Most of it is exported to Japan (where it is called *kanten*) and this probably explains why the lads who came out were learning Japanese (and English and German) at school. They had to go and get some to show us and it looks remarkably gelatinous in its natural state. And the word 'agar' comes from the Bahasa word for jelly: agar agar.

Under the volcano. Sailing past Sangeang Island in *Skylax*

Proas go out to fish on the evening breeze. These things with a crab-claw sail just fly in the lightest of breezes

the fact that Monsieur Poivre had pepper named after him. Imagine if a Wilson or a Smith had done the same and we talked about 'pass the Wilson' or 'the Smith'.

On *Skylax*, replete with nutmeg and cinnamon from the local market in Kupang, we headed north up to the chain of islands known as the Nusa Tenggara, literally the Southeast Islands. The islands run pretty much from west to east with Bali at one end and West Timor at the other end. The plan was to island hop along the chain until we headed north again. The chain includes a number of islands popular with cruisers including Flores, Rinca, Komodo, Sumbawa, Lombok and of course Bali.

One of the most striking features of the islands is that there are volcanoes everywhere. Most are dormant, at least for now, but all around can be seen the characteristic cones and craters of volcanoes past and present. Some of them are alive and well, occasionally firing up at night, though most just let off a bit of steam from fumaroles on the side.

These volcanoes all sit on the western edge of what is called 'the ring of fire' in the Pacific, on a subduction zone where the Indo-Australian plate rubs up against the Eurasian plate causing earthquakes and letting magma bubble up to the surface and explode out of weak spots in the earth's crust. And there are a lot of weak spots spawning volcanoes. Krakatoa in the Sunda Strait between Sumatra and Java is the one we have all heard of and this massive eruption in 1883 destroyed most of the original island and flung so much dust into the air that world temperatures dropped for the ensuing two years of volcanic winter because the sun was partially obscured. This region is the most active in the entire ring of fire with more volcanic eruptions than anywhere else around the Pacific basin. I have to confess to some uneasiness as we sailed around Sangeang Island at dusk, a gigantic volcano sitting in the Flores Sea, a little fumarole puffing away on its north side as the insignificant speck of *Skylax* edged westwards on a fading breeze.

Everywhere along the island chain the locals are welcoming and curious about us, politics, Europe, America, the world. Finding provisions can be a bit difficult with some of the local shops stocking just a few basics and not much else. Many of the villages have their own gardens, a bit of livestock and maybe a proa to do a bit of fishing. These proas are lightning fast even in light winds and in many of the anchorages would come zooming out past *Skylax* before disappearing out to sea. Hours later they would come zooming back in again, hopefully with some fish.

There are fishing boats everywhere which makes navigation at night a little daunting

Opportunities for eating out were a mixed bag. Local eateries were basic unless there was a night market. The few hotels along the way charged royally for some basic barbecued food and often the 'show'. Villagers were drafted in to perform traditional dance routines though they looked either bored or edged towards wanting to put a spear through some of the boorish audience. These 'shows' don't really work for me and I'd much rather just wander around a village taking the time of day with the inhabitants and watching everyday life.

Labuan Bajo, a small town on the northwest end of Flores is a base for charter boats running to Rinca and Komodo to see the Komodo dragons and go diving on the excellent coral around the islands. It is a scruffy place, but we liked it. It has all the hustle and bustle of a trading port straight out of Conrad and ashore there are a couple of good restaurants with a sort of Asian fusion menu, a big improvement on some of the fare we had along the way. And out of town there was a good bazaar though you needed to take a bemo to get there.

We headed north near the end of the chain stopping here and there for the night. Indonesia is such a vast archipelago you can easily underestimate distances and it's a fair old hike up to Singapore. At night there are fishing boats everywhere, floating villages with pressure lamps and the ubiquitous coloured strobe lights. Most of the boats using lights to fish at night are squid boats though they take anything they can get.

Throughout the archipelago makeshift Fish Attracting Devices (FADs) are employed. These are commonly a bamboo raft with some palm leaves on top and a bucket at either end to slow the rate of drift. In the morning and evening the 'owner' will come out and fish around the FAD. In places there will be a lot of them, a maze that you need to zigzag through. They are not lit and don't show up on radar so at night are a real problem. I nearly hit one and only avoided it by a matter of feet when I spotted its dark outline just in front of us. Now you might think a bamboo raft wouldn't do much damage, but in Southeast Asia bamboo is frequently used to build scaffolding on construction sites, often up to five stories and more, so if it's that strong… I don't want to hit a bamboo FAD at speed.

The jumping off point for Singapore is Batam Island on the south side of the Singapore Straits. This is a purpose built resort with a marina. It's all quite *shi shi* and a bit of a shock. From the marina you can see the constant stream of shipping in the Singapore Strait and the high-rise profile of downtown Singapore.

Small celebration for crossing the equator again. The local beer, Bintang, is quite OK

Singapore

Sitting in Nongsa Point Marina and looking out to the Singapore Strait it's not often that you don't see two or three ships passing by. I have never seen tankers as big as these with some of them the size of several football pitches. Singapore is the busiest port in the world (so Singapore MPA says) with some 140,000 shipping calls every year. I work that out to be an average of 380 shipping calls a day. On any one day there are reckoned to be 400 ships in the designated anchoring areas around Singapore. Ships transiting the strait are strictly regulated and are on average 15 seconds apart. In practice this is not how it works and you get ships overtaking in the strait, ships slowing down and turning to go into the Port of Singapore, and ships just going slowly while they take on supplies.

So the talk was of how to get across the strait to Singapore. There are two crossing zones clearly shown on all charts and any small craft like us need to cross the shipping channel as near to right angles as possible in either of these two zones. Fortunately we had 'Aussie Dean' at the bar who has been cruising around Indonesia and Southeast Asia from Darwin for the last 20 years or so. 'It's easy, no worries' he said, 'just head along the south side until you get to Batu Berhanti at the western crossing zone and then take a deep breath. Easy as ...'

It all turned out OK with a few 360s to avoid ships and then a chug along the built up coast until you get to the channel between Singapore and Malaysia leading to Raffles Marina.

One thing that will strike you is the vast extent of the oil storage tanks and refineries along this bit of Singapore. This little island has the third largest refinery area in the world. Singapore just keeps reclaiming more and more land from the sea so it now spreads out over a significantly bigger area than the original island ever did. A bit further on you will come across oil rigs in various states of construction. Singapore builds more oil rigs than anyone else in the world. To police all this fast patrol boats roar up and down all the time and call up ships that are not conforming or have not checked in with Singapore traffic control. It's a hurley-burley of organised chaos with more than enough going on to keep you occupied, but in practice it is not as bad as you might think as long as you keep your wits about you. And when you see how cool the fishing boats out in the strait potter about fishing while the behomeths of the oceans churn through then you feel a bit better about the whole thing.

Raffles Marina has nothing to do with the well-known Raffles Hotel in downtown apart from the name. It is nowhere near the eponymous hotel. The marina is part marina and part hotel and club.

Crossing the Singapore Strait

Ashore in Singapore

Provisions

Singapore has large supermarkets where you can find most things you want. Most of them are on the outskirts of downtown. It's worth stocking up on provisions here as there is little up the Malaysian coast until you get to Penang. From Raffles you can get a shuttle bus to Jugong, a local residential area with a shopping mall and supermarket. The shopping here on the outskirts is better than downtown where it's all hotels and restaurants.

Eating out

Singapore has a great mix of eateries. In somewhere like Raffles Marina the food is mostly a version of some sort of international cuisine. The same applies in many other places in downtown. Fortunately you can find good street food in all sorts of places. Most of it is on display so you don't need to be proficient in Chinese or Malay. Just point to what you want and be prepared to experiment. On the corner of the mall in Jugong there is good street food. In downtown much of the street food has been sanitised and moved into food courts. Usually there will be a whole range of food from Chinese, Malay, Indian and western-style food and in these malls it is more likely those serving you will speak English.

There is also China town, Little India and some established street food markets like Orchard Street and Lau Pa Sat in China town. One of the small problems about it all is that 10 million tourists visit Singapore every year and downtown is not that big. What I'm getting at is that you will not be discovering a very local sort of place unless you are outside downtown in a more residential 'local' area.

Raffles Hotel is usually cited as a must-visit to sit in the elegant colonial surroundings and drink a Singapore Sling. The slight problem is that everyone else will be doing this and a Singapore Sling here costs an arm and a leg. There are other restored hotels and bars that will be a little less crowded and I'd suggest having a look at Raffles and then getting a drink elsewhere.

Berth holders automatically become members which means you can use all the facilities including the pool, the showers (a beautiful fluffy white towel is provided at the desk) and a discount in the restaurant and bistro. You are miles away from downtown here, but the MRT, the Mass Rail Transport system is fast and efficient and cheap. You can get to most places or close to most places in Singapore and then take a taxi to where you want to go.

Raffles Marina has little to do with the eponymous founder of Singapore

If you read any of the media articles on piracy and a lot of the stuff on the internet you will see the Malacca Strait gets mentioned as an area where yachts need to be on the lookout for pirates. It's cited as a 'piracy risk area' which sounds authoritative but doesn't mean much at all. It neglects the fact that piracy here is much diminished and what piracy does occur is on ships and not yachts. It's not pirates you need to worry about here, but unlit hazards like fishing boats, nets and FADs, logs and especially lightning strikes. There are a lot of thunderstorms with frightening amounts of electricity arcing through the night sky.

Malaysian fishing boats. At night in the Malacca Straits there are lots of them to zig-zag through

On *Skylax* we pottered up the Malacca Strait anchoring behind islands or tucking into harbours and bays on the Malaysian coast. Every year several boats are damaged, usually damage to the propeller and shaft, when motor sailing at night and encountering nets and logs. A number of boats have been sunk from hitting waterlogged logs that float just on the surface or just beneath it. Fishing boats will usually display a light of some sort but not always as I found out. Just before Port Dickson at three in the morning we were humming along at 6½ knots under sail when I dimly saw a shape ahead of me and just managed to get the wheel over to skim by a 40 foot solid hardwood fishing boat. He was not lit at all. If we had hit him we would have sustained serious damage at the very least and quite possibly could have sunk. Not to mention injury to the fishermen and us.

From Port Klang we were racing in the Raja Muda Regatta. In Port Klang on the river berth we were in a scene straight out of Conrad's *Lord Jim*. A steaming tropical river port teeming with coasters and lighters loading and unloading cargo, the river itself full of rubbish swirled along by the current, tin-roofed houses down at the waters edge with rickety wooden jetties, a miasma of steamy mist overlaying the water… this is Conrad's river. Even in town you get a feeling of edgy goings-on, of seedy characters in dilapidated bars off the main street, of conmen and others. We were had when a car pulled to a halt and a well-groomed Indian man got out. 'Do you have any small change… I need to change 100 Ringit…' With slight of hand and the old distraction technique he managed to take a 100 Ringit off us before a friendly shop-keeper warned us to have nothing to do with this 'bad man'.

Port Klang. Like somewhere out of Conrad's *Lord Jim*

SOUTHEAST ASIA

Raja Muda

Every year in November the Raja Muda Regatta runs from Port Klang to Langkawi near the Thai border. There are three offshore legs and some inshore races. In *Skylax* we are in the fat cruising class with just three of us crewing. There are lots of hot racing boats taking part, all carbon fibre and lots of beefy crew. On *Skylax* we have everything on board as is normal for cruising which at least means we eat well and can rummage in the bilge, our wine cellar, for a good bottle of something when we finish.

If there was an unanticipated bonus to the regatta that I didn't really expect it was the hospitality and the food. At every stop a bounteous spread was laid on in the evening, a mix of local Malay, Chinese and Indian food. The highlight was the Penang stopover where an old Chinese courtyard with a shrine to the ancestors at either end was surrounded by stalls serving some of the best streetfood I have had. It was impossible to sample it all, partly because I had to go back and try the tempura prawns and the lemon pork with noodles more than once.

The Raja Muda ends up in Langkawi with a royal bash at the Royal Langkawi Yacht Club. How did we do? Well the last inshore race was a bit of a disaster when I managed to hit a coral outcrop that I had actually circled on the chart as dangerous. Even so we were still first in class. Not bad for a fat cruising boat replete with food stores and a wine cellar.

Breakfast for one of the raceboats in the Raja Muda

From the detached pontoon in the river you look across to the wonderful Royal Selangor Yacht Club, built in Malay style and open to what little wind there is. A bumboat runs you across the river and you sink into rattan chairs and order a drink from the attentive staff while fans whirl overhead. Malay style with colonial overtones.

From Port Klang we race offshore to Pangkor Island, a frustrating leg where at one point in the night we are going backwards with the tide. The leg from Pangkor to Penang involves a windy start and we do well against the racing classes as well as easily winning our class. At one point we have a fully crewed up IRC 2 boat trying to engage us in a sailing duel, the French crew ducking and diving around our stern. I shout out to them that they are wasting their time, we are fat cruising class, to no avail until Lu who is on the helm calls out 'And it's a girl driving as well.'

Royal Selangor YC in Port Klang

Start of the Raja Muda off Port Klang

Stilt fishing house built out from the coast.
They have fixed fish traps to catch fish as the tide goes in and out

Penang is one of my favourite places along this stretch of coast. It's a wonderful mix of old British colonial, Chinese mews and temples, Indian and Malay, all peppered with a few skyscrapers here and there. Fortunately it is now a UNESCO World Heritage site so all the wonderful old buildings cannot be torn down. And as I indicate in the Ashore section, it has superb street food.

The final offshore leg of the Raja Muda was our best, the wind just forward of the beam and *Skylax* at full throttle eating up the miles. The Royal Langkawi Yacht Club sits close to the ferry port for Kuah, the main town. It is a bit of a ramshackle place, spilling out in different directions with a barely focussed centre. It does have the advantage of being a duty free island where everything is that little bit cheaper than elsewhere in Malaysia.

Around the main island there is a scattered archipelago of islands and islets, all steep limestone and covered in jungle. There are 99 islands according to the tourist office, but that means counting some pretty small rocky lumps that don't really qualify as islets let alone islands. Around the shores of the main island of Langkawi there are a number of up-market hotels and a few marinas. At Telaga Marina on the northwest of the island there is a little cluster of restaurants which give you some idea of what the out-of-town developments are like: an Italian, not half bad, a Chinese, average, a Spanish restaurant, a Russian Soviet-style restaurant complete with symbols from the old days of the Communists, and a vaguely Western establishment. Fortunately around the back there is a little Indian roti shop for cheap eating. It's a bit of a drive to Kuah to get good street food again.

Downtown Penang, a mix of old colonial architecture that now has UNESCO Heritage status

The Quarterdeck at the Royal Langkawi YC is not a bad place for a drink and bite to eat

Telaga Marina. A logical jumping off point for the Indian Ocean

Ashore in Penang

Provisions

There are a couple of small supermarkets on or near the high street though the stock is not huge. There are also bakeries and greengrocers. The market on several roads off the high street and towards the Strait of Penang is amazing. You can get everything from fruit and vegetables to sausages (there will be trays of them drying in the sun), frogs (live and looking somehow stunned when plucked from the basket for a customer), chickens, cakes, just about anything local you can think of.

Little India in Penang

Eating out

Penang has just about the best street food around. Just wander up the high street and down any of the side streets and you will find Malay Halal eating houses with trays and trays of things like chicken, lamb and fish stews, satay dishes, chicken, lamb, and vegetable coconut curries, rotis, rice (try tomato rice), and things I am not even sure of but tasted delicious. Rotis, either *roti canai* or more rarely *roti tisu*, are used to mop up the curries or sometimes just to mop up curry sauce. *Roti canai* is like the thin pages of roti in a 'book' of roti. *Roti tisu* is, as its name suggests, like ripped up tissue paper piled up on a plate. Most of these places have cutlery, but at some stalls there is no cutlery and the roti is what you use to grab chunks of food with to eat.

In the high street itself there are several good Halal restaurants. The one thing you can't get in these places is alcohol, but they do wonderful fresh juices made on the spot. Eat here and then wander down towards the waterfront for a drink in a licensed bar or café.

In Little India there are tandoori restaurants serving the best tandoori chicken anywhere. I know this sounds a bit over the top, but these simple restaurants do serve wonderful tandoori as well as all sorts of curries and rotis. Most of them are owned by Muslim Indians and so no alcohol again. Don't let that put you off.

Chinese restaurants in Penang have been a bit of a disappointment and I'd steer towards the Halal and Indian restaurants and stalls. I just want to know where some of the Chinese food served at the Raja Muda dinner is for sale. Some Chinese noodle shops do lunch only and these were the pick of the bunch. Both Malays and Chinese use noodles and if you hunt around you can find a few good noodle dishes. Kampua is a noodle dish that can have just vegetables or minced chicken or pork. It's a simple dish, sometimes eaten for breakfast in Malaysia, but tasty. In places you will also get things like prawn noodle soup (*prawn mee*) and chilli crab with noodles. And *chow mein* of course.

There are also plenty of restaurants doing more western fare including steaks, pizza and the like, but don't miss the Halal and tandoori places.

Night market in Penang

Roti shop

Sausages drying in the sun in Penang market

Halal eatery on Langkawi. You need to visit a few times just to get through some of the food on offer

Not a job I'd fancy in the sometimes frenetic traffic of Penang

Roti shop

Strange fruits

Apart from all the usual tropical fruits like pineapples, bananas, mangoes and papaws, Malaysia has a whole plateful of strange and assorted fruits.

Some like the durian which smells like a sewer and tastes like sour ice cream are for aficionados only. Due to the smell, it is banned in many places like cafés and buses and ferries.

Others should be tried and tried again. The rambutan is cousin to the lychee and tastes just as good. The mangosteen is the size of an orange but with a dark purple skin concealing white segments which taste like sweet and sour strawberries and grapes. The starfruit is a pale green and when cut has a star shape. It has a cool slightly sweet lime taste and is one of my favourite fruit juices. The custard apple or zirzat has a warty green exterior over a creamy white flesh that tastes of lemon.

In the markets you can find stalls which do slices or segments of these fruits and so can taste all of them and then select what you want. You can also get a fresh fruit salad made up of those you fancy.

Ashore in Kuah

Provisions

Halfway between the Royal Langkawi YC and Kuah town there is a good supermarket in the Langkawi Fair Mall on the main road. It's easiest with a taxi to get back and forth. There are a couple of other smallish supermarkets in Kuah where you can get most things. If you want bacon and sausages you need to find one of the Chinese grocery shops where the pork is kept out at the back. Ask around. For fruit and vegetables there are numerous shops and stalls though in general the selection and freshness is not great. Most of it is imported from the mainland.

Local eatery on Kuah

Langkawi is the place to stock up on drink. If heading west you are headed for a wine desert until you get to either the Mediterranean or South Africa. Duty free prices mean everything from beer to spirits to wine is reasonably priced and you should take advantage of it.

Eating out

There are good local eateries in Kuah though you need to spend a bit of time looking for them. The Quarterdeck in the Royal Langkawi YC is the gathering place for yachties in the marina and in the anchorage. The food is western style but

not bad for all that. Down in the park with the giant eagle statue there are a clutch of little restaurants serving all sorts of local food and are just a stroll away from the marina. There is a night market on the waterfront in Kuah most nights although it may be in other parts of the island on some nights. No worry, just head inland where there are good local restaurants serving Halal Malay food, Indian and some good Chinese eateries. I had garlic prawns in a barely sanitary Chinese shack here that were so good I had to have them again. Surprisingly KFC and McDonalds are also well established here.

Christmas in Malaysia

After Thailand we cruised back down to Malaysia where a Christmas cooking duel had been arranged with the Professor. Chickens and stuffing, potatoes and vegetables, Christmas puddings and brandy butter were all to be produced on the dot of 12 o'clock on *Skylax*. Suitable vintages had been procured for the day and extras like paté de foie gras and a mature Roquefort were also on the menu. *Skylax* roast chicken with a gentle Thai inspired marinade and lemon roast potatoes pulled off a coup. The Professor (actually Emeritus Professor as Peter likes to remind us) was in with the Christmas pudding and superb brandy butter.

Christmas in the Tropics has its benefits. After the feast we piled into the dinghies with a bottle or two of red and motored over to a little islet with a sandy beach and wonderful turquoise water to swim in. After that it was home again for an early night.

Christmas in Malaysia – sun hats and crackers

Yachts traditionally leave Southeast Asia after New Year, preferably not the day after, when the northeast monsoon has kicked in for an easy passage to Sri Lanka, India or the Maldives depending on inclination.

We were in a bit of a hurry to get up to Thailand for the Kings Cup Regatta and had to pick up crew who were arriving in Phuket. So we left Langkawi for Phuket with just a couple of stops along the way. Cruising around the islands and coast could wait.

After the racing we cruised gently around the islands in Phangna Bay. There are any number of spectacular limestone islands, many of them with hongs, caves that the rain has carved out of the limestone as it filters through it. Around the islands it is so shallow everywhere that you can anchor almost anywhere. In the NE monsoon there are lots of anchorages on the west side of the islands and for the most part you can make it up by just looking at a chart. You could spend weeks around here before returning to Phuket to re-provision. Off Ko Pranak a longtail pulled up and lo and behold sold us dinner – a dozen fresh prawns.

After our rush to get up to Phuket for the racing at the King's Cup we ambled south through the islands to Malaysia. Christmas was coming up and soon it would be time to set off on an ocean passage to Sri Lanka.

Phang Nga Bay off Phuket

Ashore in Phuket

Phuket is in danger of becoming the Thai Singapore it is now so built up. Most of the tourist facilities are on the west coast though there are smaller developments all around the coast. To service all of this, and the permanent or semi-permanent population of foreigners there is a strip of shops, malls and office buildings running along the busy main road from Ao Chalong in the south to well north of Phuket town.

Provisions

To get to the various supermarkets it's probably best to be in Ao Chalong where they are within walking distance or in Boat Lagoon where they are a short ride away. You can get everything here from fancy bread to bacon and hams to fine wines. On a more basic level there are small grocery shops and greengrocers shops scattered around. Again Ao Chalong is probably the best place to be despite the long ride back to the boat in a bit of a chop while loaded down with shopping.

Eating out

There are good tourist restaurants everywhere, by which I mean Thai tourist restaurants. I recommend the tourist restaurants because the food is a bit less fiery than in local restaurants.

In Ao Chalong the Anchor Inn has long been a favourite and the Captain Hook (just ignore the name) also has good food. On the waterfront Jimmy's Lighthouse is a popular haunt for yachties and they serve reasonable western style food as well. Around the coast it's a matter of using your nose to sniff out restaurants that are likely candidates. Apart from Thai there is everything from Indian, some good if quite shi-shi Italian and French restaurants, and the inevitable pizza places. You won't be short of places to eat out on this cosmopolitan island.

Street food in Thailand is great and anywhere there are people about there will be stalls and carts from late afternoon to late. Most of the stalls are run by women and you will invariably find yourself being pinched on the bum, led by the hand or entreated in some way to patronise a stall. If you are going to a restaurant you will also probably have to run the gamut of the girly bars and here you will be entreated again. Just smile, it's the Thai way, and wander on to make your own choice in your own time.

Pad Thai noodles are probably the most common and are basically stir-fried rice noodles with some vegetables, chilli, tamarind paste and any of shrimps, chicken, pork or the vegetarian option with tofu. I usually order it with a small amount of chilli. Barbecued kebabs, usually chicken or pork, are common and usually served with a bit of rice. Tom Yam soup is also a favourite, a sweet and sour broth that may contain noodles and depending on the vendor, prawns, chicken or pork. The list of dishes could go on for a while, but I'd suggest you explore for yourself and ask for the chilli content to be toned down if at all possible.

Thai Buddhist shrine. Gifts of food, rice, fruit, something to drink, are left here every night

Dinner arrives, freshly caught prawns, in Phangna Bay

King's Cup

The King's Cup takes place at the beginning of December and is a proper racing series, though thankfully it still has a cruising class for the likes of *Skylax* laden with food and wine for the Indian Ocean passage. Mind you we were one of the few in our class with everyone living on board and fully laden for the trip. Joe from Greece was out with Graham from New Zealand to beef up the crew as this is a more high-powered event than the Raja Muda. There was also some history here. In 1995, in a previous cruise down here in the 31ft *Tetranora,* I had won my class with just Graham for crew and we thought it would be good to repeat the experience.

We had some hot competition in the racing and though we did well when there was a bit of wind, things were not so good when the wind was light. Somehow we squeaked a win in our class. Lots of the boats here have their own Southeast Asia campaign and we retrospectively got embroidered crew shirts made up featuring the *Skylax* Southeast Asia campaign to mark our win in our class.

King's Cup party after the racing. More food and drink than you can poke a spinnaker pole at

Like the Raja Muda there is a substantial amount of eating and drinking that goes on ashore after the racing, all included in the race fee. I'm not sure why more cruising boats don't take part in these racing series.

Don't believe it. First overall in class in the King's Cup

'Mouse shit' chillies

This is one of the smallest chillies, a tiny red fruit of fire. The Thai name for it, *prik kee noo*, literally means the mouse shit chilli. It is used liberally in most Thai cuisine and you don't need much of it to impart a chilli fire in your mouth that will cancel out any other spices used.

Chillies probably arrived here with the Portuguese, or maybe some Arab traders from what is now Yemen or Oman, sometime in the 16th century after Columbus had brought chillies to Europe from the New World. Over the years the Thais must have propagated the mouse shit chilli and by the 19th century it was used in most Thai cuisine.

The story behind the 'mouse shit' epithet is sweeter than it sounds. Small Thai children are often called 'noo' or mouse as a term of affection. Likewise mice are regarded as an everyday part of life in Thai villages and under the gentle Buddhist culture of the country are regarded somewhat affectionately. All that Buddhist respect for all life sort of thing. Just as you know that mice have been around by their little droppings, so the anecdotal evidence goes, you only know there are mouse shit chillies in food when you encounter a bit of it in the food and then, you know it is there.

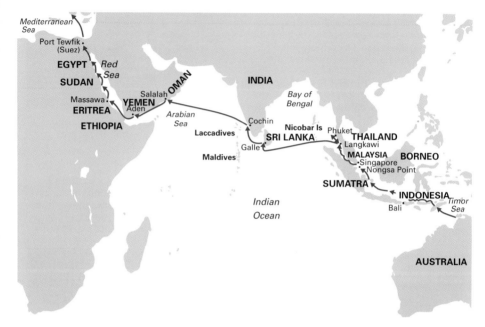

Cruising has two pleasures. One is to go out in wider waters from a sheltered place. The other is to go into a sheltered place from wider waters. *Howard Bloomfield*

So the time has come. We have visas in advance for India. Tomorrow we go to get fresh stuff, some meat, fruit and vegetables and eggs before leaving on Thursday for Galle in Sri Lanka. It's been some time since we have been on passage and like all departures we have a few butterflies about leaving Telaga Marina where life is easy. Heading out into the Big Blue seems like something utterly new after cruising the coast and islands of SE Asia. Hopefully after a few days we will settle back into the rhythm of old Mother Sea and life in a small capsule bouncing along the surface of the water will seem quite normal.

Yachts leaving from Langkawi will usually head for the Great Channel between Great Nicobar Island and the northern end of Sumatra as it is closer to the rhumb line than more northerly channels. Yachts leaving from Phuket will usually use the Sombrero Channel.

The Nicobars are the mystery islands of the Indian Ocean. You need a special permit to visit them and these are next to impossible to get from the Indian government. The reasons given are that the special ecology of the Nicobars should not be intruded upon by visitors. This includes intrusion on the tribes who live here with a veiled reference to the aggressive nature of the locals. Poison arrows are even mentioned. Most people believe the protective attitude of the Indian government has more to do with military installations on the islands and as you transit the channels between the islands you are often over-flown by military jets from the Nicobars.

Day 1

14th Jan 1000. Slipped lines at Telaga Marina. Filled up with diesel on the fuel dock. Heading for Galle in Sri Lanka.

2300. Wind ENE 6 Speed 7·7. Time for a reef? Several ships. Lightning out to starboard.

Day 2

15th Jan 1200. Wind ENE 4 Speed 4·9 knots. Gentle sailing. Reading. Sleeping. Bacon sarnies for lunch. Daily run 133M.

Day 3

16th Jan 1500. Wind ENE 3 Speed 4·0 knots. Sailing slowly goose-winged. 36°C below. Slow progress.

Day 4

17th Jan 1200. Wind ENE 4 Speed 5·7 knots. Gybed genny over. Wing and wing now. In Nicobar Channel. Daily run 177M.

Day 5

18th Jan 0600. Wind NE 5 Speed 7·0 knots. Two dolphins trailing lots of phosphorescence. Lots, lots, lots of lightning. Wind shifty.

Day 6

19th Jan 1200. Wind ENE 5 Speed 7·2 knots. Lu doing radio sched as net controller. Daily run 157M.

Day 7

20th Jan 2000. Wind NNE 5 Speed 6·9 knots. Still rattling along. Moon looking plumper.

Day 8

21st Jan 0500. Wind NNE 6 Speed 7·7 knots. Fast, wet, wild, 25 miles in less than 3 hours. Ship.

Day 9

1730. Anchor down in Galle harbour after clearing in. Drinks.

Coconut figures highly in Sri Lankan cuisine

The gas bottle terrorist

You need to be a bit careful filling gas bottles in some places. Bottles are normally filled to a set weight and somehow in Galle something went wrong when on a previous trip here in 1996 I had a bottle over-filled. As I carried it back it began hissing from around the rubber collar and the hissing got worse as I got closer to the boat. You have to remember that the civil war in Sri Lanka was at its height. Every night the soldiers rowed around the harbour dropping sticks of dynamite into the water to deter Tamil frogmen from swimming in and attaching mines to the naval boats.

By the time I got to the boat the bottle was hissing spectacularly and the only thing I could think of doing was to run up to the front of the boat and throw it in the water. The bottle erupted as it hit the water and like some demented porpoise dived down to the bottom and then up again to five or six foot above the surface before dropping down again and repeating the sequence. The soldiers on the shore clambered into one of their boats and roared over pointing automatic rifles at what was clearly a Tamil torpedo porpoising around the harbour. I shouted to them not to fire. The consequences of a bullet hitting the gas container could have produced a nice little explosion in the harbour.

Finally the bottle used up its propellant and slowed to a giddy circling motion on the surface. The soldiers retrieved it and returned it to me with more relief than admonishment at my foolhardiness. I was just happy that I hadn't set off a fire-fight in Galle harbour.

As we are leaving the Great Channel between the Nicobars and Sumatra one of the ships transiting the channel gives us a call on VHF. 'Gidday, where are you headed,' the voice with a marked South African accent asks. We explain where we have come from, where we are going, and find out he is a yachtie with a boat in the Caribbean at the moment. 'Well, we are just having a braai on the back deck,' he says. I query whether he can slow down a bit and we could tie up behind him for some barbecued steaks and a glass or two of South African wine. 'Not like that anymore,' he says, 'we have to account for every minute, any deviation from our course, anything and everything we do is clocked' he says. 'Not like the old days, not like you guys sailing free of schedules and timesheets and bosses in an office somewhere'.

This passage across the Bay of Bengal is normally a gentle one until you get closer to Sri Lanka where the wind is pushed off India and accelerates down the side of Sri Lanka with a lot more force. So it proved. We ate and drank well on a relatively benign passage until closer to Sri Lanka where a day and a night of stronger winds whooshed us down and along the bottom of Sri Lanka. We arrived off the old Dutch trading port of Galle in the afternoon and after being checked by the navy and negotiating a few little presents for odd marineros and navy officials were allowed into the port.

If you are prone to internet and cruiser rumour then the likelihood is that Sri Lanka does not figure on your list of destinations to visit in this part of the world. Sri Lanka

Pole fishing

Along the coast from Galle there are the pole fishermen often depicted in tourist photos. At Welligama and Polhenna Beach there are poles rammed or wedged into the sea bottom with surf crashing all around them. The fishermen wade out to the poles and stand on wooden supports to fish the water around. They only seem to catch tiny little fish, but they can catch quite a few in a short time. This method of fishing is reputed to be the oldest continuous method of fishing in the world.

Spices of all types in a Galle shop. Find the local shops instead of the 'tourist spice shops'

often gets bad press from those who visit by boat. To be sure there is some minor corruption, there are touts all over the place and there is always the tang of violence in the air from the Singhalese Tamil problem. Ignore all this because Sri Lanka remains one of the most spectacular tropical islands in the world and the Sri Lankans themselves, the everyday folk you meet in the street, are some of the nicest people on this planet. All this despite a devastating civil war, the 2004 tsunami and internecine political rivalry that often spills over into violence.

The old fortified town of Galle has been partially restored and is a fascinating warren of streets with old colonial buildings dating from the Portuguese, the Dutch and later the English periods. The navies of these powers took Galle in succession to control the spice trade from the island. The walled town is mostly intact, a little scarred by time, but now undergoing a sympathetic restoration. It is a magical place to wander around and you can still get that wonderful English legacy of tea and plum cake in the tea house.

Ashore in Galle

You will sometimes get advice from the agents and touts here that you should let them negotiate for provisions and other things lest you get 'ripped off' by the locals. In fact this has never really been a problem here and wandering around Galle town to do the shopping is an interesting and lively experience.

Provisions

There is a supermarket close to the harbour where you can get most things. In Galle new town there is a strip of greengrocers' shops with an excellent selection on the main road near the waterfront. Also nearby are some good spice shops and smaller grocery shops as well. You can get a tuk tuk to ferry you around.

Eating out

Restaurants here are a mixed bag. Many will take a tuk tuk to Unawatuna where around a beautiful sandy beach there are small restaurants serving everything from simply prepared seafood to curries. This beach really is one of the most beautiful around and it's worth going for a long slow lunch here.

Around the new town there are lots of small restaurants serving mostly Southern Indian (Tamil) curries and snacks. In the walled old town there is the Galle Fort Hotel, a quite stunning conversion of an old colonial building. Pop in for a cold drink or a cappuccino on the veranda or better still go for a meal. The Asian fusion food is excellent if a little more expensive than other places. Still spoil yourself with a little old world charm and good food. Also in the old town is the Rampart Hotel with mediocre food but excellent rooftop views and Mama's with good Sri Lankan curries at good prices.

Street food is also a bit of a mixed bag. Nearly everything is served with a paratha, a flat bread much like a roti. And a lot of it uses coconut or coconut milk. The most common street food you will come across is kottu where shredded paratha is stir fried with vegetables and meat, sometimes seafood. It's tasty and quite filling. There will also be pots of curries using chicken, vegetables and pork usually served with rice and a paratha. There are also other dishes along similar lines, all quite highly spiced and often chilli hot.

Sweets are usually very sweet, a legacy of English colonial rule I suspect, with cakes and jellies overburdened with sugar. The local plum cake, though, is excellent.

You will miss a lot if you don't take a trip into the Highlands. For this you can take a 'guided tour' in a mini-van or take a car. From the coastal flats you head up into the highlands, to old colonial retreats in the cool of the mountains like Nuralia at some 6,500ft (you need warm clothes), past Buddhist temples, through tropical rain forest and waterfalls dropping hundreds of feet, and of course through vast tea plantations.

Tea was introduced to Sri Lanka and India by the British. Tea plants from China had been cultivated for a while, but it wasn't until the late 19th century that plantations were established. They are still here, great swathes of hill-side covered by the very ordinary looking tea plant along with the great colonial houses with sweeping verandahs built for the owners and managers of the plantations. You can take a tour of some of the processing plants and then sample a cup of tea afterwards. This is another Sri Lanka away from the booming surf on golden beaches and proas setting out through the surf to set nets in the inshore waters.

Drying the precious tea leaves in the Highlands

Tea in the Highlands

Touts and the food con

I met Anil while looking for an auto rickshaw in Galle.

'Come with me or they will charge you tourist prices' he said. 'I know you, I've seen you around the harbour… where is your wife?'

I explained she had to go back to the UK because of a death in the family. 'So sorry', he said, 'so sorry for your wife'.

And then he proceeded to tell me about the tsunami. 'I lost my fishing boat, my young daughter was swept out to sea and drowned, for four years we have been living in a camp, but now we have a small house. Sadly my other daughter has polio.'

I listened to this catalogue of disasters and grief told to me quietly and with restrained dignity by Anil and wondered how he could still be so helpful, so warm to me, by comparison the rich foreigner.

'What can I do?' I asked.

'Tell others,' he said, 'Tell them we are still here'.

'Maybe a mosquito net,' he said, 'For my daughter. And some milk powder and flour. We will go to the shop to buy it.' I gave him

the meagre 500 rupees he needed for the net and went to the shop and bought the groceries he requested. How could you not? He blessed me and held my hand.

A small price in the face of need.

Two days later I was waiting for a friend around the same area. Up popped Martin who told me how he had lost his fishing boat in the tsunami, 'Also my wife and my younger daughter. And my other daughter has polio. Maybe you could buy me some milk powder…' Now just maybe the similarity, the almost exact 'coached' nature of the stories, is coincidence. Or not. I bought him some milk powder and really the amounts are small (1US$ is approx. 150 Sri Lankan rupees).

Touting is a sophisticated way of life in Sri Lanka and touts are adept at spotting opportunities and exploiting them. I was talking to one of the agents and mentioned the approaches by Anil and Martin. He smiled and said I had been conned. Afterwards they return to the shop and in collusion with the shopkeeper return the goods and get the money. But then again life is hard in Sri Lanka and how much did it really cost me? I'm still a little confused.

Sri Lanka to India

Lu had to return home from Sri Lanka to England due to a death in the family. I was quite happy to take *Skylax* up to Cochin in India on my own, but soon had crew. A young Israeli lad, Adam, wondered if I could give him a lift to India. He didn't have much in the way of experience, hopefully he could do a few basics and make the trip a little sweeter. He was a vegetarian which would not be a problem as we often cook vegetarian dishes at sea. It's something under 400 miles to Cochin from Galle so I figured it only involved a few nights at sea anyway depending on what the wind gods dished out.

The wind funnels out of the Gulf of Mannar between Sri Lanka and the bottom of India with a bit of violence. Adam is a plucky lad though and soldiers on in between bouts of sea sickness. When we get to the bottom of India the wind dies and the seas calm down and Adam's appetite returns with a vengeance.

We arrived off the entrance to the buoyed channel at 2300 and I dithered about a night entry. Then I spotted a ship heading for the channel and pulled in behind confident that he drew a lot more than us and would have a pilot on board.

It turned out to be one of the large dredgers keeping the channel dredged and it was operating in the buoyed channel. Less than halfway down it stopped, turned around, and began dredging. Cochin is not an easy one for a night entry as the buoys are a considerable distance apart and in the haze that afflicts this coast you need a pair of binoculars to pick up the succession of buoys.

Still we got in safely and anchored off the Taj Malabar Hotel ready to clear in on the morrow. Customs duly came out to us in the morning. They asked for a beer for the guys in the boat but were otherwise polite and helpful. Mr Bijou, the

Day 1

2nd Feb 1115. Anchors up in Galle. Everything very muddy. Heading for Cochin.

1800. Wind NNW 4 Speed 4.4. Sailing slowly. Adam thinks dinner was excellent.

Day 2

3rd Feb 0300 Wind NNE 6 Speed 7.3 knots. Adam writes: 'My stomach is not to get out into the Gulf of Mannar'.

1500. Wind NNE 6 Speed 7.8 knots. Skylax humming. Adam braving out his sea sickness. Should calm down soon as we approach India.

Day 3

4th Feb 1200 Wind E 3–4. Speed 5.6 knots. Fishing boats asking for food. Green parrot on the cross-trees. Daily run 155M. Adam's appetite back.

1200. Chugging into the anchorage off the Taj Malabar Hotel in Cochin.

Anchorage off the Bolghatty Hotel

Coracle people in the Bolghatty anchorage

Customs officer, filled in much of the paperwork or advised me on what to put where, and then was waiting ashore to help. In the office it's all quaintly Dickensian, all manilla folders tied with ribbon and dusty ledgers lining the shelves.

We were met by an 'agent', Nasir and Ibrahim, who helped us through the formalities with the harbourmaster, customs, health and immigration. Of course they had a friend with a tuk tuk to ferry us around and afterwards he guided us in his boat into the anchorage in Bolghatty Creek off the main town of Ernakulum.

In the anchorage off Bolghatty we are transported to another world. Cochin is the Indian Venice, a city connected by water and old pinnaces ferry people around, barges chug up and down the waterways carrying goods back and forth, fishermen paddle out in dugouts with throw nets catching a glittering clutch of tiny fish and the coracle people skate around the calmer reaches. This is a watery world where life is hard for some under the backdrop of the Asian Tiger ashore, all new apartments and 4x4 Tatas.

The coracle people come out at various states of the tide to fish with small surface nets, gather firewood from Bolghatty Island, and retrieve bits of discarded rubbish that might be useful to them. They live in an encampment under one of the modern apartment blocks being built in Ernakulum and their brightly coloured washing adorns the shore line. Their boats are round woven coracles almost identical to those that were used in Ireland. They are wickerwork with some sort of waterproofing between the weave and how they paddle these big baskets with a single paddle is beyond me when the boat has neither stem nor stern. Still paddle them they do, although when the tide is running strongly it takes a lot of effort to avoid being swept onto the yachts at anchor. They keep to themselves although now and then they will ask for water or a cigarette. On the shore where you leave the dinghies there will often be one of the young girls with a baby on her hip gently asking for money, I say gently because begging is banned in Cochin and you don't get mobbed the way you do in Mumbai.

In the market in Ernakulum, as well as fruit and vegetables there are beans, rice, pulses, spices and bags of things I'm not sure about.

Strange to think the chilli, so pervasive in Indian cooking, only arrived here with the Portuguese in the late 16th or early 17th century

The words India and curry are virtually synonymous. You might think you could find the sort of westernised curries you are used to in abundance in India. The reality is somewhat different though not surprising when you look at the history of food in India and the recent origins of much of the cuisine. India is made up of different regions which have been influenced in different ways by the various nations that have invaded the country. In the Middle Ages the Moguls brought Persian style cooking, dry rice dishes and slow-cooked meals like biriyani to India, as well as the Muslim faith.

When the Portuguese arrived they brought ingredients from the New World that radically altered Indian cuisine. The potato is commonly used throughout India for samosas and sag aloo. Tomatoes are now widely used in different curries. And the chilli is now ubiquitous and used to flavour many Indian dishes.

The arrival of the British and the period of the British Raj again radically transformed Indian cuisine and gave rise to new dishes – mulligatawny soup is an Anglicised version of a Tamil recipe for 'pepper water', or kedgeree which is an amalgam of a rice and pulse dish that was combined with fish and eggs as a breakfast dish. Even the term 'curry' we are all so familiar with is derived from the Tamil 'kari', meaning a spicy sauce. By Victorian times Indian dishes from the Raj were in Victorian cookbooks and 'Indian' curry paste was being produced in England. It's instructive to know that outside large hotels and western orientated restaurants that you are unlikely to find a tandoori (so no tandoori chicken) or dishes like jalfrezi or a vindaloo. And as for a balti and chicken tikka masala, these are British inventions.

There will be some who disagree with me, but in many ways British Indian food is more refined and tastes a whole lot better than Indian food in India. I have travelled the length of India trying out food in local eateries, on the trains and even in some more expensive restaurants and off the top of my head I can name a dozen Indian restaurants in the UK that do it better.

Lu returned to Cochin and after a bit of pottering about and stocking up on provisions we were ready for the trip across the Arabian Sea and into the pirate zone off Somalia.

Pepper

Most of us regard it as an everyday condiment on the table. We trot along to the shop and buy a jar or packet of the stuff and think little of it. When you actually see how pepper is cultivated and gathered your respect for it will increase 10-fold.

You can take organised trips into the waterways south of Cochin and it is a 'must do'. A number of agencies can arrange a tour and even if you are averse to tour parties (I am) it is still worth doing. You are bussed to an area south of Cochin and then loaded onto open boats that are poled up the shallow canals.

Outside of Cochin much of what goes on is small scale agrarian with smallholdings growing everything from market vegetables to spices like pepper and cinnamon, a bit of rice and small mixed orchards with fruit, cashews, and coconuts. The pepper vine is grown up and around other trees in the orchard. The tiny fruits are individual drupes on spikes, that is individual fruit the size of a peppercorn. Every peppercorn is picked by hand and then dried.

Black peppercorns are the unripe fruit soused briefly in boiling water and then dried in the sun. White pepper is the ripe fruit put in a sack and immersed in water so the outer husk rots. The peppers are then dried. Green and red peppers use the fruit pickled in vinegar or brine and then dried.

Pepper has been exported from this part of India since antiquity. The ancient Greeks and the Romans were familiar with pepper that had been transported from here to the Mediterranean. The Arabs long held a monopoly trading pepper to Europe and the impetus for the great European voyages of discovery was this simple little black spice. Fortunes were made and lost and wars were fought to control the trade.

Ashore in Cochin

Cochin is made up of islands and peninsulas split by waterways and connected by ferries that run until dusk. Ernakulum on the shore across from the anchorage in Bolghatty Creek is the 'new town' and is the place to head for to provision up.

Provisions

There are several supermarkets in Ernakulum town though the selection of items is not great. You can get the basics but imported and specialist goods are scarce. What there is here is one of the best markets in the world. Once you get to the bridge over the grubby canal the market is hard to miss. It meanders into the back streets parallel to the waterfront and you can get all the fresh fruit and vegetables you need here: pineapples, bananas, mangoes, papaya, apples and even strawberries at times, potatoes and onions, chillies, green beans, cabbage and occasionally lettuce, tomatoes and peppers, just about anything you can think of. There are also cashews, dried fruit, and bottles of spicy sauce of indeterminate origin. The market buzzes with colour and life, you need to squeeze between customers buying big bags of fruit and vegetables, and if you can't find something just ask. The stall-holders are a friendly lot entreating you to buy from them, but if they don't have something you will be escorted to a friend or relative who has just what you want.

On the waterfront there is a butcher with fresh meat and you can also get frozen chicken. There is also a bakery in town that does very good plum cake.

Eating out

In Ernakulum there are some excellent hole-in-the-wall lunchtime eateries mostly doing vegetarian food. Just wander around the back streets and make a choice – they are very cheap. Many of these eateries do not open in the evening.

Commonly you will get rice, a roti and a choice of curry sauces to go with it. You will be eating with your hands in these backstreet places which as always takes a bit of doing. If rotis are served tear off a strip and use it like pincers to pick up rice and sauce. Alternatively with rice make a little ball of rice and dip it in the sauce. You will also get rice cakes which have been steamed with coconut and spices and are delicious. Thalis are often sold in railway stations and the like as well as in backstreet eateries. You get rice and a selection of curry sauces and pickles in (at the railway station) or on (in eateries) a banana leaf. You may get just a couple of sauces or in some places a selection of six or eight.

There are several restaurants on MG road including the Pandhal and Renaissance that offer reasonable food. You can always take the dinghy across to the Bolghatty Hotel that does a buffet of Indian dishes in the evening that is quite good. The best food, Indian and vaguely western, that I had in Cochin is the Sunday buffet at the Taj Malabar Hotel on Willingdon Island. They also serve in the evening but it is a bit of a problem to get back as the ferries stop at dusk. You will get a selection of meat curries and likely Keralan fish curry, maillee, which combines coconut, ginger and curry leaves and fish. My old favourite, the masala dhosa, where a crunchy rice crepe is filled with a spicy potato mixture and served with a dipping sauce and chutney will also be found in the restaurants and in some back street eateries.

The warren of alleys that is Ernakulum market has all the fruit and vegetables you might need

India to the Red Sea

As we get ready to head off for Salalah and the Red Sea we decide not to post position reports... not that I think too many Somali pirates are looking at them on the internet anyway, but just in case. In addition I've taken other precautions. The radar reflectors have been taken down so we don't show up well on radar. At night we will be running just a small white all-round light above the cockpit instead of the usual full navigation lights. Any radio schedules have coded positions with the code agreed on beforehand. Despite or perhaps because of the precautions I'm getting a rumbly feeling in my stomach. Even though I've done this trip a couple of times before, I still get a few butterflies and a bit of queasiness thinking about it. Still, we have a bottle of champagne on board to toast the gods on a safe arrival in the Red Sea.

On previous voyages across the Arabian Sea I've set out from Cochin and curved around with the wind towards the Gulf of Aden and Salalah. Now the Somali pirates are operating further offshore that option is more dangerous and so we plan to go north through the Laccadives and stay north. This is a light wind route, but hopefully a pirate-free one.

This patch of sea was once the preserve of Arab traders. The Romans certainly came this way and the ancient Greeks may also have traded across this stretch of water. Skylax was commissioned by the Persians in 500BC to map out the boundaries of the Persian Empire and travelled overland to the Indus and then down it to the Arabian peninsula. Hippalus is credited with discovering the seasonal swing between the northeast monsoon and the southwest monsoon that allowed a voyage from the bottom of the Red Sea on the southwest monsoon and the return voyage on the northeast monsoon. The likelihood is that Hippalus simply wrote down what was already known to Arab and Indian traders in the region.

The ancient Greeks and the Romans were certainly familiar with many of the spices to be found in India. Pepper, cinnamon, ginger, cassia (Chinese cinnamon), and possibly even nutmeg and cloves which must have been carried from the Spice Islands in Indonesia. In early Greek times much of this trade was overland across the Arabian Peninsula. Later trade moved to the sea and Arabs living in the south of the Arabian Peninsula built up fleets of ships and dominated the trade routes across to India. Places like Mukalla in Yemen under the Hadramaut and in Muscat in Oman became important trading ports pushing the boundaries of the routes beyond India and Sri Lanka to Southeast Asia.

The Arabian Peninsula and India is a region where there is a dearth of iron ore which ruled out constructing boats with nails. Even as late as the 1990s I watched small forges in Mukalla turning old scrap iron, bits of reinforcing iron and iron rod, into hand-made nails for the boat builders. In the Middle Ages boats here were built of planks bound together with coir and the seams waterproofed with fish oil and fat. In India boats in the south of the country are still built in this way. Around the Arabian Peninsula even large trading craft were all built this way in the past when iron nails were not to be found. In Oman, in 2009–10, a replica of a 9th-century trading ship was built using coir to hold the planks together. In 2010, *The Jewel of Muscat* sailed to Singapore via Cochin, Galle and Penang.

Day 1

20th Feb 0645. Anchor up in Bolghatty anchorage. Heading for Salalah Oman.

1800. Wind WNW 3 Speed 3·9 knots. Sailing slowly. Five ships around. Fishing boats.

Day 2

21st Feb 1500 Wind NNE 3 Speed 5·2 knots. Sailing gently up through Lacadive Islands. Ships and fishing boats around.

Day 3

22nd Feb 1200 Wind NE 3—4 Speed 5·2 knots. Ducking around the bottom of Bitra Point. Daily run 129M.

Day 4

23rd Feb 0500 Wind NNW 4 Speed 5·5 knots. False dawn over India. Something smelly in the sea?

Day 5

24th Feb 0800 Wind NE 3 Speed 5·1 knots. Wind up and down but light. Under 900M to Salalah.

Day 6

25th Feb 1500 Wind ENE 3 Speed 3·9 knots. Lu lands nice mahi mahi. One ship eastbound. Wind light again.

Day 7

26th Feb 1500 Wind ENE 2 Speed 6·1 knots. Another mahi mahi landed. One ship nearby. Motor-sailing.

Day 8

27th Feb 1200 Wind E 3 Speed 6·1 knots. Still motor-sailing. Wind comes and goes, but not much of it. Daily run 133M.

Day 9

28th Feb 0800 Wind E 2 Speed 6·0 knots. Rosy fingered dawn. Booby came to visit. Yanni the engine doing sterling service fingers crossed.

Day 10

1st Mar 1500 Wind ESE 4 Speed 5·9 knots. Sailing, sailing, sailing again. What a relief after so much motoring.

Day 11

2nd Mar 2200 Anchor down in Salalah port.

With the European Age of Discovery and the arrival of Vasco da Gama in India the Arab hold on the spice trade was loosened and the larger trading vessels of the Portuguese, the Dutch and English carried the spices directly to European markets. The ancient ports on the Arabian Peninsula are still there and in places like Mukalla you can still see the wonderful Hadramaut architecture ashore. Other ports like Al Baleed near Salalah have crumbled into oblivion.

So we headed north through the top of the Laccadives and then west for Oman along 15°N. This involved being pretty close hauled up through the Laccadives. In practice we shaped our course to the wind and wriggled our way through the islands. Once clear of the northern Laccadives it was a matter of sailing pretty much along the rhumb line climbing up towards 15°N and towards Salalah. The wind was patchy and fickle though the sailing was easy in relatively flat water. We ate, read books and even managed to catch a couple of small mahi mahi. It needed patience to sail the distance in light winds where we often only averaged 3–4 knots.

Overall it was an easy trip with the seas slight and even flat calm at times. We had a couple of visiting birds including a little swallow or flycatcher that decided it was much better off inside the boat than outside and made itself completely at home before flying off for land when we were close to Salalah.

One thing that was obvious was that ships and fishing boats were pretty wary of us, no doubt wondering whether we were a pirate skiff. We carried only a small all round white light above the bimini except when ships got close and we turned on the navigation lights. Two ships must have picked us up on radar even though we had taken the radar reflectors down and made 90° turns to avoid us. Fishing boats also tended to give us a wide berth.

Salalah was just a brief stopover before we left in company, in convoy, with 20-odd other yachts. 2010 was the last year it was safe to come this way, but effectively until 2011 it was relatively safe as long as you hugged the Arabian Peninsula. This the convoy did and we arrived safely in Aden. We even caught a nice little tuna on the way. There is much I could say about sailing in convoy, but much of it is summed up in a joke doing the rounds in Aden which went something along the lines of: Did you know that the pirates in Somalia are getting T-shirts printed up that say 'I survived the convoy'.

Dinner and a bit on the way to Aden

Hitch-hiker en route to Oman

Aden is one of those signposts of the sea that once seen will not be forgotten. The razor-back ridge of Krater rears up out of the sea and provides a safe haven and a huge natural port behind it. Krater, as its name suggests, is an extinct volcanic crater. The dry basalt slopes of Aden shimmer in the heat and seem to radiate heat right out to sea and as you get nearer you can pick out white houses dotted around the slopes. It is a welcome sight whether you are coming from the east or the west.

Ashore in Aden

Years ago Omar the taxi driver used to be the 'fixer' here and I mentioned he was a useful contact in a book on the Indian Ocean. Sadly he died eight years ago. However you will come across a lot of taxi drivers ('I am Omar'... 'No, I am Omar'... a bit like something out of *Spartacus*) and 'guides' who can show you around and drive you to where you want to go.

Provisions

In Krater a new mall has opened, the Aden Mall, which has a huge LuLu supermarket. The fruit and vegetables are best bought from the carts around the port area and are excellent considering they are grown on the edge of the desert. They keep well since they haven't been refrigerated.

Market day in Aden. The variety of fruit and vegetables you can get in Yemen constantly surprises me. It's mostly desert...

Eating out

There are local eateries around Aden and as long as you are not too fussy about hygiene, you can get wonderful local food here. Much of it is cooked on a gas burner which looks and sounds a bit like the afterburner on a 737 jet engine. Meat and other things are flash-fried and served with pilaf. Other eateries have grilled fish and meats which are also good.

There are several hotel restaurants around serving 'international' fare, but personally I like the local hole-in-the-wall places better. There is, of course, good coffee, strong and black Arab-style, everywhere.

We stayed a week here getting some provisions in and pottering around Aden. At times it seems a bit edgy, but the people are friendly and the food ashore is good. Not to mention the coffee. Coffee is believed to have originated in the highlands of Yemen from where it was exported to the eastern Mediterranean and then via the Ottoman Empire throughout Europe. Mocha is a small city on the Red Sea coast that gave its name to the prized mocha beans, celebrated today just as much as in yesteryear.

Qat

Pronounced '*gat*'. This is the national narcotic of Yemen and it seems that the majority of the male population indulge in it. It is a small evergreen bush, *Catha edulis*, cultivated in the highlands and trucked down daily to the markets on the coast. The leaves are chewed to produce a mild stimulant effect and every afternoon you will see Yemenis sitting around chewing qat. The stated attributes are a peaceful disposition and heightened sexual prowess... apparently. Stories of wild-eyed Somali pirates fuelled by drugs are not fuelled by qat.

The leaves are chewed into a mulch and by the end of the afternoon the user will have a large pulpy ball of the stuff extending the cheek pouch. It has no immediate effect and it was explained to me that the couple

Qat. It tastes like it looks and you need to chew a whole wad of it to get the mildest narcotic effect

of leaves I tried were not enough and I should continue chewing for a few days until a cumulative effect kicked in. It is not cheap and it would appear that a good deal of the income of the average Yemeni goes on the stuff.

Salalah in Oman

With the locals in an Aden café

Rice and … more rice in Aden

Market day in Aden

Baked fish in clay ovens

I first came across clay ovens, a sort of dustbin shaped tandoori oven I guess, in the market in Mukalla in the Yemen back in the 1990s. We had stopped in Mukalla before setting off for India on what turned out to be a long slow trip against the prevailing NE monsoon. Next to the oven was a pile of fish, whatever the fishermen had caught that day. You chose a fish which was then smeared all over with a spicy paste and literally stuck on the side of the clay oven. A freshly made roti was stuck on the inside as well. These ovens were so hot that the fish and the roti literally 'stuck' to the side of it when the man with asbestos hands reached in and whacked it onto the clay side of the oven.

When the fish was done out it came and was served up on a plate with the roti. The fish was wonderfully succulent contained as it was by the spicy paste on the outside which kept all the moisture in. For a dollar you got a fish, tuna, snapper, bream and others I couldn't identify, and the roti and maybe a small salad as well.

It took me a while to find someone who spoke English so I could find out what the spicy paste was that covered the fish before it went into the oven. It turned out to be mashed banana with spices like turmeric, cumin and other spices mixed into it. This was what gave the fish a wonderful spice and fruit covering. Pudding, if you wanted it, was mashed banana with shredded roti through it.

Since then I have looked for these clay ovens in other places. They exist in the market in Aden in the Yemen, in Massawa in Eritrea and in Port Sudan. It seems to me that they are less common now than they were in the 1990s. They still exist in Mukalla, in Massawa in Eritrea and no doubt in other places in the Yemen and Oman. We tried it again in Massawa, but those ovens and the fish in Mukalla still do the best baked fish in a clay oven anywhere.

Bab El Mandeb is the southern entrance to the Red Sea. It's called the Gate of Tears and not without reason. In December 1996 I left Massawa for Aden on an eastabout trip. It was the wrong time of year and I knew it. Passages down the Red Sea are best made in July or August during the southwest monsoon. Once around to Aden or Salalah you then catch the tail end of the southwest monsoon in September or the faltering start of the northeast monsoon in October across to India. Hippalus in Roman times knew this as do the Arab traders who have criss-crossed this sea for centuries. If you miss this window then you have strong winds and contrary currents all working against you.

When I say there are strong winds blowing up the Red Sea I mean up to gale force winds. The trip down to Bab El Mandeb is one of the worst trips I have done, beating to windward against a 35 knot true wind and being pushed back up the Red Sea by the current. By the time we got to Aden we were all bruised and battered and I had to send one of the crew back home as he was exhausted.

Going the right way and heading north up through Bab El Mandeb into the Red Sea is definitely the easy way to do it. We had 35 knots for around a 6–8 hour period after the strait along with up to 2 knots of north-going current and flew up here with just some genny out. Lu had eaten something that didn't agree with her in Aden so I was on my own for the night and opted to keep things simple with just the roller-furling genoa. As it was we did close to a 185 mile day helped by all that favourable current.

When I first visited Eritrea in 1995 and then again in 1997, the Civil War with Ethiopia, all 34 years of it, had just ended in 1994. The city was a bombed and pock-marked place with the bare minimum of services. But the people were over-joyed the war had finished, Eritrea had won, and everyone had great hopes for the future. An interim military government was in place and democratic elections were promised in two or three years.

Sadly the military are still in power and have tightened their grip on keeping power and keeping the ordinary people in line (what's that they say about absolute power...). Their foreign policy has also become somewhat bizarre. When I was in the Hanish Islands in 1995 Eritrea invaded the islands which had traditionally belonged to Yemen. Some sort of rapprochement with Yemen is now in place. They have also been accused of helping Somali insurgents which seems odd given a large proportion of the population is Tigraen Christian. Then again its not so odd

Massawa still pock-marked after the long civil war

Ashore in Massawa

Happily the people are still wonderful. Poor maybe, but welcoming and friendly. Mike the 'laundry man' is still around after all these years and is the 'fixer' for things. He now has a café, the Café Jasmine, on the waterfront. As ever he is immensely helpful at organising things in a country where most things are hard to come by. And he does a wonderful espresso.

Provisions

There is not much to be found in Massawa or Eritrea generally. It is hard to get water, let alone food. There are a couple of small grocery shops with limited stocks. Even getting bread, through Mike, can be difficult at times even if a new bakery had finally been built.

Eating out

There are fewer hole-in-the-wall restaurants than there used to be some years back. Away from the waterfront there is the Salaam fish restaurant that does fish in a clay oven. No cutlery and little sanitation, but the fish is good. Mike in Café Jasmine does some snack food but not much. Over the bridge there are a couple of hotels including the Hotel Luna though don't expect too much from them. If you can find it, hot goat stew known as 'zigny' is worth a taste though it is invariably really, really hot. The chillies go in towards the end of cooking so doesn't gently blend in and the chilli heat can be overpowering.

Old Italian colonial and modern Eritrea café life in Massawa

when you know that the Ethiopians are helping the provisional government in Mogadishu and Eritreans just love to hate anything to do with the Ethiopians.

Sadly Massawa seems nearly as pock-marked from the war as it did 14 years ago with the exception of a few of those memorials that military governments like to erect for themselves. The people still lead a life blighted by shortages of just about everything including diesel, good sanitation, communications and food.

From Eritrea it is a matter of beating up the Red Sea against the prevailing northerly winds blowing down. It can be a bit tedious, but once you know what you are up against it is really a matter of settling in and patience. As the boat crashes off the waves hard on the wind the motion and angle of the boat can make things difficult, especially in the galley. This is where you need those simple pasta and risotto meals, easy to prepare and cook, to keep things going. You have no idea how good this simple fare tastes as we bang, wallop and crash northwards.

Ashore in Port Sudan

In town there is a whole bazaar area with shaded walkways in Italian art deco that house little grocery shops, bakers, greengrocers, hardware shops, spice shops and friendly people.

Provisions

There is not a lot in the grocery shops though after Eritrea it seems like a wondrous selection. The small hole-in-the-wall bakeries produce scrumptious little bread rolls. On the outskirts of town (take a tuk-tuk) is the souk under canvas with fruit and vegetables galore and freshly butchered meat (and flies), a whole market supplying Port Sudan with fresh produce. It always seems a bit unusual that after sailing past 500 miles of desert there should be such an abundance of fresh fruit and vegetables on the edge of the sands. The people are friendly, though women should dress appropriately with arms and legs covered and a headscarf. Expect the locals to be curious and a little reserved as you will likely be the only Europeans there.

Eating out

Around the waterfront and along the High Street are lots of little eateries. You can get all sorts of grilled meat and poultry, salad, and wonderful big puffy bread, the sort that looks like a rugby ball with air in it, cooked on the premises. You also get a sort of Sudanese take on pizzas akin to the Turkish *pide* which are excellent.

In the souk in Port Sudan

Snack bar in Port Sudan

Most yachts headed towards Sudan go to Suakin. There is more room to anchor and it's a more picturesque place than Port Sudan. More picturesque but not really the heart of Sudan. Port Sudan is crowded, noisy, you are tucked in with a giant container port on one side, and it's a bit dirty and frenetic. And there are lots of beggars. What is surprising in countries like Sudan, seemingly always at war and repressing the rights of the population, is just how normal life is. Everyone has to make a living, has to eat, has to try and make the best of things even if the things are not easy to get on with.

You get much of North Africa through the town. Port Sudan is a magnet for refugees from surrounding countries – Daniel the Ethiopian, Eritreans. Ahmet and Mustafa, Nubians from near Aswan. You get a feel for the country here that is outside the desert trips to see some tame Berbers and camels, a feeling for the turmoil of the region and of long journeys to escape conflict and find a better life.

Heading north up to Egypt, still bashing to windward against the northerlies, we zigzag slowly north. We head over to Saudi Arabia on one tack and then tack over to starboard and head back towards the African coast. Early on the second morning Lu has a plan. She shows me Sharm Luli, an enclosed bay on the Egyptian

Port Ghalib on the Egyptian coast. It's surreal to arrive at a 5-star marina built in the middle of the desert

coast, and bribes me with the promise of roast chicken with all the trimmings if we just bear away a little bit and head for the anchorage. After all it's called Luli Lu pointed out. The promise of roast chicken does the trick and by 1100 we are swinging to anchor in the coral fringed bay.

We get to Port Ghalib a couple of days later. Port Ghalib is a vast hotel and apartment complex built on the desert coast. Incorporated into the resort is Port Ghalib Marina, an intertwining system of waterways and basins around which the hotels and apartments are scattered. It is huge and we are only talking about Phase 1 here. The project is backed by Kuwaiti money and when it is finished there will be 27 hotels. It has its own power plant and reverse osmosis plant to provide fresh water. Behind the resort there is the workers 'town', a dormitory suburb to provide accommodation for all the people who work here.

Although the architecture is well done in a quasi-Egyptian / Mediterranean style, the resort could really be anywhere: on the Spanish Mediterranean coast, in the Bahamas, in Dubai. Somehow there is an anonymity to it and also a touch of the global reach of large corporations with a TGI Fridays and Costa Coffee. Many of the people in the hotels are here for the diving, there are more than a dozen large dive boats operating out of here, or they are here for winter sun and lying around the hotel pool.

For yachts coming up the coast Port Ghalib is a welcome respite from the northerlies blowing down and a logical place to clear into Egypt. It also offers that miracle of water and electricity on the quay, something most boats will not have had since Malaysia and Thailand. It's a culture shock, a strangely bizarre though oddly pleasurable experience sitting in the Grand Café sipping a cappuccino in the middle of the desert.

From Port Ghalib it is a long haul up to Port Suez at the southern end of the Suez Canal. As you head up to Port Suez you get to the Gulf of Suez where the northerly winds are funnelled down the narrow gulf and increase in strength.

We left Port Ghalib with a forecast for light northerlies and later on light easterlies and even southeast winds. For the day and through the night we had light northerlies and were able to make good northing by motor-sailing. By the second day the wind was still light and then started to go NE and even ENE in the Gulf of Suez.

And then the wheels fell off. By early evening we had 20 knots on the nose and a short sea, but we were still making progress. By 2200 we had 25 knots and things weren't looking great. An hour later off the reefs at Sheratib we had 30 knots continuous and more in the gusts. Things weren't looking bright as we were making just 2 knots at fairly high revs and water was cascading down the side decks – and elsewhere. At midnight we turned around and ran off to the anchorage at El Tor about 30 miles south.

Running south under a pocket handkerchief of jib we were trying to go as slowly as possible so it would be light when we hung a left through the oilfields to get to El Tor. Fortunately dawn, or at least the false dawn was just after 0500 and we turned between some capped wells and navigated tentatively through the oilfield.

El Tor was a little haven once we got in and anchored in the outer part of the harbour. The inner part had five other yachts who had given up the unequal struggle as well. We waited two days before deciding to head off again. We were happy just to have 15–20 knots and to plug on overnight up to Suez.

Everyone feels a sense of relief at getting up the Gulf of Suez and into Port Suez itself. And it really is a quite pleasant place to be. The area immediately behind the Suez Yacht Club, emphasis on 'club' and not 'yacht', is the old colonial area with wonderful villas where the English and the French formerly lived. The streets are lined with trees that some topiary man regularly shapes into spheres. The people are friendly and everything pretty much works. Wonderful.

Tied up in Port Suez at last. The 'boatman' organises laundry, beer, bread, all the essentials

Once the paperwork is done in Port Suez you are allotted a time and a pilot and a little convoy of yachts set off up the canal. At some point you will meet up with a big ship convoy coming the other way and so it was with huge container ships and tankers trundling down towards us. At the end of the day we get to the Bitter Lakes and Ismailia. Like Port Suez, this is a bit like stepping into the old colonial days of the French and English, only more so.

Ismailia is a convivial spot to stop over for a few days. In many ways it makes sense to stop here to wait for a weather window in the Mediterranean and then just transit the second half of the canal and keep on going straight into the Mediterranean.

The Yacht Club at Ismailia is all art deco with the ghosts of the old colonial past seemingly still present. The old yacht club has been restored to its former glory, but nothing goes on here. There is a small tea house and the yachts tied up on the dock, but otherwise you can roam around the building at will. In the 1930s and 40s this would have been the social hub of Ismailia, all frilly layered dresses and formal attire, all gossip and scandal and Pimms and Pernod.

We leave Ismailia late which means that by the time *Skylax* pokes her nose into the Mediterranean it is dusk. Large ships, tugs, work boats and a number of oil rigs complicate the passage north, but we are back in the Mediterranean. It's difficult to describe my feelings on getting back to the Mediterranean. Its not just another sea, it's home. A few tears, a slow exhalation of pleasure, and as it happened a gentle sail hard on the wind in a Force 3–4 and relatively flat water. We point *Skylax* towards Kaş in Turkey and let the girl gobble up the miles. *Skylax* is in her element and almost smelling the hay and the stable. And so here we are after some 30,000 miles since we left, catching our breath and meeting old friends, all of us a little older and none the wiser.

Ashore in Ismailia

You are in a customs compound at the YC and so have to pass in and out through the customs post to get to town and back. Sometimes they will have a poke around in the bags of stuff you have brought, but generally any *baksheesh* is low level. The town itself is quite safe to wander around and the locals generally friendly.

Provisions

There is the Metro supermarket in town which has pretty much everything you need including lots of western goods and if you buy a lot they will run you back to the customs gate in the supermarket van. Alternatively you can get a cab. There are also small grocery shops.

Eating out

There are local hole-in-the-wall eateries serving good local food, just cast an eye over what the locals are eating and order 'one of those'. There are also a few more formal restaurants which are quite OK and not expensive. Only a few of the more formal restaurants have alcohol.

Egyptian food always comes with Arabic bread (*Eesh baladi*), unleavened bread that you rip bits off to eat with the food. It usually comes in a large hollow bun sized round rather than bigger solid loaves. Most of the food you will come across is typical Levantine food, so falafels, donor kebab (Shawarma), Ful Medames (Mushed Fava Beans), and various lamb or chicken stews. Local eateries often do sandwiches Egyptian-style where you get a bun of Arabic bread filled with fillings of choice – falafel, kebab, salad, omelette, whatever the vendor has displayed on his stand.

The wonderful art deco Yacht Club in Ismailia

No man will be a sailor who has contrivance enough to get himself into a jail; for being in a ship is being in a jail, with the chance of being drowned. A man in a jail has more room, better food and commonly better company. *Samuel Johnson*

Skylax's voyage through the Mediterranean is really about the beginning of the voyage around the world. It's also about the beginning of a long personal history of sailing in the Mediterranean, writing about this wonderful inland sea, and spending decades going ashore and sampling the cuisine. Many of the recipes in this book have a Mediterranean flavour if not always an authentic take on a recipe. In all sorts of ways these are home waters, waters we have cruised extensively over the years and while this chapter roughly follows our meandering track from Turkey to Gibraltar, it can't help but digress to other bits of the Mediterranean and my experiences there over more than 35 years.

Elizabeth David and her books on Mediterranean food probably did more than anyone to introduce the Anglo Saxon north to Mediterranean cooking. In the austere years after the war these recipes glowing with the warmth and sun of the Mediterranean were a splash of the exotic on the drab tables in the north. Bright salads and stews smelling of herbs and sunlight grabbed the imagination of many cooks and supplanted grey over-cooked meat and vegetables boiled to death. And yet trying to understand Mediterranean cuisine, when so many cultural influences, so many spices and herbs from the Orient and fruit and vegetables from the New World have arrived in this area makes untangling it all seem an impossible task.

A short introduction to Mediterranean food

At first glance it might appear that there is no unifying factor in the cuisine and foods of different Mediterranean countries, between Turkish and Italian or between Spanish and Greek cooking. To be sure the word 'Mediterranean' encompasses very different cultures and the history of the area spans millennia, but there is an underlying theme and that is climate. The classic definition of the Mediterranean climate, as the area between the northern limit of the olive tree and the northern limit of the palm grove, gives us the first element of this unity, the olive. The arid summers all but rule out pasture for cattle and consequently dairy products. Butter, milk and cream rarely feature in the cuisine and are replaced by olive oil. Bread is not buttered, but used to mop up the olive oil from salads, meat and fish, and from the numerous other dishes covered liberally with it. Sauces using olive oil with tomato paste, onion, peppers, lemon, herbs and spices replace the butter and milk-based sauces found in northern countries. Yoghurt made from goat or sheep milk is used instead of cream, which is almost never found in sauces or desserts.

A second consequence resulting from the lack of pasture is the virtual absence of beef from the diet. In recent years cheap beef has been imported and substituted for the veal, goat and lamb which have been commonly used in Mediterranean dishes.

Seasonal vegetables provide the variety and colour found in Mediterranean cuisine

The arid land cannot sustain mature cattle and so calves are eaten as veal. Sheep and goats can survive on the sparse vegetation that remains through the summer, and their milk is used instead of cows' milk to produce yoghurt and cheese, both of which last better in a hot climate than the milk itself.

As well as the olive, wheat and vines are cultivated all around the Mediterranean. It is hard to imagine how the desert sands in Libya and Tunisia once produced vast yields of wheat, but in the heyday of the Roman Empire what is now desert was the bread-basket of Italy. Today the wheat grown is not used exclusively for bread. The hard durum wheat for making pasta is cultivated extensively in the northern Mediterranean countries, and while the Italians are the pasta wizards of the world, many other countries also use pasta in their diet.

Pastry dishes range from the fancy creations of the French to the paper-thin *filo* pastry of the Greeks and Turks. *Filo* is wrapped around anything from cheese and spicy minced meat to nuts and raisins soaked in honey. Rice is also an important crop, used in the *paella* of Spain, *risotto* in Italy, and the *pilav* of Turkey and the Middle East.

These, then, are the essence of Mediterranean food. Olive oil replaces the dairy products used in northern Europe. Meat is basically veal, lamb and poultry. Seafood is prized, but costly. Bread, pastry, pasta and rice provide the staple carbohydrates. Seasonal vegetables – tomatoes, aubergines, green peppers, courgettes, cucumbers, carrots, lettuce, cabbage and the essential onion and garlic – provide the variety and colour found in the dishes. It all sounds rather basic compared to the dairy-based cuisine of the north, but as Arabella Boxer points out in her excellent *Mediterranean Cookbook*, the basic ingredients are combined in appealing and interesting ways and spiked with herbs and spices.

'Taken as a whole, the average diet of the Mediterranean countries, particularly in the east, is austere but supremely healthy. Based on grilled meat and fish, raw salads, bread, fruit, herbs and yoghurt, it provides a limited but to me very appealing diet. It would be hard to suffer a liver attack or a cardiac condition in a true Mediterranean area, for the animal fats consumed by the north Europeans and the Americans simply do not exist. The potential monotony of such a limited diet is offset by the use of herbs on the northern shores of the Mediterranean, and spices in the south.' Arabella Boxer, *Mediterranean Cookbook*

The different countries around the Mediterranean have different preferences for the herbs and spices most commonly used. In the North African countries spices predominate: coriander, cumin, caraway and saffron are used in Egypt and the countries of the Mahgreb, Tunisia, Algeria and Morocco. Chilli peppers are also extensively used and are most often encountered in *harissa*, a powder or sauce made of tomato paste and hot piri-piri chilli peppers. It is usually toned down for the tender palate unaccustomed to its normal fiery strength. In Spain the centuries of Arab rule significantly influenced the cuisine and spices are the important additives flavouring Spanish food. *Paella* would be incomplete without saffron to give it its distinctive flavour.

In France and Italy, herbs are the important flavouring. In *bouillabaisse*, a dish Arabella Boxer describes as 'more truly typical of the Mediterranean than any other', parsley, thyme, fennel and the bay leaf are used. French cuisine utilises herbs and also spices in a rich and varied way for which it is justly famous. In Italy basil and oregano are the favourites. In Greece oregano is supreme, along with the lemon. With everything from a lamb chop to *avgolimoni* sauce, the acid juice of the lemon imparts a unique taste to the food. In Turkey, the Middle Eastern preference for certain herbs becomes evident with parsley the favourite, closely followed by chervil and dill. In the Middle East parsley and mint are used in everything from meat dishes to desserts.

Fish has traditionally been part of the Mediterranean diet and figures in the cuisine of all the countries around its shores. But lately it has become something of a luxury and prices, especially for prized fish and lobster, have rocketed. The reason has to do not so much with a depletion of fish stocks in the Mediterranean, though that is a factor, but with the increased demand for fish by both the locals and the increasing numbers of foreign tourists. Added to this is the demand of foreign markets for fish like Bluefin tuna for sushi in Japan and sea bass for the tables of northern Europe. This is a great shame as many countries, Spain and Italy especially, have novel and delicious fish dishes.

In recent years the exodus of sun-starved northerners to the shores of the Mediterranean has distorted the traditional cuisine. In the popular tourist spots snack bars serve up hamburgers that taste like cardboard and miserly portions of cold chips. Pizza restaurants have sprung up from Gibraltar to Turkey. And Coca-Cola and Pepsi slug it out for the lion's share of the market from the Mahgreb to Turkey. The traveller can ignore or embrace this food pollution according to his or her tastes.

Food can be a lot more expensive if you choose fish and a *shi shi* location *Kadir Kir*

Skylax returns to the eastern Mediterranean *Yusuf Civelekoglu*

Coming up the Red Sea *Skylax* was limping along. Not mortally wounded, but licking her wounds. After over 30,000 miles on her circumnavigation there was general wear and tear and worse, some wounds we had inflicted on her.

In Malaysia in the last race of the Raja Muda an insane moment of adrenaline inspired red mist racing put her briefly up on a coral outcrop. Even worse was the fact that I knew it was there and stopping dead from five and half knots was chilling. In Ao Chalong in Thailand we dragged anchor in a squall and came to a stop on a robust aluminium boat and scratched the gel coat and mangled the aft starboard toe-rail.

As we beat our way up the Red Sea, happy that the Mediterranean was near, but tired of body and soul, we needed somewhere to park *Skylax* for some necessary care. So we headed up to a new marina in Didim on the Turkish Aegean coast to repair the known knowns and to find out about a few known unknowns.

Turkish cuisine has been praised as the best in the eastern Mediterranean, and so it is. The traditional cuisine scores from combining a wealth of basic raw ingredients in novel ways to make dishes which often have novel names. The most memorable of the names are *imam bayaldi*, 'the Imam fainted' (aubergine with tomatoes and onions) and a sweet pastry soaked in honey called 'lady's navel'. Aubergine features a lot in Turkish cooking and it was said that in Istanbul you could tell when the aubergine season started from the fires that swept through the city – fires caused by the hot oil from fried aubergine dishes spilling over and igniting. Over 40 dishes are attributed to this purple vegetable. Females also figure a lot in the naming of dishes, particularly desserts, with names like 'lady's thigh', 'lady's breasts', 'lady's fingers', and so on through most of the anatomy.

Ashore in Turkey

Some things have changed massively in Turkey as it emerges into the 21st century, though thankfully some things have not changed. The development along the coast means there are now big supermarkets with all sorts of goodies and a proliferation of restaurants serving more 'international' fare.

Not for nothing is Turkey called the market garden of Europe

Village bread (unleavened) being cooked at Kapi Creek on the Lycian coast

Provisions

In the larger centres there will be a supermarket not too far away, usually a Migros or a Carrefour, with a good selection of local food and imported items. In general prices are quite high for any imported items.

In all but the smallest villages basic provisions can be found and fresh produce is excellent. Imported goods can be found in large towns and tourist centres. In the large villages and towns there is a market day once a week, usually on Fridays, where all manner of fresh produce, fruit and vegetables, dried fruit and nuts, poultry, cheese, herbs and spices are brought from the surrounding countryside for sale.

The quality of the produce, especially the fruit and vegetables, would be hard to better anywhere in the Mediterranean. Not without reason is Turkey known as the market garden of Europe. In small villages you may find individual farmers selling locally produced vegetables off the back of a truck and you often come across small roadside stalls selling almonds and seasonal fruit such as apricots and pomegranates, as well as honey, molasses, herbs and spices.

Simple meal, soup, bread, salad in a shady nook

Spices are still to be found all over Turkey

Eating out in Turkey

Mezes are superb in Turkey and can make a meal in themselves. You will commonly come across *cacik* (yoghurt with cucumber and garlic), *patliçan salata* (pureed aubergine mixed with yoghurt), *taramasalata* (red fish roe with yoghurt and garlic), *pilaki* (white beans in a vinaigrette sauce), *dolma* (stuffed vine leaves), *borek* (white cheese or mincemeat wrapped in filo pastry and deep-fried), *Amerikan salata* (potato salad with mayonnaise, also called Russian (*Rus*) salad), *coban salata* (a mixed salad meaning literally 'shepherd's salad'), and many more – depending on the chef's inclination and ability – such as fish salads, pickled octopus, fiery tomato and onion purees, and the celebrated *imam bayaldi*. Soups are usually on offer at lunchtime and the most popular are lentil and rice soups, meat broths, and vegetable soups. Special shops serve only *Iskembe corbasi*, tripe soup, which is a sovereign remedy for hangovers in the eastern Mediterranean. Friends who live in Turkey swear by it, but however bad my hangover I've steadfastly refused to believe that tripe soup could cure it.

Cooked dishes like stews and oven dishes are prepared at lunchtime and kept hot until the evening, so the best time to have them is at midday when they are fresh. Most of the dishes combine meat, usually lamb, with vegetables to produce dishes like *salcali kofte* (meatballs in a sauce with vegetables), or *kuzu ve patliçan guveç* (a lamb and aubergine stew). This is usually accompanied by pilau rice or bulgur (*pilav*). Some restaurants specialise in *kebap*, of which there are several varieties depending on where they originated. The *doner kebap* is cooked on a slowly revolving vertical spit and the cook slices meat off it with a long knife. Usually the meat comes on a bed of rice with a salad garnish and a piquant tomato sauce or yoghurt according to your taste. *Adana kebap* is spiced with hot peppers, *Urfa kebap* comes with sliced

Doner kebab, but superior to any kebab you will have outside Turkey

Lahmaçun is a type of *pide* – roll it up with a salad filling inside and enjoy

onions and black pepper, and *Bursa* or *Iskender kebap* comes on chopped *pide* bread with yoghurt and butter. Beef usually comes as *bonfile* or *biftek*, small steaks grilled over charcoal. *Şiş kebap* is grilled lamb on a skewer and *şiş kofte* is meatballs.

Fish is not cheap in Turkey and you should enquire about the price beforehand. It is sold by weight, so before it is cooked the *patron* will weigh it and give you a price. Usually it comes fried or grilled, though in some places more ambitious dishes and sauces are prepared. Enquire to see if one of my favourites, a lemon and dill sauce, can be prepared. Usually your grilled or fried main course will come with French fries, a legacy of increasing tourism in this area. Instead you may like to order rice or bulgur *pilav*.

Sadly, in some of the larger resorts the traditional cuisine is being subordinated to blander 'international' dishes that the restaurateurs think the tourists want (unfortunately some of them do like their steak-and-eggs-and-chips). Fast-food places have also sprouted in the resorts and the Turks have taken to these with a vengeance, ensuring that they are here to stay.

Desserts are not generally served in restaurants and for the traditional sweet sticky desserts you will usually have to go to a patisserie. However, a restaurant will usually have fresh fruit; depending on what is in season it may be peaches, apples, pears, grapes, oranges or melon. As far as I am concerned a plate of honeydew melon beats sticky sweets any day. The sticky sweets are almost identical to those found in Greece and parts of the Middle East: *baklava* (flaky pastry stuffed with nuts in a honey syrup), and *kadayif* (shredded wheat with nuts in the same sweet syrup). Some of the patisseries make a variety of chocolate and sponge cakes, but on the whole these are too sweet for my taste. *Dondurma* (ice cream) is also popular and is often sold on the streets by colourfully attired vendors who make a great show of their prowess at flicking scoops of ice cream into the cone.

Greece

Although Turkey was where we crossed our last track to complete the circumnavigation in 2010, in fact it was in the Ionian in western Greece that we made last minute preparations and repairs before setting off for Gibraltar. We checked all our gear, had the engine checked over and got a new set of sails sorted. That was back in 2007.

From Turkey routes across the Aegean are to some extent a matter of choice. Magically most of the islands dotted across the Aegean are within sight so you can see where you are going to next. At worst you can head off in the vague direction of the next island and it will eventually materialise on the horizon. Millennia ago the ancients sailed these seas in the same way, picking off the landmarks that guided them on their way. Even at night under the starry skies you can see the outline of islands from some way off.

Greece is often mistaken for the place where white-washed cubist houses are built up organically around the turquoise waters of a bay or harbour. Not surprisingly Greece is a mish-mash of influences from all of the invaders who trammelled down through the mainland and islands from the Romans through the Slavic hordes to the Turks and the Venetians, and even the English before independence. The architectural heritage is still visible with lots of theatres, city walls and the occasional acropolis, Venetian castles dotted strategically around sea

Location, location. Many Greek tavernas have wonderful settings

Ashore in Greece

Things have changed massively in Greece and these days you can find most things you need in the large supermarkets and even a lot of smaller ones. How this will all change as more austerity measures are heaped on the Greeks is difficult to know, but there does seem to be an inclination to stock less.

Provisions

In all but the smallest villages you will have few problems obtaining the basic provisions. In the larger towns and popular tourist resorts there are big-name supermarket chains like AB and Lidl. Unfortunately these are often on the outskirts of town so it is a long walk to get to them. Familiar brands for many foods are available, but imported items naturally cost more than local produce. Don't forget the small shop owners for fruit and vegetables, and the butchers and bakers. In addition some towns will have local produce markets one or two days a week, where you can buy locally grown fruit and vegetables and sometimes fish and meat.

Fish is expensive. Large fish such as red snapper and grouper are very expensive and the prices of prawns and lobsters are considerable - certainly comparable to or higher than in Italy and France. Fish from fish farms is a lot cheaper than the wild variety and farmed shellfish, predominantly mussels, are also available.

Bakers are a growth industry in Greece and even small villages often have a good bakers with all sorts of bread from white through all shades of brown. They will also often have mini-pizzas, cheese or spinach pies, bacon and egg pies, filled croissants, in fact whatever the baker reckons he can sell.

Wine has improved massively in Greece in recent years. New methods and new equipment have ensured that the wine is a lot more consistent than it used to be. Bottled wines are numerous and vary from excellent to just quaffable. Local wine can often be bought cheaply from the barrel, but taste it first. The ubiquitous retsina is an acquired taste. Wine is on the whole cheap. Local beer such as Mythos or Amstel is good and cheap. Local spirits, ouzo (akin to Pernod) and brandy (sweetish) are also good value.

Market day in Kavala in northern Greece

Ashore in Greece

Eating out

Eating out is a part of life in Greece as in other Mediterranean countries, but the food is not the sophisticated fare found in Italy or France or the carefully prepared food of the Levant. Not that the Greeks don't eat well - they do. The food is invariably fresh, simply cooked, and appetising, but the choice will often be limited and the garnishing meagre. In the larger towns and cities a wider choice will be found on the menu than in the smaller islands and villages. In recent years the quality and variety of dishes has got much better and you can find some excellent Greek cooking. Many of the old dishes have been revived and often given a twist here and there with some interesting combinations of ingredients.

There are still the old style Greek restaurants serving grilled everything with chips. In the more touristy areas, you still get the 'kidnap and hustle' tavernas where waiters stand outside the taverna and actively and often physically attempt to hustle you inside. Some of these will proffer enticements like a free drink or free entertainment. Generally these tavernas have to resort to hustling because their food is mediocre and the prices high. Those offering a freebie of some sort will make sure it is recovered by charging more for other items. My advice is you pass them by and resist being kidnapped until you have inspected the

Anton's simple steamed courgettes with a vinaigrette dressing for lunch

other tavernas nearby. You can always go back if you decide the taverna-with-hustle was worth visiting anyway.

Now that increasing numbers of tourists arrive in the summer the bigger tourist areas have to import considerable amounts of foodstuffs for the bulging taverna tables. Often your calamari will come frozen from Californian waters, your lamb will come frozen from New Zealand, your feta was probably manufactured in Denmark, and even the aubergines in your moussaka may have come from Spain. Only in the smaller, more out-of-the-way places or those who are trying a lot harder will you get locally grown produce tossed into the salad or grilled over the charcoal.

You can eat well in Greece and by looking around and some local advice you can eat very well in wonderful settings. Tavernas are often perched on the harbourside, many have tables on the beach, with views out over the water and with the open sky above you in the summer you should just sit back and enjoy it all. Eating out in Greece is very much a social occasion and there will be a hubbub of noise from nearby tables as mezes are shared over animated conversation about everything from the follies of the local mayor to international politics.

Grilled octopus

Wine in the Mediterranean

The Greeks and the Romans were both fond of a good tipple. Odysseus on his travels pined for what he described as 'the best of all occasions' when the guests and feasters were assembled and 'the wine steward draws wine from the mixing bowl to pour into each cup in turn'. The Romans were famous for their excessive feasts washed down with copious quantities of wine. Their love of wine was such that wherever Roman rule spread viticulture quickly followed, providing wine to slake the thirst of foot soldier and general alike. In this way the vine spread from a few isolated parts of the Mediterranean across to the far boundaries of the Roman Empire.

Wine in the Mediterranean varies tremendously in quality from one country to another. The Côtes du Rhône and Côtes du Provence of France can be superb and reasonably priced wines. The *vin ordinaire* has probably been blended with wine from Sicily, though the French vehemently deny it. Italy produces excellent wines and gives the best value for money in the cheaper range. The *vino corriente* of Spain is eminently drinkable, but Spain produces excellent quality wines as well, not to mention the fine sherries of Jerez, its distinctive brandy and good liqueurs. As you move farther east to Croatia, Greece and Turkey the quality deteriorates. Slovenia produce some excellent white wines in the north, and from Macedonia come some good reds, and in Turkey a few good reds can be found from the vineyards on the Aegean coast. This is changing as modern methods are introduced to the eastern Mediterranean. Greece in particular now produces some very good wines using a large number of grape varieties unfamiliar to those more used to French, Italian or Spanish wines. But overall the quality and consistency cannot match the wines of France and Italy. In Turkey you can drink a bottle of quaffable wine, order another identical bottle and find it virtually undrinkable. The ingredients and the enthusiasm are there, but not the expertise to turn the grapes into consistently good wine.

Good quaffing Greek wine

In North Africa the wines of Tunisia, Algeria and Morocco vary immensely and again are not consistent. When the French administered this part of the world they planted extensive vineyards and produced some good wine. After the French departed the vineyards deteriorated and the expertise to turn the grapes into good wine was, alas, lost. Some quaffable wine at reasonable prices is bottled, but don't expect the variety and consistency of the products from the countries directly across the Mediterranean. Individual and distinctive wines such as the *retsina* of Greece can be an acquired taste. *Retsina* is made by adding pine resin to the wine during fermentation, giving it a distinctive resiny flavour described by some as imparting a taste not dissimilar to certain brands of turpentine; others consider it a unique tangy wine. You either like it or hate it. The ancient Greeks appear to have liked it, or perhaps all wine then tasted of resin. In ancient amphorae and wine jugs traces of pine resin have been found, and it may have been used to seal the containers to prevent the wine going off, imparting the unique sappy taste.

At the other end of the Mediterranean, the blended wines of the Jerez region in Spain are known worldwide. The various sherries – more than just the familiar dry pale *fino*, dark nutty *amontillado*, and the sweeter *oloroso* and cream sherry – are produced from subtle blends of wines of different types and ages. They are made on the *solera* system, where some of the oldest wine is mixed with the next oldest and so on down to the new, so that the newest wine absorbs some of the flavour and character of the older ones.

In the oldest wine producing area in the world, you will have no difficulty finding wine of some description. There are few countries around the Mediterranean that don't produce large quantities of wine for their own consumption and some of it is excellent; and whatever its merits or demerits, it is all comparatively cheap.

Cheers, Santé, Yammas, Sharife, Saluté!

A short sail across to an island and then lunch

Cool spot to read a paper

routes and Turkish towers added onto Genoese forts. The various influences on the cuisine are less obvious but still evident. Italian and Turkish influences predominate, but you also get odd remnants of other cultures like fruit cake and ginger beer in Corfu or Cephalonian pie which likely owes its origins to Shepherds pie.

In the Ionian we have been getting the boat ready, but there comes a point when boat jobs have to finish. Otherwise we would be here forever fixing that, making this better or ensuring that is more than strong enough. The job list gets smaller but then collects scribbled notes around the margins between cups of tea.

What doesn't help is going racing just before the big off, even if it is a friendly informal race. Still we had to do the Ionian Regatta one more time before leaving the Med. It was a windy old race with the wind hitting 29 knots at one stage with everyone struggling to hold on to all sail. Eventually, we put a reef in the main up the side of Arkoudhi Island, but kept the full 140% genny. And did *Skylax* fly. Remember we are heavily loaded up with spares and food and all the paraphernalia needed to head west. Catching the boat in front we tacked over quickly and the genny got caught on the radar. There was a lot of adrenaline and until the genny was half winched in we didn't notice that the radar was sitting at a jaunty angle. We tacked back over, went backwards while we pulled the genny out and then finally got going again after losing time and places.

When we got in the next day we whipped the sails off and sent them to the sailmaker in Levkas Marina. Then I started on the radar and bracket. Fortunately the cable was still intact and so I bundled the radar up in a bag hanging from a halyard and unbolted the bracket. It was a twisted mess, but good old Pip took it to the workshop and gave it back the next day, straightened and beautifully painted.

In many ways this hop-skip-jump from Greece to Gibraltar is more like a delivery trip than our usual leisurely tours of the Mediterranean. We need to get to Gibraltar where we will sit and wait for a weather window to the Canaries and so can't really dally too much in places we know and love. So the next leg is to Sicily rather than a cruise around the boot of Italy.

In a few remote places like Manganitis you get whatever the patron has for lunch or dinner

Yesterday we finally managed to snap the bit of elastic holding us to Levkas and sailed down towards Sivota for an early morning departure from Greece. Or so we thought. After the incident with the radar and the torn genny in the Ionian Regatta, Robby at CYS just had to trot out the old homily about things happening in threes. Sure enough when the wind went light off Nidri I turned the key to start the engine and nada, nothing happened. True to my missed vocation as a car thief I got hold of a screwdriver and with a lot of sparks connected the main power to the ignition solenoid wire and bingo, the engine started.

At the time we were drifting around in circles and a charter boat chugged up to us. 'Gee, what sort of boat is that', one of the Americans on board called out, 'she sure is beautiful'. Sure, I thought to myself, but she would be more beautiful if the engine started.

We were up at 0730 and had breakfast underway as we motored down the Meganisi Channel in the early morning calm. There is a light mist over the mainland hills. A few caiques are collecting their bottom nets and long-lines. It seems like the elastic tying us to Levkas might finally part.

Motoring out into the Ionian there is a two metre plus ground swell from the strong southerlies of the last few days. It makes for an uncomfortable start towards Sicily. By afternoon a solid NW 4–5 has kicked in and *Skylax* heels on a close reach at 7–8 knots. We are going to Sicily.

Seafood figures prominently in Italian cuisine, in fact all over the Mediterranean

Ashore in Italy

Provisions

Most items are readily available in even quite small towns and local brands are of high quality. Fresh meat, fish and fruit and vegetables are generally of good quality and there will often be a local market with fresh produce, fish and shellfish.

In many of the larger towns there are supermarkets (Standa, Upim, Famila) which have a wide range of goods with all prices clearly marked so you can work out at leisure how much things cost.

Every morning in every town, village and city there is a marvellous aroma of freshly baked bread. All sorts of loaves and buns as well as sticky buns and pizza are freshly baked and likely other goodies as well. Italy has also kept all those wonderful small shops where you can get your parma ham, fresh mozzarella and Parmesan cheese without resorting to supermarket shopping.

Wine and liquer shop.
Mind the innocuous looking limoncello

Eating out

When you mention Italian cooking most people automatically think of pizza and spaghetti. This is a sad oversimplification because Italian cuisine is as diverse as it is delicious. The centuries during which the country was a collection of separate kingdoms, duchies and republics have given modern Italy as many subtle variations in cuisine as in language.

Italy's historical position at the crossroads of the Mediterranean made it an entry point for foods from Africa and the Near East. In Sicily ice cream and sherbet arrived with the Arab occupation of Sicily. Delicacies like almond paste and marzipan were also introduced by the Arabs. A typical Italian meal, if we could isolate such a thing, now represents the best of a long tradition of cooking which whole-heartedly embraced new ingredients and incorporated them into Italian cuisine. Just think of the tomato which was introduced by Columbus from the New World and it's difficult to think of Italian cooking without tomato paste, passata and tomatoes themselves.

Meals often begin with an antipasto such as the rosy, thin slices of prosciutto, mortadella, a kind of Bolognese salami, or caponata, the aubergine appetiser from Sicily. Pasta opens the next course and is the basic Italian staple. There are estimated to be about 100 different pasta shapes, most pasta names being colourful descriptions of shapes, for example cannelloni are big pipes, vermicelli little worms, farfale are butterflies, bucatini little holes. There are many delicious ways pasta can be prepared which range from elaborate lasagne to the simplest linguini with olive oil and fresh basil. In Italy, pasta is cooked *al dente*, which means it should be cooked but have some bite to it and should never be the gluey mess sometimes called spaghetti outside of Italy. Many of the recipes at the end of this book feature on pasta, one of our favourite carbs.

Veal is the principal meat and is excellent throughout Italy. Veal and chicken, less commonly lamb, beef and pork may simply be grilled, perhaps with an accompanying sauce, or cooked in a casserole in which there may be novel, always delicious, combinations with other ingredients. Fish, now considerably more expensive than it was, may simply be grilled or baked with a sauce or in a casserole. Some of the swordfish dishes in Calabria and Sicily should not be missed. In Sicily I have had the most wonderful swordfish casserole with mozzarella, peppers, tomato and oregano that tasted simply divine.

Café life is integral to the Italian way of life

At night a big old waning moon comes up illuminating the eastern horizon with a watery yellow colour. Starry sky. The NW wind lasted through the night until midday on the morrow, then slowly died and clocked N–NNE. Slow sailing and in the late afternoon we turn the engine on (with my magic jump lead wire Lu has found for me).

Eventually a bit of wind returns and we sail slowly with the wind on the quarter. Then in the early morning it dies. Lu calls me up at 0900 to say the boat is caught on a line, maybe it is around the prop. We cut it loose and all is OK. Earlier she had negotiated a huge mess of floating net, probably part of a drift net that had been chopped up by a ship. Drift nets are a menace at night, not just to yachts, but to all the creatures that dwell in the sea: dolphins, small whales, sun fish, and of course the intended victims, tuna and swordfish. Several years ago the government banned drift nets, but relented after the fishermen blockaded the Strait of Messina and stopped the ferries from running and ships from transiting the strait.

Several yachts in the distance look as if they are headed for Malta. And with the fresh NW'ly we have made good time and are heading for the south side of Sicily.

We have decided to press on to Licata on the south of Sicily. We do need to get a bit of a move on to get to Gibraltar. It is lumpy for the last 50 miles to Licata. We sail hard on the wind a bit, motor a bit, sail some more, and arrive just before midnight. We anchor in the basin on the east after some delicate work getting through the new sheltering breakwaters, part of which are underwater and marked only by small buoys.

The south side of Sicily is not a bad way to come late in the season. The winds are generally OK and it is reasonably warm, at least T-shirts and shorts in the daytime. The coast is beautiful, there are enough secure harbours and anchorages to tuck into, and the people are friendly souls.

Still it's getting late in the season and the weather is not looking great just at the moment for the passage to Sardinia or a leap over to the Balearics. We are weatherbound in Trapani on the NW corner of Sicily with strong NW and west winds forecast for the best part of the next week. Still Trapani has it's charms, a lot of them, and we eat out, wander around the streets, take a trip to Erice on the cablecar, and do some boat jobs. Lu fixes the solenoid connection so now, wonder of wonders, the engine starts with the ignition key.

Blue fin tuna

Bluefin tuna stocks have fallen by 75% from a peak in 1975, with a drop of nearly 40% between 1998–2007. Scientists suggest that it is likely that a collapse in the stock will occur in the near future.

Atlantic blue fin tuna return to their breeding grounds and for the majority of the Atlantic population that is the Mediterranean. They follow set migratory routes and consequently are easy to catch. Most blue fin tuna goes to Japan for sushi (and sashimi) and in recent years the prices have risen dramatically as stocks decrease. According to the International Consortium of Investigative Journalists (ICIJ) the black market trade in Eastern North Atlantic bluefin tuna was worth $4 billion between 1998–2007, and comprised one in every three (some say up to half) bluefin tuna that were caught. This black market has been overlooked by a host of officials, from overworked local inspectors to international regulators, most notably the International Commission for the Conservation of the Atlantic Tunas (ICCAT), a regulatory body set up to protect the bluefin stocks. It frequently ignored its own scientists' recommendations for smaller fishing quotas and tighter controls. The Mediterranean bluefin tuna population have been subject to an almost complete disregard for quotas, illegal use of spotter planes, woefully inaccurate estimates of the numbers being transferred to fattening cages, undersized catches of juveniles, shady transshipments on route to Japan, and a highly mobile and poorly monitored fishing fleet throughout the Mediterranean.

Fleets routinely overfished their ICCAT established quotas, sometimes by 100%, and fattening 'ranches' hid what they were doing. The ranches, in effect, 'laundered' the extra fish by under-reporting the amount they took in and manipulating fattening ratios to account for the weight of the off-the-books catches, according to interviews with ranchers, inspectors and officials.

In May 2008, a Turkish vessel reported catching 580 tuna, and transferred those fish into cages belonging to Sagun, a leading ranch in Turkey. But when Sagun reported the harvest of those fish five months later, the Bluefin Tuna Catch Document Scheme (BCD) data show that it pulled out 2,866 fish – nearly five times the number that went in.

By this time, criticism from environmentalists and warnings from scientists about plummeting bluefin stocks were starting to have an impact, prompting a public pledge by top buyer Mitsubishi to support a sustainable fishery. Mitsubishi, a corporate giant best known for trading in cars, steel and chemicals, owns subsidiaries that control about 40% of the bluefin market in Japan. The Japanese, who helped to finance and shape the ranching industry, were now trying to distance themselves from the system, and their no-questions-asked policy finally began to change. Relying on the BCD, which gives each catch a unique identifying number allowing regulators to track a catch from vessel to market, Japanese officials started to closely scrutinize suspicious shipments. By the end of the year, they had taken the unprecedented step of refusing entry to more than 3,500 tonnes of Atlantic bluefin – a sixth of their entire supply that year.

An international attempt – sponsored by Monaco and backed by the EU and US – to ban Atlantic bluefin trade by listing it under CITES, the Convention on International Trade in Endangered Species, was ultimately blocked by aggressive lobbying from the Japanese, but Japan's chief ICCAT delegate has warned that his country will consider supporting a temporary shut down of the ranches. How far Japanese officials will go remains to be seen. Demand for the prized bluefin will remain in the markets and sushi bars of Tokyo and Osaka, and Japan remains by far the world's biggest buyer. Despite concern by some ranchers, few believe the Japanese will support a moratorium on bluefin fishing at the ICCAT annual meeting.

It is not just the tuna which are under threat. Tuna being fattened in ranches are fed exclusively on high grade mackerel, sardines, squid and shrimp, further decimating these vital feed fish and threatening the food supplies of other marine species such as dolphin, swordfish and seals, who feed on them. It takes 25 tonnes of feed fish to raise just one ton of fattened tuna.

It is hard to see how the situation can improve, but there is hope on the horizon in the form of Maria Damanaki, the new EU fisheries minister, who appears to be taking the threats to the fisheries seriously. But without a sea change in attitude from the various European governments I don't rate her chances too high.

We left Trapani early in the morning and headed vaguely in the direction of Sardinia or Mallorca depending on weather. It wasn't a great start as we tacked off Sicily until the promised NE winds kicked in and we sailed slowly towards Sardinia. Off the bottom of Sardinia a nice strong easterly arrived and by late evening we were flying towards the Balearics.

The wind died in the early morning and we entered what the Italian forecast called an 'area di instabilite'. Between thunderstorms, light variable winds and an overcast sky we motored for a fair chunk of the time. On her watch Lu even had a couple of waterspouts off in the distance. By night a good Force 4–5 N–NE had kicked in and *Skylax* picked up her skirts and was sitting on a comfortable 7½–8 knots headed directly for the Balearics.

By evening we were approaching Mallorca still sitting on 6–6½ knots and early for a berth in Palma. Happily I'd phoned ahead for a berth though at a bit of a price. €90 a night as it turned out. Wish I'd known beforehand.

On the third day here a tornado brushed the east coast causing torrents of water to wash cars and houses away and killing one person. This was the second tornado in a week which sort of hints at some pretty dramatic changes to weather patterns. In Palma we had horizontal rain and the harbour turned liquid brown with all the soil and debris washed down off the hills.

After the tornado in Palma, Mallorca. Definitely time to get out of the Med

Almerimar is a good place to provision up before leaving the Mediterranean

We left Palma for Cartagena with light winds that steadily increased through the day until we had a healthy 25 knots plus pushing us on and a disproportionate cross-sea. Lu even had the top of a wave dump in the cockpit on her watch. We flew down to Cartagena and were off the bay and outer entrance by nightfall. Lu was worried about catching the Rugby World Cup final between England and South Africa the next day, but I persuaded her we could carry on to Almerimar and easily be there in time for the evening kick-off. And so we were. *Skylax* flew and we tied alongside the arrivals quay at 1400 the next day.

We stayed a week in Almerimar relaxing and provisioning. Lu got to see the South Africans beat England, only just, and we read English papers and had a few big English breakfasts. It's that sort of place, but easy on the brain and relatively cheap to boot. A week here cost a tad more than one night in Palma. The local supermarket has most of the things you need to get for the transatlantic and at good prices. And it's only a short trolley trundle back to the boat.

We fuelled up and were soon sailing slowly down the coast. A nice norther gradually kicked in and we arrived off Europa Point on Gibraltar early in the morning. A couple of months before a cargo ship was rammed off here and sank just off the point with about half of the hull out of the water (at an angle). At the time we didn't know what was going on with large ocean going tugs holding it in place and isolated danger buoys all around it. We worked our way around and finally pottered up to Marina Bay at dawn. This was it. Gibraltar and what felt like the real beginnings of the circumnavigation.

Ashore in Spain
Provisioning and eating out are covered in the Atlantic chapter.

Cooking on passage is an art that needs to be learned. The ultimate passage food is one-pot cooking. If it's all in one pot then it can go in a dog bowl which makes eating it a lot easier when you are rolling/bouncing/bucketing around on the sea. Of course not all our cooking at sea is like that, but it's handy to have a repertoire of dishes for those occasions when the motion of a little ship at sea makes cooking a difficult chore. And there is very little in the way of washing up compared to multi-pot cooking. There are more complicated recipes as well, some really only suited to a harbour or anchorage or very calm weather. The Beaufort number should help a bit in deciding on what to cook.

All the recipes here are simplified to some extent and I also suggest variants on the ingredients and garnishes for the simple reason that you can't wander into your local supermarket or delicatessen and pick up the wang-gooly ginger or mosharabi fermented bean curd that some complicated ingredient list demands. In most of these recipes I have tried to cut down on the ingredient list because boat galleys do not feature the work surface and storage of even a modest kitchen on the land. If you do have that size galley you probably have a chef on board as well.

As I've said before: the ingredient list and the recipe itself should be treated as a broad outline for constructing the meal. If you don't have a particular ingredient think of something that tastes the same, has a similar texture, blends in with the sort of recipe it is. If you don't have chopped fresh chilli then hot chilli sauce, chilli powder, harissa, or sambal can all be used. If you don't have UHT cream then plain yoghurt works fine. If you don't have sausages to chop up for a risotto try chopped chorizo, salami or at a pinch chopped bacon. If you don't have fresh mint use mint sauce for something like minted

Vegetarians

Meals that are suitable for vegetarians are marked with a

There are vegetarian options scattered through pasta, risottos, beans and pulses, and just vegetables.

Beaufort Force

A number is given for the suggested maximum Beaufort Force a recipe can be used in. To a large extent this depends on the sea state and the wind angle. Going to windward in a Force 5 is a bit different to off the wind in the same force so adjust your ambitions depending on the sea state and motion of the boat. For an approximate conversion from Beaufort Force to knots multiply the Force x4. So Force 4 is 16 knots, Force 6 is 24 knots, etc. Works up to around Force 7.

Moroccan beef or a raita. It's not long before you adapt to slightly changing recipes or adapting the ingredients to what you have or can get ashore. And there is something strangely satisfying and liberating in all this amateur culinary alchemy.

All this talk of cooking on passage and simple meals omits the fact that much of our cooking is done in harbour or at anchor. So some of the recipes are a little more complicated than you might want them to be on passage. All the recipes are marked with a maximum Beaufort force that is a guide to what sort of weather you might cook a recipe in and to what you might want to leave for calmer conditions in harbour or an anchorage. And it all works on dry land as well.

A few tips

Onions When finely chopping onions take half an onion and slice 'along the grain', as it were, and then holding it together with your fingers chop 'against the grain'. That way you get easy finely chopped onions.

Finely chopped onion.
Cut it in slices holding it together and then cut it at right angles the other way

Base tomato sauce A number of the recipes have the same basic ingredients where you sweat some onions and garlic and then add tomatoes and whatever spices/herbs are being used. In lots of cases I use a tin/Tetra Pak of chopped tomatoes, but if you have fresh tomatoes going off then you can chop these up instead of tinned/Tetra Pak. I don't bother skinning them as that is a pain whether on the water or on land. If you have a freezer this basic tomato sauce can be packed into zipped plastic bags in portions for two/three or however many people are on board for a passage. In the absence of a freezer some of those ready made pasta sauces in bottles are well worth carrying. Surprisingly they can be found in most places around the world.

Base stock sauce Along the lines of the above a base stock sauce can be made up of sweated onions, carrots, celery, maybe mushrooms or other vegetables, and is sweated for at least 10–15 minutes. This can also be packed up in suitable portions and put in the freezer.

Burning the skin on peppers on a burner

Peppers (capsicum) If you want to skin peppers you can burn the skin on the stove burner, let them 'rest' inside a plastic bag for a few minutes, and then scrape the skin off with a knife.

Coating with flour When you need to cover bits of meat or fish with flour, put the flour in a plastic bag and then drop the cut up meat or fish in and jiggle it around to cover with flour. As well as a bit of salt and pepper in the flour it's worth experimenting with spices like paprika, cumin, chilli flakes and the like to get 'flavoured' coatings. I usually put the bag in the garbage as trying to wash it out is tedious to say the least.

To coat meat or fish in flour put the flour mixture in a plastic bag and add the cut up meat or fish and jiggle around

Garlic Some of you may not like garlic. If that's the case then just leave it out of the recipe. I use Easy Garlic, it goes under various names, which is just crushed garlic in a jar ready to go. It works well on board without the mess of peeling and squeezing garlic and tastes just as good. Of course I use fresh as well.

Chilli Different chillies have different degrees of heat. So a Scotch Bonnet or a Thai bird's eye chilli can be blindingly hot. In general small chillies are hotter than big chillies. I always de-seed the chilli as most of the heat is in the seeds. If you like things super hot then leave some seeds in. At sea I often use some hot Caribbean chilli sauce as I have a fair idea how hot the stuff is so will put 3–4 drops or maybe 10 drops for more heat in a recipe depending on the sauce.

Starch

That includes potatoes, pasta, rice and couscous.

Potatoes To some extent it depends on the quality as to how you cook them. Boiled new potatoes are a treat, especially with fish. Good, small new potatoes only need a bit of butter on top when cooked. On bigger boiled potatoes a squeeze of lemon works well and maybe some chopped parsley or chives. If they are a bit older, sautéed potatoes are one of my favourites, depending on the weather. And a roast would hardly be a roast without roast potatoes. I love good fluffy mash, but you can also part mash it so you get 'lumpy' mash or scrunched potatoes. Scrunched mash goes well with lots of recipes. You can also add various things to mash: chopped parsley, chives, finely chopped onion. Also try a tablespoon of Dijon mustard for 'mustard mash' or a level tablespoon of horseradish sauce for 'horseradish mash'. Experiment with quantities to get the right balance.

Pasta Pasta needs boiling water in an open pan and ideally as much water as possible. On most boats this is not practical so you need to have enough water in a big enough pan without being really Italian about it. Cook as per the instructions on the packet, usually 8–12 minutes, so it is *al dente*. Don't over-cook it.

Rice Cooking rice is a bit of a minefield. My friend Anton won't use anything except Basmati rice and as he says, it's dead simple with two measures of water to one of rice. Let it boil right down until nearly dry then turn the heat off and put a lid on and leave it to sit for 10 minutes by which time any other water should have been absorbed. I must confess to sometimes adding a bit of oil to the rice when the water goes in, a practice frowned on by many. Anyway Anton's Basmati method works well and can be used with most types of long grain rice. Short grain rice nearly always ends up as a bit of a sticky mess. Boil in the bag rice works pretty well although you need to be careful hoiking the bag out of the boiling water and when opening it. Around ⅔ of a mug of rice is right for two hungry people.

Couscous So simple and so easy on a boat even in bad weather. Simply add the same volume of boiling water to the same volume of dry couscous. A measuring jug is useful or do it by eye. Before you put the boiling water in you can add a little bit of stock, a little dribble of roasted sesame or walnut oil to it, or a small knob of butter. Afterwards you can add other things – see couscous salad. Around 80–100ml/mg of couscous is about right for one hungry person.

Conversions

You really don't have to worry too much about quantities as long as they are about right. In any case you may want to add say a bit more chilli or less garlic depending on tastes to some of the recipes.

By Weight (dry)

1 level teaspoon	⅓ tablespoon	⅙oz	5g
3 level tsp	1 tbsp	½oz	15g
1 heaped tbsp	⅛ cup	1oz	25g
2 heaped tbsp	¼ cup	2oz	55g
4 heaped tbsp	½ cup	4oz	110g
8 heaped tbsp	1 cup	8oz	225g
16 heaped tbsp	2 cups	16oz/1lb	450g

By Volume (liquid)

16 tablespoons	1 cup	8 fluid oz	½ pint	235ml
32 tbsp	2 cups	16 fluid oz	1 pint	475ml
64 tbsp	4 cups	32 fluid oz	1 quart	945ml

When I mention a mug for quantities I mean around 300ml which is around a cup and a half. We don't have any cups on board so I use around ⅔ of a mug. When I mention a large handful I have largish hands so just accommodate. A bit more or less for handful measures of things like fresh herbs is neither here nor there. A good glug means a good glug, probably around a tablespoon full.

RECIPE CONTENTS

Pasta

Putanesca
Tuna pasta
Pasta pesto
Salmon and cream
Spicy sausage pasta
Roquefort and walnut pasta
Spinach and cream tortellini
Spinach and poached egg pasta
Roast vegetable pasta
Spaghetti carbonara
Special ragu
Oven baked feta and tomato pasta
Baked ham and vegetable pasta

Risotto

Basic risotto
Variations: Vegetarian, tuna, ham
  and bean, squash
Prawn risotto

Chicken

Simple Mediterranean chicken
  stew
Fruity chicken curry
Thai green chicken curry
Moroccan lemon chicken
Teriyaki chicken and noodles
Chicken with spinach and feta

Beef

Moroccan minted beef
Chilli con carne
Beef stew
Goulash
Corned beef hash

Pork

Sausage and mash
Easy hot pot with sausages or ham
Sausage and bean or lentil stew
Cassoulet

Lamb

Lamb curry
Lamb tajine

Fish and fishy things

Fresh catch
Ceviche
Satay fish
Fish and white bean stew
Lu's coconut fish
Easy fish stew
Spicy fish stew
Baked fish and spicy lentils
Fish cakes
Kedgeree
Poisson cru
Fish and chip salad
Dealing with crayfish

RECIPES

Prawns

Prawns with feta
Prawns with peppers and sweet
   chilli
Prawns with chorizo

Stir Fry

Vegetable stir fry
Hot sherry squid

Pies

Beef and Guinness pie
Bacon and egg pie
Chicken and leek pie
Fish pie

Barbecues

BBQ beefburgers
Marinades (for chicken, beef
   and lamb)

Beans and pulses

Turkish borlotti bean stew
Chickpea curry
Bean burgers
Spanish bean stew
Easy lentil soup
Anatina dahl
Bean dip
Hummus

Just vegetables

Vegetable curry
Cabbage with potatoes and coconut
Spicy potato cakes
Ratatouille

Eggs

Omelettes
Frittata
Menemen
Huevos rancheros
Eggs Benedict
Egg curry

Salads

Basic green salad and dressings
Salad Niçoise
Moroccan couscous salad
Rice salad
Potato salad
Bean salad
Coleslaw
Carrot salad
Avocado and lettuce salad
Potato and halloumi salad
Hot chicken salad

Snacks and other food

Crostini (or bruschetta)
Instant noodle soup
BLTs
Toasties
Frank's pikelets
Stovetop pizza
Breakfast muesli
Drop scones

Bread

Desserts

Ready-mix cookies and muffins
Baked fruit
Fruit clafouti

Pasta

We eat a lot of pasta, both on passage and at anchor or in harbour. In general we try to buy a well-known brand such as Barilla as some 'own' brands can produce slimy slushy pasta when cooked. It should always be cooked *al dente* as per the time on the packet, usually about 10 minutes in boiling water. Commonly we will have penne (large and small), linguine, spaghetti, tortellini, tagliatelle, and some conchigliate and spirals. We carry a lot of the stuff!

On passage we use a bit less water per serving than in harbour where we can refill the water tanks, purely to save water. It's important that the water is boiling vigorously when you put the pasta in. In harbour use a bit more water as pasta likes to be in a big pan of boiling water and do not put the lid on once the pasta is cooking.

Generally we drain it in the galley sink with a little bit of cold water pumped in so that the boiling water doesn't cook the sink outlet pipe. You can drain it over the side from the cockpit, but that can be dangerous if the boat lurches and you may also loose the pasta overboard. If you are not too keen on pasta some of the sauces for these recipes can be used with rice or couscous, though they work best with pasta.

For portions three large handfuls of penne or similar, or a small bundle (3cm diameter) of linguine or spaghetti for two people is about right. If the boat is bucking around a bit break the bundle of spaghetti or linguine in half to make it easier to eat.

Apart from the pasta recipes below we always carry a few jars of pasta sauce, something like Putanesca or Arrabbiata, for quick and easy pasta meals.

For 2

Olive oil

Small onion finely chopped

2 cloves garlic, crushed, or level tsp Easy Garlic

400g tin of chopped tomatoes

Small handful of chopped olives

½ chilli, de-seeded and finely chopped or small slosh hot
  chilli sauce or pinch of chilli powder

Parmesan

Pasta such as spaghetti, tagliatelle, penne or twirls

- Put a good splosh of olive oil in a pot and sweat onion until transparent.

- Add garlic, chopped tomatoes, chopped olives and chilli. Cook gently while pasta is cooking, usually 10 minutes.

- This basic sauce can be used as a base for other dishes. Add finely chopped peppers, chopped olives, chopped ham, chorizo or salami. Incidentally pasta putanesca means whore's pasta. Serve with grated parmesan on top.

For 2

Ingredients for Putanesca recipe above
1 tbsp capers
Small tin (200g) tuna

- Use the basic putanesca recipe with the addition of the capers. Open and drain a 150–200g tin of tuna.

- About 3 minutes before you serve the sauce add the crumbled tuna to the sauce. If you put it in too early it will turn to tuna mush.

- Serve with grated parmesan and chopped parsley if you have it.

- To the basic mixture before the tuna is added you can also add chopped sun-dried tomatoes, finely chopped green pepper (sauté with the onion) and a smidge of hot chilli sauce depending on taste. I have some basil-flavoured sambal which is the business. The basic mixture can be adapted to your own tastes.

Not all tinned tuna is the same. It should be line caught and if it is that will be mentioned on the tin. There are a number of brands found all over the world, but in Spain, Portugal, the Azores and a few other places, mostly in South America, you will find some lesser known brands. Often the tins are a bit larger and the price a little more than the well known brands, but the tuna inside is a world away from the other stuff and if you find good tinned tuna, stock up on it.

Some people adore pesto, others hate it.
We are solidly in the adoration camp.

For 2

Knob of butter or glug of olive oil

Green basil pesto

Parmesan grated

Fresh parsley or basil chopped (optional)

Pasta such as penne, twirls or linguine

- Cook the pasta and while it is draining put a little butter or oil in the same pan on low heat.
- Put the pasta back in and add two tablespoons or more, depending on inclination, of pesto. Stir it around so it coats the pasta and put some grated parmesan on top of each serving.
- A one-pot dish if you disregard the colander.
- You can also add finely chopped fresh tomatoes or cherry tomatoes with the butter, and chopped basil or parsley at the end if you have any.

RECIPES

For 2

Small pack (150–200g) of smoked salmon shredded into bits

Capers – a couple of teaspoons from the jar

Chopped sun-dried tomatoes – small handful

Parsley or chives, chopped (optional)

Knob of butter or margarine

Small (200ml) pack of UHT cream or yoghurt

Pasta. Tagliatelle, spaghetti, linguine, shells or penne work well

- Cook pasta *al dente* as per instructions on the packet.
- While it is draining add butter or margarine to the pan on low heat. Add drained pasta and all the other ingredients: salmon, capers, sun-dried tomatoes and cream. Warm through on low heat.
- Add lots of freshly milled black pepper. Warm through and serve with grated parmesan and chopped parsley or chives if you have them.

Smoked salmon often has a use-by date of 2–3 months on it and keeps well in the fridge.

Lu sometimes puts a small tin of peas (150g) in as well (drained).

RECIPES

For 2

4 large or 6 small sausages, chopped into bite-sized pieces. Spicy sausages
   are good but not essential

Small onion finely diced

Small chilli finely chopped

Olive oil

1 tbsp wholegrain (Dijon) mustard

Glass of white wine

200ml cream or plain yoghurt

Handful of fresh basil leaves chopped. Or parsley

Pasta. Penne, shells, tagliatelle are all good

- Put a pan of water for the pasta on to boil.
- Cook sausage chunks in a pan until they start to brown.
- Add a small glug of olive oil and gently sweat the onion. When
  soft add the chilli and cook for a few more minutes.
- Stir in the mustard and the wine and bring to a simmer. Add a bit
  of water if it gets too dry.
- Let it all simmer for 10–15 minutes while pasta is cooking. Drain
  the pasta and add it to the sausage mixture.
- Add cream and heat through for a minute or two and serve with
  basil on top.

ROQUEFORT AND WALNUT PASTA *Up to Force 6–7* ⓥ

For 2

Olive oil

Knob of butter

150g (small pack) Roquefort or any other blue cheese will do

Good handful of crushed walnuts

Pasta such as shells, twirls or penne

- Put pasta on to cook.
- In a pan splosh a bit of olive oil and the butter. When the butter has melted stir in clumps of cheese until it has just melted.
- Throw in the walnuts and add the drained pasta. Stir around with the sauce until it is coated.

SPINACH AND CREAM TORTELLINI *Up to Force 6–7* ⓥ

For 2

1 tin (400g) tin of chopped spinach, drained or frozen spinach if you have it

200ml (small carton) cream or yoghurt

½ tsp grated nutmeg

Tortellini of choice

- Put tortellini on to cook.
- In another pan empty chopped spinach, add nutmeg and gently heat through.
- When pasta is nearly cooked put cream or yoghurt into spinach and heat through.
- When tortellini is cooked, drain and put into pan with spinach mixture and stir around. Serve with a few shavings of parmesan on the top.

For 2

Olive oil

Bag of fresh spinach or tin of spinach, drained (or frozen spinach if you have a freezer)

Juice of ½ a lemon

100ml cream or plain yoghurt (4 tbsp)

Small handful grated parmesan (optional)

½ tsp grated nutmeg

4 eggs

Pasta of choice. Tortellini is also good here.

- Cook pasta in a pot of boiling water as per instructions. Drain.
- Put a pan of water on to boil for the poached eggs. A dash of vinegar in the water will help to cook the whites and keep them in a compact shape.
- Wash fresh spinach and remove any tough stems. Put the spinach into a large pan with ½ cup of water and cover. Cook over a medium heat until the spinach is 'wilted', about 5 minutes. Drain off excess liquid. If using frozen spinach it will take a little longer. If using tinned, omit this step and just drain the spinach.
- Add the nutmeg, lemon juice and cream or yoghurt and parmesan to spinach mixture on low heat and stir through.
- When the water for the eggs is boiling, reduce the heat to a simmer and break the eggs gently into the water. Cook for 2½–3 minutes until the white is firm and the yolk still runny.
- Combine pasta with spinach mixture, ladle onto plate and put poached eggs on top.

Any of the following vegetables: onions, garlic (roasted garlic is fruity sweet), squash, peppers, tomatoes, courgettes, aubergine … anything similar. For example onions, garlic, peppers and tomatoes works well. Cut squash, aubergine, peppers, etc., into chunks.

Olive oil

Any dried rosemary, thyme or oregano

Balsamic vinegar or juice of half a lemon

Seasoning and grated parmesan (optional)

Pasta of choice: penne, shells or twirls are good.

- Slice up the vegetables into bite-sized bits and put into a baking tray (except for tomatoes).
- Drizzle with olive oil and season. Some dried rosemary, thyme or oregano over the top works well.
- Bake in a moderate oven for 30 minutes. Put the tomatoes in after 15 minutes.
- Put the pasta on before the vegetables will be finished and cook until *al dente*. Drain.
- Mix in the vegetables with the pasta and if you want to drizzle a little lemon juice and/or balsamic vinegar over the top. Sprinkle grated parmesan over.

SPAGHETTI CARBONARA *Up to Force 7*

For 2

150g grated hard cheese: Cheddar, Edam, Gouda

4 rashers bacon cut into bits or lardons

3 eggs

Olive oil

200ml cream or plain yoghurt

Handful grated parmesan (optional)

Pasta of choice: spaghetti, linguine or penne

- Boil water and put pasta into cook.
- In a high sided pan fry bacon bits. When done put bacon bits in a bowl but leave a little of the fat in the pan.
- While pasta is cooking break eggs into a bowl, add grated cheese and some ground black pepper. Whisk with a fork until eggs are nicely beaten in with other ingredients.
- Drain pasta and put into high-sided pan on low heat. Pour egg and cheese mixture over the pasta.
- On a low heat stir mixture into pasta until egg is cooked. When nearly cooked add cream or yoghurt and warm through.
- Serve with cooked bacon bits and parmesan sprinkled over.

I often make this as the first passage meal the night before we leave. If there are two of you it can always be recycled the second night into chilli con carne with the addition of a 400g tin of kidney beans (drained) and a splosh of hot chilli sauce or chilli flakes to taste.

For 4 hungry people

Small pack lardons or several rashers of bacon chopped

2 small or 1 big carrot finely sliced

2 sticks celery finely sliced

3 bay leaves

250g pack mushrooms sliced. At a pinch you can use a 200g tin of sliced mushrooms (drained)

500g minced beef

400g tin or pack of passata or chopped tomatoes

300ml (mug) of chicken stock (dissolve a cube in a mug of hot water)

2 glasses of white wine

Good pinch of nutmeg

Pasta, penne, linguine, tagliatelle or spaghetti

Small pack of UHT cream or yoghurt

Grated parmesan

- In a large pan sizzle the lardons or chopped up bacon. Add the sliced carrots and celery and bay leaves and gently sweat for 10 minutes or so until soft.
- Add the mushrooms and cook for another 5 minutes.
- Turn up the heat and brown the mince in the same pan, about 5 minutes.
- Then add passata, stock, wine, nutmeg, and salt and pepper to taste and turn heat down.
- Leave to simmer on low heat for at least an hour without a lid. Add water if it starts to dry out.

- Cook pasta and serve with the sauce and a good splodge of cream (or plain yoghurt) on the top and parmesan. A simple green salad goes well with it.

For 4

200g feta cheese

300g (6 medium sized) tomatoes roughly chopped or equivalent in cherry tomatoes

Brown sugar

Olive oil

Balsamic vinegar

Handful fresh basil

Cup of chopped olives, green or black

Handful of pine nuts or pepitas. Slivered almonds or crushed walnuts will also work if you don't have pine nuts.

Pasta of choice – penne or farfale are good

- Put oven on at 180°C (about).
- Roughly crumble feta into aluminium foil square and drizzle some olive oil on it then wrap into a parcel closed at the top.
- Wrap chunks of tomato (or whole cherry tomatoes) in foil, sprinkle with brown sugar, drizzle with olive oil and close parcel.
- Seal foil packets and put in the hot oven for 30–45 minutes. Half way through open the top of the tomato packet.
- Toast the pine nuts or pepitas, in a small frying pan on a medium heat until they brown. Keep jigging the pan as they will burn easily.
- Cook pasta and drain. Put pasta in a large salad bowl and crumble oven baked feta and tomatoes (with juice) over pasta.
- Sprinkle olives, a handful of torn basil leaves and the toasted pine nuts over and splash a good dollop of olive oil and balsamic vinegar over. Instead of olive oil you can use a vinaigrette salad dressing.

RECIPES

For 4

Pasta. Penne, farfale or shells work well.

150g of ham, preferably thick cut, cut into chunks. Cooked bacon will work OK

200g peas, preferably frozen but tinned will work, or 200g mushrooms chopped

Bunch of spring onions chopped

Large knob of butter

50g plain flour

500ml of milk

120g grated hard cheese like Cheddar, Edam, or Gouda

Seasoning

- Cook pasta according to instructions.
- While pasta is cooking put the butter in a pan on moderate heat. Add the flour and mix together until it is a paste. Slowly add the milk continually stirring until you get a nice white sauce. Mix in cheese and spring onions and add seasoning to taste until you have a cheese sauce.
- Drain pasta and put in an oven dish and sprinkle ham and peas or mushrooms over. Add cheese sauce and gently stir until pasta and other ingredients are mixed through.
- Cook in moderate oven (180–190°C) for 25–30 minutes. It

might be useful to cover with aluminium foil for 10–15 minutes at first so the top layer of pasta doesn't burn.

- You can also add chopped tomatoes, sliced peppers or anything else you think will work.

RECIPES

Risotto

Risotto is an easy one-pot dish that can be cooked in arduous conditions. It also has the big advantage of being able to swallow up all sorts of ingredients you might have in the boat. Any 'proper' cookbook will tell you, you must use Arborio rice, short grain, but I've always cooked risotto with par boiled long grain rice. My friend Anton suggested it should be called 'Rodotto'. Risotto also has the advantage of being a bit 'sticky' making eating it easy when the boat is rolling around.

For 2

Olive oil (say 1½ tbsps but I just glug some in)

Parboiled rice (2 cups)

1 onion finely chopped

2 cloves of garlic thinly sliced or teaspoon of Easy Garlic

200g tin of peas

Stock cube (chicken or vegetable, dissolved in a cup of hot water)

Chopped ham/bacon/salami/chorizo or lardons (around 200g or more)

Small UHT cream (usually 200ml carton) or equivalent in yoghurt

Cup of grated cheese. Parmesan is best but use what you have

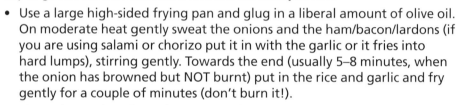

- Use a large high-sided frying pan and glug in a liberal amount of olive oil. On moderate heat gently sweat the onions and the ham/bacon/lardons (if you are using salami or chorizo put it in with the garlic or it fries into hard lumps), stirring gently. Towards the end (usually 5–8 minutes, when the onion has browned but NOT burnt) put in the rice and garlic and fry gently for a couple of minutes (don't burn it!).

- Tip in the stock and another 2 cups of water, then the drained peas, and leave on low heat to cook. After 20 minutes or so, just before all the water has been absorbed by the rice, tip in the cream or yoghurt and the cheese and continue cooking until the risotto is just moist.

- You can omit the cream/yoghurt and the cheese if things are bit hairy on board.

Variations

Wine
Substitute some of the stock with white wine.

Vegetarian risotto
Sweat onion, rice and garlic. Then use a 400g tin of chopped tomatoes, tablespoon of capers and small handful of chopped olives.

Tuna risotto
Same as vegetarian option but put a small tin of tuna in 3–4 minutes from the end and stir into the mixture.

Ham and bean risotto
Sauté ham/chopped bacon/lardons and onion, rice and garlic as per main recipe. Then add a 400g tin of cannelloni, borlotti or similar beans. Cook then go to cream and cheese at the end as per the basic recipe. Lu's speciality and tastes excellent.

Squash risotto
Cut half a small squash into segments, slosh a bit of olive oil on it and roast squash in a tray in a moderate oven for 30–40 minutes. Sweat onions, rice and garlic. Add stock and water and diced squash. Put cream in at the end if you wish. Again one of Lu's specialities.

Other ingredients
It's pretty easy to see you can add all sorts of things on board that need using on a passage. Finely sliced green or red peppers (gently fry), fresh tomatoes (sliced or diced), mushrooms (fresh or tinned), leftover chicken, fresh fish, sausages (fry up first), carrots (sauté or tinned), tinned mushroom or chicken soup (no cream or cheese or stock as this thickens it up nicely).... Use your own creative powers to conjure up a special risotto out of what's available.

For 2

Olive oil
Knob of butter (optional)
1 tsp of tomato paste
Small handful of chopped sun dried tomatoes
4 spring onions sliced or ½ onion finely chopped
250g shelled small prawns
Glass of white wine
Vegetable or fish stock cube dissolved in a cup of hot water
Parboiled rice (2 cups)
Handful chopped parsley

- Put oil and butter in a pan over gentle heat and sweat onions and rice. Stir in tomato paste and sun dried tomatoes towards the end when onions are translucent.
- Add stock, wine and 2 cups water. Reduce over low heat until rice has absorbed the water. You may need to add a little more water if rice is not cooked properly. The rice should be plump but not hard.
- A good trick is to take the pan off the heat when it appears cooked and give it a stir. Add the prawns then put a lid on for 3–4 minutes off the heat.
- Or a few minutes before the end stir in the prawns and cook for 3–4 minutes until prawns turn pink.
- Serve with chopped parsley over.

Chicken

Many of these recipes are good with beef or lamb as well.

On passage we normally take a frozen chicken or two wrapped in newspaper and popped into a zipped plastic bag. These will last at least five days in the coolest part of the fridge and a lot longer if you run a proper freezer. We often do a roast chicken with roast potatoes and vegetables which leaves plenty over for chicken sandwiches for lunch and something like a chicken stir fry or curry the next evening. That's with two of us. Roast chicken is 20 minutes a pound (half a kilo) plus 20 minutes. Leave to stand for 10–15 minutes after cooking.

If you have a small oven then you will need to spatchcock the bird. This is easy to do by putting it breast side down and using kitchen scissors to cut down either side of the backbone, cutting through the ribs on the way before removing the backbone. Then turn the bird over and squash it down so it is flat – you will hear a few more ribs breaking when you do this. The chicken will cook quicker than a whole bird going in, around 45 minutes for an average bird.

Marinades for chicken

Simple Olive oil, juice of 1 lemon, oregano or rosemary, salt and pepper. Rub it all in.

Honey and mustard Olive oil, juice of 1 lemon, 2 tbsp honey, tablespoon Dijon mustard, salt and pepper. Mix into a paste and spread on.

Oriental Olive oil, juice of 1 lemon, good glug of soy sauce, 2 tbsp sweet chilli sauce, 1 tbsp brown sugar. Mix up and spread on.

Indian Olive oil, juice of 1 lemon, 1 tbsp of curry paste, 150–200ml coconut milk, dash of hot chilli sauce or pinch of chilli flakes to taste. Mix into a paste and spread on. I quite like this but it is not to everyone's taste.

The chicken should marinade in the fridge for a minimum of an hour and preferably several hours. Overnight is not too long. For these marinades spatchcock chicken works well. You can stuff your whole chicken with things like a peeled onion cut into quarters, squeezed lemon halves, and a bunch of rosemary.

All these marinades are also good with chicken bits, the bags of thighs, legs, wings, or breast. With a sharp knife score the skin and then leave the bits marinading for a good hour or more.

Note Though it sounds a bit strange, roast chicken served on a bed of salad with the juices dribbled over the salad works well.

For 4

Olive oil

450–500g chicken. Cut into bite-sized bits. Can be thighs or breast. De-bone thighs if you want to.

2 tbsp flour

2 medium onions chopped

2 carrots sliced

2 celery stalks chopped

2 cloves of garlic crushed or 1 tsp Easy Garlic

1 400g tin of chopped tomatoes

Handful of green olives or black (optional)

2 bay leaves

1 level tsp oregano or thyme

Small glass of white wine

250ml (large mug) chicken stock (dissolve 1 cube in boiling water)

- Use a high-sided pan or a pressure cooker on gentle heat. Sweat onions, garlic, carrot, celery, oregano or thyme and bay leaves. About 10 minutes.

- Put flour in a plastic bag with a bit of salt and pepper. Put the chicken bits in the bag and shake it around to coat chicken.

- Turn heat up a bit and add chicken bits to vegetables and brown. If thighs are not de-boned this will take a bit longer.

- Add tinned tomatoes, wine, stock (and olives if using them) and scrape bottom of pan to get any sticky bits into the stew.

- On low heat let it simmer for a good 40 minutes to an hour or about 30 minutes in a pressure cooker. Add a little water if it reduces too much.

- Serve with mashed potato, rice or couscous.

FRUITY CHICKEN CURRY *(also good with lamb) Up to Force 5–6*

For 4

Glug or two of vegetable oil
500g chicken bits (thighs, breast, legs) cut into smaller bits if large
2 onions sliced
2 cloves garlic finely sliced or 1 tsp Easy Garlic
1 tin chopped tomatoes
2 tbsp mild curry powder
1 tbsp coriander seeds
Big thumb finely chopped or grated fresh ginger
10 dried apricots chopped or dates or dried figs
1 mango preferably not ripe (then it doesn't go all mushy) diced
1 banana sliced
400ml tin of coconut milk

- Fry chicken in hot oil in pan until cooked through and browned over and then put aside in a bowl on paper towel.
- Sweat onions until soft. Add garlic, curry powder, coriander seeds and ginger, stirring until the onions are covered in spices, for another 3–4 minutes.
- Tip in tomatoes, coconut milk, put chicken back in and add apricots (or dates or figs) and simmer for a good 30 minutes.
- Then add diced mango and sliced banana and return to a low heat for another 10 minutes.
- Serve with rice and naan bread if you can get it.

For 4

Glug or two of vegetable oil

400g chicken fillets sliced into bite-sized chunks. If you are using thighs and wings with the bones in then you will need around 550g

Handful of spring onions chopped. Otherwise a small onion finely chopped

2 cloves of garlic minced or 1 tsp Easy Garlic

6 new potatoes cut into bite-sized pieces. Or 2 or 3 ordinary potatoes chopped

100g green beans chopped into 3 or a can of sliced beans

400ml can coconut milk

1 lime with zest grated off

4 tsp Thai green curry paste. Or other mild curry paste but Thai green is best

2 tsp Thai fish sauce or soy sauce

1 tbsp brown sugar

Vegetable or chicken stock (dissolve a cube in 400ml hot water)

Handful chopped basil leaves (or coriander or parsley)

- In a high-sided pan add some oil and brown chicken. Remove and put in a bowl with paper towel.
- Put potatoes in boiling water for around 5–8 minutes until partially cooked and then drain.
- Heat up a pan with the oil and swizzle spring onions, garlic and Thai green curry paste around on low heat for a minute or two.
- Add coconut milk, fish or soy sauce, stock, sugar and lime zest. Heat through and mix up for a couple of minutes.
- Add chicken and potatoes. Simmer and cook for 15 minutes or until chicken is cooked. Chicken on the bone will take longer, at least 20–25 minutes.
- A few minutes before the end add the green beans.
- Sprinkle chopped basil (or coriander or parsley) over curry when served. Serve with rice.

RECIPES

This is a variation on a fairly standard recipe that can be adjusted depending on what you can get. I usually make it in harbour (it's a good dish you can prepare ahead if people are coming to dinner on board) though I have also made it at sea.

For 4

Glug or two of olive oil

500g chicken bits (thighs/breast/even wing all on the bone is fine although cut bigger bits in two). Around 4 thighs and 4 other bits – two big chicken breasts can be cut in half or even three)

Large onion sliced

4 cloves of garlic finely chopped or 2 tsp Easy Garlic

Tin of chopped tomatoes (400g)

1 tbsp tomato paste

Rind from 1 lemon (use a vegetable peeler on a lemon) finely chopped into small bits

Juice from 1 lemon

1 tsp turmeric

1 tsp of ground cumin

2 cinnamon sticks

Garnish: good handful of slivered almonds (or chopped whole almonds or chopped walnuts or pine-nuts at a pinch), cup of chopped black olives, chopped coriander (or parsley)

- Use a high-sided pan and brown chicken bits in olive oil on medium heat. When browned both sides put in bowl with paper towel to soak up excess fat/oil.

- Sweat onions in the same pan and then add garlic, lemon rind, turmeric, cumin and cinnamon sticks and heat for another 2 minutes or so, stirring occasionally.

- Return chicken to pan. Add tomatoes and lemon juice and a bit of water so it's all covered.

- Leave to cook for 40–50 minutes on low heat. Can be reheated later.

- When you serve sprinkle chopped olives, slivered almonds and chopped coriander over each serving.

- Serve with couscous. I usually make this ahead as well (it's fine cold) and make up a couscous salad. *See section on salads.*

For 2

Vegetable oil

300g chicken bits (breast cut into strips or thighs with the bone out)

2 tbsp Teriyaki sauce

½ a chilli de-seeded and finely chopped

2 cloves garlic finely diced or 1 tsp Easy Garlic

Small knob of ginger grated

1 tbsp soy sauce

Squirt of sesame seed oil

300g vegetables finely sliced or diced: carrots in fine sticks, green or red pepper sliced, celery finely sliced, cabbage or bok choi finely sliced, anything that you have that works.

100g noodles

Handful of chopped coriander (or parsley) chopped for garnish

- Put chicken in a bowl and marinade for at least 20 minutes with teriyaki sauce and finely chopped chilli.
- In a high-sided pan glug a bit of oil in and cook chicken and marinade until brown, around 10 minutes on moderate heat should do it. Remove chicken and put in a bowl with paper towel.

- Turn heat down and gently sauté ginger and garlic.
- Cook noodles in boiling water, usually a few minutes.
- Add chicken and vegetables and turn up heat and cook for a bit.
- Add noodles, sesame oil and soy sauce. Mix through and serve.
- Serve with coriander on top.

RECIPES

For 2

Olive oil

2 chicken breasts or 4 chicken thighs (de-boned)

1 small onion chopped finely

Clove of garlic finely chopped or crushed or tsp Easy Garlic

125g feta

Good bunch of spinach chopped or 400g tin of chopped spinach

1 cup dry white wine (optional, use cup of water instead)

Nutmeg

- Put a glug of olive oil in a pan and cook chicken browning both sides. Put chicken to one side.
- Sauté onions and garlic in same pan then add wine or water and simmer for 5 minutes.
- Crumble feta in and let it melt and mix through.
- Add chicken and spinach, pinch of nutmeg and let it all simmer for 10–15 minutes.
- Serve with rice, couscous or pasta. (If serving with pasta it's better to chop chicken into smaller pieces).
- A variation on this is to stuff chicken breasts with a spinach and feta mixture and fry or grill the chicken breasts with the stuffing. Also works well with lamb.

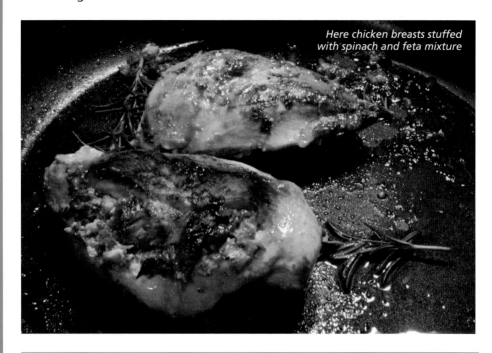

Here chicken breasts stuffed with spinach and feta mixture

RECIPES

Some of the chicken curry recipes work well with beef as well.
Cut the beef into long slivers and use in place of chicken.

Beef goulash

MOROCCAN MINTED BEEF *Up to Force 3–4 Also a good passage meal prepared the night before but double the quantities*

OK, you need a bit of steak, but all the other ingredients are easy to find or adapt.

For 2

Olive oil

400g of beef cut into narrow strips about 10cm long
(just cut it into strips)

1 onion sliced

1 tsp ground cumin

400g tin of chopped tomatoes

Small bunch of mint or two teaspoons of mint sauce

1 tsp of finely grated or chopped lemon rind (or lime)

Dash of lemon or lime juice

½ cup of slivered almonds

Chopped parsley or coriander (or the mint) if you have it to garnish

- Sauté beef in the oil in a high-sided pan until cooked through. Put aside on paper towel in a bowl.
- Sweat onions in the same pan.
- When onions are soft add cumin and lemon rind.
  Let them cook gently together.
- Put the beef back in with tomatoes, lemon or lime juice, and the chopped mint or mint sauce. Add a bit of water if too dry. Cook slowly for 20 minutes.
- Sprinkle with some chopped mint (if using it) and slivered almonds.
- Serve with rice or couscous.

RECIPES

CHILLI CON CARNE *Up to Force 4–5,*
but good passage meal prepared in advance

For 4

Olive oil

1 large onion sliced

2 cloves garlic crushed or 1 tsp Easy Garlic

1 chilli, de-seeded and finely chopped

500g mince

1 carrot sliced

2 sticks celery finely sliced

2 bay leaves

1 tsp ground coriander

400g tin of chopped tomatoes

2 tbsp tomato paste

1 glass red wine

Worcester or HP sauce

1 mug beef stock (or vegetable or chicken).
Dissolve a beef cube in a mug of hot water

400g tin of kidney beans

Sour cream or yoghurt to serve

- In a pressure cooker or high-sided pan put a glug of olive oil and gently sweat onion, chilli, sliced carrot and celery and the bay leaves, about 10 minutes.
- Turn heat up and add mince. Brown, stirring for around 5 minutes. Add garlic, coriander and tomato paste.
- Turn heat down and add tin of chopped tomatoes, kidney beans, Worcester or other sauce, stock and red wine. Season with salt and pepper.
- Simmer gently for 40–50 minutes, 30 minutes in a pressure cooker, topping up with a bit of water if necessary. Cooking a bit longer or leaving to stand won't hurt it.
- You may need to add a bit of hot chilli sauce or pinch of dried chillies if you want it warmer.
- Serve with rice and a dollop of sour cream or plain yoghurt on top.

Variation Any leftover chilli is good in tortillas with some grated cheese, salsa and a dollop of plain yoghurt.

RECIPES

Beef stew is one of those recipes that can swallow up all sorts of vegetables you might have on board. This one has just onion, potatoes, and carrots (and a bit of garlic), but you can also put in some sliced celery, mushrooms (a tin of sliced mushrooms is OK), sweet potato cut into chunks, squash peeled and cut into chunks, green beans (add fresh and tinned later on), anything along these lines that will work.

For 4

Olive oil

Knob of butter

400–500g beef. Cheap cuts like stewing steak or beef skirt work fine. Cut into bite-sized chunks

3 rashers of bacon cut into bits

2 onions sliced

3 cloves garlic crushed or heaped tsp Easy Garlic

2 carrots sliced

2 large potatoes halved and cut into chunky slices

1 glass red wine or small can Guinness or other dark beer (not lager)

2 beef or chicken stock cubes dissolved in a large mug (300ml) hot water

1 tsp dried oregano or thyme

1 tsp dried rosemary

Flour

Salt and pepper

- Put a good splosh of olive oil and the butter in a high-sided pan or pressure cooker and add bacon bits and beef lightly coated in flour (use the plastic bag method).

- Brown beef lightly then add onions and garlic and simmer over a low heat until onions are translucent, about 5 minutes.

- Add carrots and potatoes, herbs, stock, wine or Guinness, and season to taste. Put a lid on pan or pressure cooker and let it cook slowly for a good hour.

- If necessary add a little water. You can thicken the stew with a little cornflour paste or some instant mashed potato mix.

- Serve with crusty bread or rice or couscous.

Variation Add 400g tin of baked beans towards the end and stir in until warmed. Sounds naff but is surprisingly yummy.

GOULASH *Up to Force 5, but good passage meal when prepared in advance*

For 4

Olive oil

400–500g beef cut in bite-sized chunks – sirloin is best but otherwise use stewing steak

3 cloves garlic crushed or heaped tsp Easy Garlic

1 large onion sliced

1 red pepper seeded and sliced or diced

1 green pepper seeded and sliced or diced

400g tin of chopped tomatoes

1 tbsp tomato puree

2 beef or chicken stock cubes dissolved in a large mug (300ml) of hot water

1 tbsp flour

3 tbsp paprika

Handful chopped parsley

Sour cream, cream or plain yoghurt

- Put a handful of flour and salt and pepper in a plastic bag and add the beef bits and shake it all around to coat with flour.
- Put a good glug of olive oil in a high-sided pan or pressure cooker and brown steak chunks.
- Add onion, garlic and diced peppers and simmer over low heat for around 5–10 minutes or so until onion and peppers are soft.
- Add tomato paste and paprika and mix around a bit so everything is coated with the paprika and tomato paste.
- Add stock and chopped tomatoes and cook for a good hour over a low heat with the lid on, or 30 minutes in a pressure cooker. Add extra water if it starts to dry out. Can cook longer and can always sit for a bit.
- Serve with rice, couscous or mashed potato and with a dollop of sour cream or yoghurt and chopped parsley (if you have it).

I'm not a fan of corned beef and rarely use it, but I know some of you are. This is the fourth variation on a theme that I've put together and I think it works the best.

For 2

1 tbsp olive oil

1 400g tin corned beef

1 onion sliced

1 stick celery sliced

2 medium sized potatoes peeled and sliced

1 pepper de-seeded and finely sliced into ribbons

1 chilli, de-seeded and finely chopped

1 clove garlic crushed or 1 level tsp Easy Garlic

Juice of 1 lemon

2 bay leaves

1 tsp oregano

Glug of Worcester sauce or HP brown sauce
    or tomato ketchup at a stretch

Salt and pepper

- Heat oil in a pan and gently sweat onion, celery, chilli, garlic, bay leaves and pepper.

- Add sliced potatoes and add just enough water to cover. Add lemon juice, Worcester sauce, oregano and salt and pepper to taste.

- Gently simmer with the lid off until potatoes are soft, around 20–25 minutes.

- Add corned beef and break up through the mixture with a wooden spoon. Do not mash into a goo, you need chunky bits of potato in it. Heat through, about 5 minutes.

- You can add other ingredients and mix and match depending on what you have, though the onion and potatoes are necessary. Sliced carrots, cabbage or broccoli should all work.

RECIPES

Pork

You obviously need to be in non-Muslim areas to get the basic ingredient, though sometimes wild boar is available in Islamic countries. You can also get beef or chicken sausages, though these vary from terrible to just OK.

Sausage and bean stew

SAUSAGE AND MASH

You don't need a recipe for this, but if you are cooking the sausages in the oven try putting a pepper in cut into strips with a drizzle of olive oil over them and a bit later a few tomato halves with a bit of dried thyme or oregano over the top and maybe a bit of grated parmesan. Mash can be just mash or you can adulterate it, in the nicest possible way. Try putting a tbsp of whole grain mustard in and mash it

through for mustard mash or a level tbsp of horseradish sauce for horseradish mash. You can also use some finely chopped onion mixed through it and chopped parsley always goes down well.

EASY HOT POT WITH SAUSAGES OR HAM *Up to Force 6–7*

For 4

Olive oil

Pack of sausages or 400g diced ham, chopped chorizo, lardons or chopped bacon

Tin of beans (baked beans work well)

1 onion sliced

1 stick celery chopped

1 orange peeled and cut into segments

1½ tbsp tomato paste

2 medium sized potatoes diced/sliced

1 tbsp paprika

1 tbsp brown sugar

2 tbsp white wine vinegar (or lemon juice)

- In a large pan or pressure cooker sweat onions, celery and sausages/diced ham/lardons or chopped bacon in olive oil. Chorizo can go in towards the end or it gets a bit tough. About 10 minutes, though take care not to burn the onion

- Stir in tomato paste, paprika, sugar and white wine vinegar or lemon juice. Add beans and potatoes and enough water to cover ingredients.

- Add orange segments if using. Simmer slowly with a lid on for around 30 minutes until potatoes are cooked.

SAUSAGE AND BEAN OR LENTIL STEW   *Up to Force 4–5*
Good passage meal prepared in advance

For 4

Olive oil

Pack of sausages (about 6). Beef sausages will do if you can't get pork

Small pack of lardons or 3 rashers streaky bacon cut up into bits

1 onion sliced

3 cloves garlic minced or 1½ tsp Easy Garlic

1 small carrot finely sliced

1 can (400ml) of beans like haricot, borlotti, cannellini or even lentils work (or ¾ cup dry Puy lentils)

1 can (400ml) chopped tomatoes

Juice of ½ a lemon (1 tbsp)

1 mug chicken stock (dissolve 1 cube in mug of hot water)

1 tsp dried rosemary (or oregano) or a couple of sprigs of fresh rosemary

Salt and pepper

Handful of chopped parsley

- Put a little oil in a high-sided pan and cook lardons/bacon and sausages for about 10–12 minutes.
- Remove sausages and cut into bite-sized chunks.
- Add onion, carrot and garlic to pan and gently cook until onion is translucent.
- Return chopped sausages to pan and add beans or lentils, tomatoes, chicken stock, lemon juice and rosemary.
- Cover and cook for 30–40 minutes and top up with a bit of water if it gets dry.
- Serve on couscous with parsley scattered over.

Do not show this recipe to les Français or you will be in for a lecture on what a cassoulet should or should not include and how far removed from a real cassoulet this recipe is.

For 4

6 sausages (or 4 large)

200g of salami or chorizo cut into small chunks

100g lardon or bacon cut into small bits

Olive oil

250g of white haricot beans soaked overnight or cheat and get 2x 400g tins. You could also use borlotti or canellini beans

2 cloves of garlic crushed or 1 tsp Easy Garlic

2 carrots sliced

1 large onion chopped

1 400g tin of chopped tomatoes

1 tbsp thyme or oregano or rosemary

2 bay leaves

Small glass of cognac or sherry or large glass of red wine

Salt and pepper though remember the lardon/bacon and salami/chorizo are salty

- Put a good glug of olive oil in a large pan or pressure cooker and gently fry the sausages. When mostly cooked remove and cut into chunks.
- Sweat onion and lardons/chopped bacon, around 10 minutes. Return sausage chunks to pan.
- Pour in a litre of water, less in a pressure cooker, and add all the other ingredients except the salami and alcohol. Simmer for 2 hours or 50 minutes in a pressure cooker.
- Add salami and cognac/sherry/wine and cook for 30 minutes or 15 minutes in the pressure cooker.
- Serve with rice or boiled or mashed potato.

Lamb

We don't do much with lamb except roast a leg or shoulder and grill or sauté lamb chops. For me mint sauce is essential, while for Lu it's redcurrant jelly. The lamb curry recipe below is one I only cook in harbour for superstitious reasons regarding lamb curry. On two occasions crossing the English Channel I've had lamb curry as the passage meal on the first night and it hasn't gone down well. I'm not usually seasick, but even the thought of it makes me feel queasy at sea. It's surprising how many places around the world you can buy New Zealand or Australian vacuum packed leg of lamb at pretty reasonable prices.

Lamb curry

RECIPES

For 4

500–600g of lamb cut into bite-sized cubes.
  You can use cooked lamb left over from a shoulder
  or leg previously roasted.

2 tbsp vegetable oil

2 onions sliced

1 large carrot grated

3 cloves garlic crushed or 1½ tsp Easy Garlic

1 chilli, de-seeded and finely diced

Good sized knob of ginger grated

Big handful of chopped dried apricots or dates

2 tbsp mild curry powder or paste

1 tbsp ground cumin

Juice of 1 lemon

500ml of chicken or vegetable stock
  (dissolve 1½ cubes in big mug of boiling water)

- In a high-sided pan or pressure cooker splosh in some oil and brown lamb cubes over a medium to high heat for 4–5 minutes. Remove lamb into bowl with paper towel to blot up fat. If using leftover roast lamb cube and omit this step.

- In the same pan add a bit more oil and gently sweat onions, chilli, garlic and ginger and soften for 3–4 minutes.

- On low heat add curry powder, cumin and lemon juice and mix into a paste for a few minutes.

- Put the lamb back in and swish around to cover with spicy paste and then add grated carrot and stock. Gently stir and then cover and cook over a low heat for 1 hour, stirring occasionally.

- 10 minutes before the end add chopped dried apricots or dates.

- Serve with rice and chutney of choice.

This is a lot easier to make than the ingredient list makes out. Also good with chicken instead of lamb.

For 4

2 tbsp olive oil

500g (1lb) lean lamb cubed

1 onion chopped

2 cloves of garlic crushed or 1 tsp Easy Garlic

700ml chicken or vegetable stock. About 1 stock cube in
2 large mugs hot water

Grated zest and juice of 1 orange

1 cinnamon stick

1 tsp of clear honey

1 tsp cumin

175g dried apricots chopped in half

3 tbsp chopped fresh mint, about a handful.
Alternatively use 1½ tbsp mint sauce

25g ground almonds (optional)

25g toasted flaked almonds

- Heat oil and fry the meat for 4–5 minutes until brown and then remove to a plate with paper towel on it.
- Add the onions to the pan and fry gently for a few minutes until softened, about 5 minutes.
- Add the crushed garlic, stir and add back the lamb.
- Add in stock, orange zest, juice, cinnamon, cumin, honey and seasoning. Bring to the boil and simmer gently for about an hour.
- Add the apricots and 2 tbsp of the mint or mint sauce and cook for a further 30 minutes.
- Stir in the ground almonds if using.
- Serve with chopped mint and toasted almonds on top and couscous.

RECIPES

Fishing is a matter of luck with
Although not the most dedicated fishermen, we do troll a line regularly and have a reasonable selection of lures. And we catch fish when Poseidon decides to allow us one of his own.

Catching and killing fish

Killing and bleeding a fish after catching it is an art in itself. The following is based on our experience and should be useful to any other dilettantes out there who have not invested a small fortune in high tech gear to catch fish.

- Initially I used a simple line with a bungee on the line to take the sting out of a strike. Lu decided we needed something a bit more sophisticated and bought a nice reel which is mounted on the pushpit. With the reel tension half on the line will reel out when there is a strike.

- We don't mess around with light line, but use 200lb line with a stainless steel trace on the end. Our lures are a mixture of Rapalla-type lures that look like blue or red mackerel or exotically coloured squiddy things. We also make some simple lures out of shiny tinfoil (crisp and nut packets are good) tied on the shank of a hook with thread and trailing a plastic streamer. It's caught fish! (Thanks James.)

- When you have a fish on the line and it's tired itself out you can reel it in. Some fish like mahi mahi and some small sharks will start to fight aggressively when they see the back of the boat. The best policy with these is to let them out a bit and they will eventually tire. Fish like tuna and

Once you get it onboard spray some alcohol (ethanol or methanol) into the gills (clearly shown here) to subdue the beast

You can make your own lures with some silver foil (crisp packets are good), a bit of thread and a plastic streamer tail on the hook

wahoo don't seem to struggle as much when they get close to the boat.

- Once you have the fish on board give it a squirt of alcohol in the gills. We use denatured wood alcohol (methanol) that you buy for the first aid box. You can use drinking alcohol (ethanol), though it seems a bit of waste to use a nice rum or the gin to subdue the fish.

- To kill the fish I used to just chop the head off and let it bleed. Severing the spinal cord kills it and it can then bleed, which is important to let the nasty toxins in its blood produced in its death throes drain out. It also leaves some tuna flesh less red in colour.

- Small tuna can be chopped laterally into steaks across the backbone. Larger tuna, mahi mahi and wahoo are best filleted. Put the fillets in plastic zipped bags and keep them in the fridge. Those with freezers can freeze some as well.

You need a pair of gloves, gardening gloves are fine, to get the lure out

After bleeding, gutting and filleting the fish (use lots of buckets of salt water to wash down) cut the fillets into handy sizes for cooking. Pack them into zipped plastic bags or Tupperware type boxes and get them into the fridge as soon as you can.

Lu on how to kill and prepare a tuna, wahoo or mahi-mahi

Lu deals with most of the killing, bleeding, gutting and filleting Japanese-style. It's more complicated than my basic 'cut-the-head-off' method, but it gives a better result.

Bringing a thrashing fish on the end of a line into the boat is a fraught moment. Teeth, hooks and surprisingly rough scaly skin are best dealt with wearing a pair of those orange rubbery gardening gloves.

1. Stun the fish

Give it a sharp bang on the head using a small baseball bat or a winch handle. Some people use alcohol sprayed into the gills which is less brutal. Either way the fish should lie still enough to remove the lure.

2. Destroy the brain

Take a sharp knife or spike and aim into the area between and slightly behind the eyes and wiggle the knife around. You know you have destroyed the brain when the dorsal fin flexes, the jaw relaxes and there is a final spasm. This stops the fish producing toxins which affect the flesh quality.

3. Bleed the fish

Cut a short vertical slit 2cm long and 2cm deep about 4cm behind each pectoral fin.

Slice around the white membranes which run around the back edge of the gills.

In both cases blood should run freely from the cuts.

Put a line securely around the tail and either trail the fish behind the boat, or suspend the fish and flush with water until bleeding has stopped, about 10 minutes.

Gutting

A very sharp knife makes gutting and preparing a fish not just easier and quicker, but safer too.

1. Slice open the abdomen from level with the pectoral fins towards the tail, and finish by cutting a small circle around the anus.
2. Use your hands to free the digestive tract and slide them whole out of the cut.
3. Cut the gill attachments at the top and bottom, and slice around the white membrane of the gill collar.
4. Free the spinal cord and various organs from the abdominal wall using a sharp knife then fingers.
5. Pull on the gills to remove all the bits in one piece.
6. Give the fish a good rinse – it is now ready to fillet or cut into steaks.

Filleting

1. Lay the fish on its side on a board.
2. Cut about 1–2cm into the flesh around the head and down to the belly.
3. Gently, with a sharp knife, work the flesh away from the bones along the top of the fish down to the pectoral line, then do the same working up from the belly.
4. Use a combination of a sharp knife, and then use your fingers to 'feel' your way along until the flesh comes away in one piece.

5. Turn the fish over and do the same on the other side.
6. Don't worry if you leave some flesh on the bones. You'll leave less every time you do it. These bits make good sushi snacks.

Fresh catch

There is nothing like the taste of fish on the day it is caught. Just grab a frying pan and drizzle in some olive oil. When the pan is warm, pop in your fish and sear both sides. Season with salt and pepper, and a squeeze of lime or lemon juice and serve with some fresh bread. For a more substantial meal serve with sautéed potatoes and a green salad. Trappas Restaurant in Antigua serves fresh tuna with some wasabi sauce and pickled ginger. Just superb and we do it all the time now.

Some people talk about eating flying fish. In my experience they are too small, really bony and don't even taste that great

CEVICHE *Up to Force 4, but best at anchor with a glass of white*

Ceviche is a South American dish which at its simplest is bits of fresh fish marinated in lime juice for a half hour or so. The fish must be fresh. You can also use lemon or even grapefruit juice to marinate it. Typically in South America some finely diced chilli is added and other variations include chopped coriander or parsley, finely diced fruit like avocado, mango or papaya and coconut milk where it starts to stray into poisson cru territory.

Fresh fillets ready for marinading for ceviche

SATAY FISH *Up to Force 4*

One of my favourite dishes with fish is borrowed from Scott Bannerot's *Cruisers Handbook of Fishing*. I've amended it slightly but it is basically his recipe. It's a good recipe for anyone who doesn't like fish.

For 2
Several fillets cut into large chunks
4 tbsp peanut butter
Good splosh of peanut oil or other vegetable oil
1 tbsp of soy sauce
1 tbsp each of grated/chopped garlic and grated fresh ginger
1 tbsp sweet chilli sauce
1 tsp of brown sugar

- Heat the oil and stir in peanut butter, soy sauce, garlic, ginger, sweet chilli sauce and sugar.
- Some people might like more soy sauce and/or more sugar. Taste it and see.
- When the sauce is bubbling gently put the fish fillets in, put a lid on the pan, and let it cook slowly for 10 minutes. Turn the heat off and let it cook for another 5–10 minutes in the hot sauce.
- Serve with rice or couscous and a green salad.

Chicken is also good with the sate sauce. Just sauté chunks of chicken until cooked and then put into the sate sauce to cook for 10–15 minutes and let sit for 5–10 minutes.

A fish and white bean stew in a single pot. It might sound a little strange to combine fish with beans, but it is delicious. It's easier to make than the ingredients list might suggest.

For 4

500g fish cut into bite-sized chunks (any white fish or tuna)

100–150g mussels. Out of shell and cleaned or use a tin or jar of mussels in brine. If using tinned/jar of mussels wash them through with water a few times to make them less salty. If you don't have mussels it is still good without them

400g tin of chopped tomatoes

400g tin of white beans (borlotti, canellini or other)

250ml of fish stock (Dissolve a cube in hot water. If you don't have fish then vegetable or chicken stock is OK)

2 medium red onions finely chopped

1 carrot finely sliced

2 sticks of celery finely sliced

2 cloves of garlic crushed or teaspoon Easy Garlic

½ small chilli de-seeded and finely chopped (or a bit of hot chilli sauce or pinch of chilli powder)

2 bay leaves

Sprig of rosemary or teaspoon of dried (or oregano or mixed herbs)

1 tsp brown sugar

2 tbsp olive oil

Handful of chopped fresh parsley (or coriander)

- Use a high-sided frying pan on low heat and glug in olive oil and add chopped onions, garlic, celery, carrot, chilli, bay leaves, sprig of rosemary and sugar. Cover and simmer for 10–15 minutes.
- Remove sprig of rosemary and bay leaves (if you leave them in it won't matter too much though they will end up on someone's plate).
- Add tomatoes, beans, white wine and stock and simmer with lid off for 15–20 minutes until liquid has reduced by a half or more.

- Add fish and mussels and simmer for 10 minutes or until mussels and fish are well cooked.
- Sprinkle with parsley when served. Serve with rice, couscous or pasta.
- If you want to be a bit fancier put a dollop of plain yoghurt on top of each serving.

Fish and white bean stew

For 2

300g fish fillets cut into bite-sized chunks

Salt and pepper

Flour

1 tsp paprika

1 tbsp olive oil

200ml coconut milk

2 tsp curry powder

1 finely chopped onion

2 medium sized tomatoes chopped into small bits

Enough pasta for 2, shells, penne or twirls work best. Also good with couscous, rice or potatoes

- Put pasta on to cook.
- Get a plastic bag and put the flour, salt and pepper to taste and paprika into it. Put the fish chunks into the plastic bag and shake gently so the fish is coated with flour and spices.
- Heat oil in a pan and sauté fish for 2 minutes each side, then put aside.
- When pasta is cooked, drain and in the same pan heat up coconut milk, chopped onion, and curry powder. Simmer for several minutes then add fish and tomatoes and simmer for a couple of minutes.
- Remove fish again and add pasta to the pan and simmer with coconut sauce for a couple of minutes.
- Serve pasta and put the fish on top.

This is easy to do when it is a bit bumpy or you can't be bothered with messing about too much.

For 2

Olive oil

200g white fish cut into chunks. Tin or bottle of mussels in brine washed. Prawns also work well.

400g tin chopped tomatoes

1 medium onion finely chopped

2 cloves garlic crushed or 1 tsp Easy Garlic

1 tbsp capers

1 tsp sugar, preferably brown

Good glug of Pernod, ouzo or similar. Or sherry or Marsala. Or ½ glass of white wine. Really whatever you have in the stores though aniseed flavoured spirits work best.

Handful of chopped coriander or parsley if you have it.

- Put a dollop of oil in a frying pan and sweat onions over low heat. Add garlic towards the end.
- Add tomatoes, capers, sugar and Pernod/sherry/Marsala or wine and let it simmer for 10–15 minutes.
- Add fish and mussels (or prawns) and let it simmer for another 10 minutes.
- Serve with coriander or parsley over the top with couscous or rice.

RECIPES

This is very easy to make and provides a variation on other fishy stews. Really it is spicy light. You can be creative with the ingredients and even add a few compatible vegetables to the basic stew depending on what is on board. We make it without even really thinking about it these days when you don't want to go to a lot of trouble getting ingredients together or think too much about cooking when it is a bit bumpy at sea.

For 2

Olive oil

250–400g cubed fillets of white fish. Whatever you happen to have like snapper, tuna, mahi mahi, whatever

A large potato cubed into bite-sized bits

Large onion finely chopped

2 cloves garlic or 1 tsp Easy Garlic

400g tin of chopped tomatoes

1 tsp paprika

1 tsp ground cumin

½ tsp ground coriander

Good glug of ouzo, Pernod or other aniseed flavoured alcohol or glug of marsala (optional but good)

1 tsp of sugar

Chopped parsley or coriander (to garnish but optional if you don't have them)

2 tablespoons flaked almonds (or toasted pine nuts or chopped cashews at a stretch)

- Put a glug of oil in a high-sided pan and sweat onion.
- Add spices and garlic and stir until well mixed in.
- Add tomatoes, sugar, ouzo (or alternative), potatoes and a bit of water if necessary.
- Simmer for 15–20 minutes until potato is cooked. Add fish and cook over low heat for another 5 minutes.
- Serve garnished with parsley and flaked almonds scattered over the top. Serve with couscous. When you make the couscous add a bit of sesame oil and a sprinkle of stock powder. Rice or mashed potatoes also work well.

RECIPES

I think Chrissy when she was on *Tillymint* first cooked this or similar.

For 2–3
175g puy or brown lentils
600ml vegetable stock
Olive oil
1 onion, finely chopped
2 celery sticks, finely chopped
1 red chilli, de-seeded and chopped
½ tsp ground cumin
4x 150g pieces of white fish
Juice and grated rind of a lemon
25g butter
Salt and pepper
Lemon wedges

- Rinse and drain the lentils. Put in pan with the stock. Bring to the boil and simmer gently for 30 minutes, until cooked *al dente.*

- Heat a glug of olive oil in a pan. Add the onion and sweat until soft. Add the celery, chilli and cumin and cook another 4 minutes until the celery has softened.

- Put the lentils with any remaining liquid into an oven-proof dish, add the onion mixture and stir together.

- Lay the fish on top of the lentil mixture skin side up.

- Mix the lemon zest with the butter and season with salt and pepper. Spread the lemon butter over the fish, and drizzle with lemon juice.

- Cover and cook for 20–30 minutes in a moderate oven (180°C), until the fish is cooked. The flesh should be firm and translucent, but flake apart with a fork. Serve with some crusty bread to mop up the juices.

Baked fish and spicy lentils. Here Lu used some sole we had got

RECIPES

You can make these with fresh fillets or if you have had no luck fishing they are arguably as good or better with tinned tuna or salmon.

For 2

400g fish flaked. You can also use 2 small tins of drained tuna if you don't have fresh fish. Tinned salmon works OK too.

2 medium potatoes cooked and mashed. If you have leftover mashed potato that works fine. Essentially the quantity of fish and mash should be about equal.

1 egg beaten

1 chilli, de-seeded and finely chopped (optional but good)

Handful of chopped parsley or coriander if you have it (optional)

Handful of chopped chives or at a stretch small onion finely diced.

Juice of ½ a lime or lemon

Handful of grated parmesan cheese or half a handful of ready grated parmesan (the 'dusty' stuff). This gives a really good taste to the fish cakes but leave it out if you don't have it.

Salt and pepper

Vegetable oil

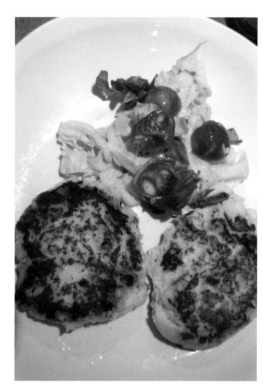

RECIPES

- In a bowl combine fish, mashed potato, chives or chopped onion, chilli if using, lemon juice, beaten egg, grated parmesan, salt and pepper to taste and parsley or other if using.

- Mix all together with your hands and then shape into cakes. Don't make them too thick. Makes 6 medium sized cakes.

- Heat a splosh of oil over moderate to high heat until hot and then fry fish cakes until nicely browned either side. Put on a plate with paper towel to mop up excess oil.

- Serve with green salad or couscous salad.

This is a variation on a Jamie Oliver recipe.

For 4

Olive oil and knob of butter

250g white fish fillet cut into chunks

250g smoked fish cut into chunks (if you can't get smoked use all white unsmoked)

1 onion finely chopped or a bunch of spring onions chopped

2 big handfuls of cherry tomatoes or 3 large tomatoes cut into wedges

3 hard-boiled eggs sliced

Large thumb of ginger grated

1 small chilli, deseeded and finely chopped

2 bay leaves

2 tbsp medium curry powder

1 tbsp mustard seeds

2 cloves garlic crushed or 1 tsp Easy Garlic

Big handful of fresh coriander chopped

Juice of 1 lemon

Mug of rice (150g), preferably basmati

Natural yoghurt

- Put rice in a pan (1:2 rice to water) with water and a little splash of oil and cook on low heat.
- In a high-sided pan put a glug of oil and the butter. On medium heat sweat onions with bay leaves.
- When onions are translucent add chopped chilli, ginger, garlic and cook for another few minutes.
- Add curry powder, mustard seeds and lemon juice and mix into other ingredients.
- Add tomatoes and fish and cook for 5–8 minutes.
- By now the rice should be cooked. Add to pan and mix gently through.
- Add sliced boiled eggs on top.
- Serve with chopped coriander and a blob of natural yoghurt on top.

A Polynesian take on fish that is cooked by marinating in lemon or lime juice. It differs from ceviche in that there is coconut milk and a few other vegetables in it.

For 4

500–700g (about 1–1½ lbs) of fresh fish like tuna, wahoo or mahi mahi cut into bite-sized cubes

1 tin (400ml) coconut milk

2 lemons or 3 limes squeezed for juice (about 1½ cups)

1 cucumber diced

Small bunch spring onions chopped

2 tomatoes chopped

1 small chilli finely chopped (optional)

1 carrot grated

Salt and pepper

- Combine all ingredients except tomatoes in a bowl, season, and leave in the fridge to marinate for 1–1½ hours.

- 10 minutes before serving add tomatoes.

- Good on it's own with a baguette to soak up the juices. Also a good starter for more than 4.

RECIPES

A variation on a Nigel Slater recipe. It tastes so much better than it sounds … trust me.
I cook it in harbour or at anchor.

For 4

300g white fish fillets cut into
bite-size pieces

300g squid cut into rings (you can
breadcrumb the fish and squid if you like –
just put some breadcrumbs and a bit of
flour in a plastic bag and throw the fish
and squid in and then jiggle around until
the bits are all coated)

3 medium sized potatoes cut into sauté
sized slices and parboiled

Salad: frisée, other lettuce, rocket,
watercress – whatever salad leaves you
have

- Sauté potatoes in pan until cooked
  and nicely browned. Put aside in
  paper towel to keep warm and blot up a bit of oil.

- Turn up heat and put squid rings in. They will crackle and pop.
  After 3–4 minutes put fish in as well.

- Put salad on bottom of plate. Arrange sautéed potatoes on
  salad. Put squid and fish on top. Pour dressing over.

Dressing

4 tbsp olive oil

Juice of 2 limes or small lemons

Handful of mint

Handful of parsley

1 tbsp Dijon mustard (or other)

1 tbsp capers

4–6 anchovies (if you have them, tinned are OK)

A blender is really necessary. I use the big 12V blender we have
on board. Put oil, lemon/lime juice, mint, parsley, mustard, capers
and anchovies in and blend to a lovely green mush.

You could conceivably use mint sauce (1½ tbsp), chop parsley
finely, and mush it up with the other ingredients with a fork. As
a last resort use a vinaigrette with mint sauce if you can't get all
the bits you need.

Dealing with crayfish *(spiny lobster)*

In many parts of the world you can get crayfish at bargain prices and in some places you can catch them yourself. Dealing with them is another matter. After some experimentation we have found the following works for us.

1. When you get them stick them in the freezer or the fridge and they will calm down with a bit of hypothermia.

2. When you want to cook them get a big pot of water on the boil with a lid. Don't believe the cuddly stories of mercy killing by putting a knife in the brain of a crayfish – it doesn't really have one. It has a bunch of ganglion serving as a central nervous system, but the chances of you piercing it with a knife are slim and the crustacean will still move about even if you chop it's head off. Horror movie stuff.

3. Once the water in the pot is boiling stick the comatose crayfish (or however many will fit) into the pot and put the lid on. Turn the heat off and leave for 10 minutes. Then pull it (them) out and they will be perfectly cooked.

4. Once the crayfish has cooled a little break the tail off by twisting the head,

but taking care to keep and pull out the white meat that is tucked into the head end of the carapace.

5. You can then work your thumb down inside the tail and remove the meat in one piece.

6. Down the back of the crayfish will be a thin black line (it's nervous system!) which you need to carefully peel out.

7. Serve with mayonnaise and a slice of lime or lemon… and white wine.

In parts of the world you can get excellent fresh prawns. In the USA, Australia and India they are large. In other places, like New Caledonia, Southeast Asia, Spain and France, prawns tend to be smaller. Frozen prawns are widely available.

See also Prawn Risotto under Risottos.

Prawns and chorizo

This is a quick and simple recipe based on the Greek classic Garithes saganaki. One of my favourites.

For 2

Glug of olive oil

1 small onion finely chopped

2 cloves of garlic or 1 tsp Easy Garlic

400g tin of chopped tomatoes

½ glass of white wine

½ mug (125ml) vegetable or fish stock (crumble ½ a cube in ½ mug of hot water)

1 tsp of brown sugar

200g of feta

200g peeled prawns, if frozen defrost

Handful of chopped coriander or parsley or basil

- Sweat onions and garlic in olive oil.
- Add tomatoes, wine, stock, and sugar. Simmer for a good 5 minutes.
- Crumble feta in and let it melt and mix through. Simmer until reduced a bit. I like the feta mixed in but some people like some lumps of feta in the sauce.
- Put prawns in last and cook for 3–5 minutes.
- Sprinkle chopped coriander/parsley/basil over individual servings.
- I like this dish with tagliatelle or linguine but you can serve with any pasta. Alternatively rice or couscous.

RECIPES

PRAWNS WITH PEPPERS AND SWEET CHILLI *Up to Force 4*

For 4

1 tbsp vegetable oil

400g shelled prawns

1 red and 1 green pepper sliced into thin slivers

2 cloves garlic crushed or 1 tsp Easy Garlic

3 tbsp sweet chilli sauce

Good handful of crushed peanuts (put whole nuts in a bag and bash on the chopping board with a blunt object like a hammer or knife handle until crushed)

Pasta: linguine, spaghetti or tagliatelle.

Handful of chopped coriander or parsley

- Put oil in a high-sided pan and sweat peppers on medium heat, about 10 minutes, until soft.
- Put pan of water on and cook pasta.
- Add garlic and sweet chilli sauce to peppers and mix through for a minute or two.
- On moderate heat throw prawns in and cook, around 3–4 minutes.
- Serve on pasta (or rice or couscous) with crushed peanuts and coriander on top.

PRAWNS WITH CHORIZO *Up to Force 3–4*

Sounds a bit weird but prawns go well with spicy chorizo. The recipe is sort of Spanish in origin though much mucked about with here.

For 2

Olive oil

250g prawns

Small chorizo with outer skin off and sliced

2 small potatoes parboiled and sliced

2 tomatoes chopped or 8 cherry tomatoes (latter are best)

Small splash of sherry or Pernod (or ouzo, raki)

Handful of chopped coriander or parsley

- Glug a bit of oil in a high-sided pan and sauté potatoes for a bit, about 10 minutes until light brown.
- Put chorizo in pan with potatoes and sauté for another 5 minutes or so.
- Throw in tomatoes and sauté for another 4–5 minutes.
- Put prawns in pan with a splash of sherry or Pernod and cook until prawns are pink, about 3–5 minutes.
- Sprinkle chopped coriander or parsley over and serve with crusty bread.

Stir-fry

Stir fries are great for using up odd vegetables. Any of the following work well: mushrooms, green beans, broccoli, carrots, peppers, onion, garlic, cabbage, bok choi, celery, really anything that has a taste and texture you think will work. Chop them up into bite-sized pieces.

It's worth keeping some jars of ready-made sauces in the stores like black bean or sweet and sour sauce. Alternatively make up your own with soy sauce, teriaki, sweet chilli and sesame seeds.

Stir fries really just involve flash frying vegetables with bite-sized bits of chicken, beef or pork. Chilli and ginger also go well here. This all happens at fairly high heat so you need to constantly stir it so nothing burns.

Serve with noodles or rice.

For 2

Vegetable oil

400g squid cut in rounds, tentacles and all

1 small onion finely chopped

1 green pepper sliced

½ a chilli, de-seeded and finely chopped

1 level tsp dried oregano

Salt

2 cloves garlic crushed or 1 level tsp Easy Garlic

½ glass of sweet sherry, or Marsala or even an aniseed tipple like pastis or ouzo

Small handful of chopped coriander or parsley

- In a bowl combine a good glug of oil, chilli, oregano, good pinch of salt, garlic and sherry or other. Whisk with a fork.
- Put squid in the marinade and refrigerate for an hour. Longer is better.
- In a high-sided pan put a good glug of oil. Add onion and peppers and cook over a moderate heat for 3–4 minutes or until onion is translucent.
- Turn up heat and add squid with marinade. There will be a fair bit of sizzling so be careful of getting splashed with hot oil.
- Cook squid until translucent, about 4–5 minutes. Do not over-cook the squid or it will become rubbery.
- Serve with chopped coriander or parsley with rice or crusty bread.

RECIPES

Pies

Pies are not the easiest thing to cook on board and they use a fair amount of cooking gas. I always buy frozen ready-made pastry as making it on a boat is messy and takes ages. These four pies are miles removed from ready-made varieties like Fray Bentos . They can also be made in advance for passage meals, but are difficult to make when things are even a little bit bouncy at sea. You don't need specialised pie dishes, just use oven-proof dishes which are the right size and depth.

Beef and Guinness pie

Good passage meal when prepared in advance. You could conceivably make the filling in advance and cook the pie underway, not that I have.

For 4

Olive oil

1 onion chopped

2 cloves of garlic crushed or 1 tsp Easy Garlic

1 carrot diced

2 sticks of celery diced

6 medium sized mushrooms chopped. A tin (400g or so) of chopped mushrooms will work.

1 level tsp dried rosemary (or oregano)

Ready made puff pastry

500g stewing or brisket steak cut into mouth sized cubes

1 small can (400ml) Guinness or other dark ale. Lager does not work

½ cup plain flour

Salt and pepper

Bit of milk (optional)

- In a pan put a glug of oil and sweat onion for 5–6 minutes until it is soft.
- Add the garlic, carrots, celery, mushrooms and rosemary. Let it all stew together on low heat for a good 10 minutes or more. You might need to add a little water if it dries out too much.
- Put the beef bits in a plastic bag with the flour and jiggle around to coat the beef.
- Turn the heat up to medium and put the beef bits into the mixture. Cook for 5 minutes or so until browned then pour in the Guinness. Season to taste.
- Cover the pan and let it all simmer for 45 minutes. Towards the end you may have to uncover and reduce the mixture a little so it is nice and thick for the filling.
- Get out your pie dish and rub a bit of butter around the bottom and edges or a thin film of oil to stop it all sticking.
- Put the pie mixture in and cover with rolled out puff pastry. Use a fork to push down the edges around the pie dish and prick some holes in the top. If you want a glaze brush the top with some milk.
- Pop into a moderate oven (180°C) for 40–50 minutes until the pastry is cooked.
- Serve with peas or other green vegetables. Peas need to be fresh or frozen as tinned just don't work here.

BACON AND EGG PIE *Up to Force 4–5, but good prepared in advance for passage meal*

This pie contains ingredients used in a fry-up and hence has tomatoes and mushrooms in it. I wouldn't suggest you put baked beans in it, but you can leave out the tomatoes and mushrooms if you want and you could add things like chopped peppers or onion. Traditionally these pies have a shortcrust pastry, but I prefer puff pastry. It's also very good cold for lunch the next day.

For 4

Vegetable oil

10 rashers bacon chopped into bits

6 eggs

A handful of cherry tomatoes or 2 medium tomatoes chopped

10 button mushrooms sliced. A tin (250g) of chopped mushrooms will work (just)

Puff pastry

Salt and pepper

Bit of milk (optional)

- Fry up the chopped bacon for a few minutes.
- Get out your pie dish and rub a bit of butter around the bottom and edges or a thin film of oil to stop it all sticking.
- In the pie dish arrange bacon, tomatoes and mushrooms (or other ingredients).
- Break the eggs over the top and roughly mix in so the yokes are all broken. Season to taste.
- Arrange rolled out pastry over the top and press down around the edges with a fork and prick a few holes in the top. If you want a glaze brush the top with some milk.
- Cook in a moderate oven (180°C) for 40–45 minutes until pastry is golden.
- Serve with salad and ketchup.

A good passage meal prepared in advance. Like the beef and Guinness pie, you could conceivably prepare the filling in advance and then make the pie later.

For 4

Vegetable oil

6 boneless chicken thighs or 3 small breasts cut into bite-sized chunks

2 leeks chopped (if you can't get leeks do a variation with fresh mushrooms chopped and change the name to chicken and mushroom pie)

Small pack of lardons or 3 rashers bacon chopped

Puff pastry (though filo pastry works well)

Thumb-sized lump of butter

½ cup plain flour

Big mug (350–400ml) of milk

2 tbsp cream (optional)

Salt and pepper

- Make the white sauce first. Melt butter in the bottom of a pan and then work the flour in with a wooden spatula or spoon. Don't bubble the butter. Add the milk and stir slowly over a low heat. After a while it will begin to thicken. Don't stop stirring. Add cream if using it and season to taste.

- Take the white sauce off the heat and add leeks or mushrooms and leave to one side.

- In a pan add a little oil and brown lardons or chopped bacon bits. When browned add chicken bits and brown also. Put to one side.

- Get out your pie dish and rub a bit of butter around the bottom and edges or a thin film of oil to stop it all sticking.

- Put bacon and chicken mixture in the dish and pour white sauce with leeks/mushrooms over and gently mix together.

- Arrange rolled out pastry over the top and press down around the edges with a fork and prick a few holes in the top. If you want a glaze brush the top with some milk.

- Cook in a moderate oven (180°C) for 30 minutes until pastry is golden.

- Serve with a salad or peas (not tinned).

For 4

600g fish. Ideally you do half white fish and half smoked fish, but use whatever you have

3 large potatoes or 6 small, peeled and cut into chunks

2 big knobs of butter

2 tbsp plain flour

2 cups of milk

3 hard-boiled eggs sliced

1 leek sliced OR small punnet of mushrooms chopped

Juice of ½ a lemon

Salt and pepper to taste

Some grated cheese (optional)

- Put potatoes on to cook for mash.
- Make up the roux for the white sauce by melting butter and mixing the flour in over a low heat. When the flour is thoroughly mixed in with the butter add milk bit by bit and keep stirring gently until it thickens into a white sauce. Season to taste. Remove from heat and add leeks or mushrooms and let it sit.
- When potatoes are cooked mash with the other knob of butter and a splash of milk.
- In a greased dish flake the fish evenly into the bottom and pour lemon juice over. Pour white sauce and leeks or mushrooms over it. Arrange sliced boiled eggs over the top. Layer mashed potato over the contents and rake with a fork so it looks pretty. Sprinkle grated cheese over if using.
- Cook in a moderate oven, 190–200°C for 45–50 minutes until the mash top is nicely browned.

RECIPES

A significant number of boats have a BBQ on the pushpitthe smell of barbecuing drifting across the anchorage can be wonderful. If you don't have a BBQ on the boat there is always the possibility of barbecuing ashore, if it is safe to do or permitted. In some places it is prohibited because of the fire risk. In some countries like the USA, Australia and New Zealand there are barbecue areas ashore which are sometimes quite sophisticated.

Growing up in New Zealand we always constructed the BBQ ourselves. Some stones piled up in a semi-circle and a bit of fine wire netting (the sort used in fences around chicken runs) across the top served the purpose.

In early charter days I remember organising this sort of BBQ for a charter group of 40 or so and a concerned Dutchman coming up to me and expressing concern about where the BBQ was. He meant a proper BBQ of the sort you might have in the back garden. When I explained to him that the pile of rocks and the wire netting was 'it', he informed me it was impossible to BBQ in this way. After his barbecued lamb, Greek sausages and a few seared green peppers he came up to me and declared this was emphatically the best BBQ he had been to.

As a last resort, and it isn't going to taste the same, you can always stick things under the grill. Below the suggestions for the BBQ really involve marinades and some suggestions for side plates.

Portions

Meat is best cooked in smaller portions on the BBQ. Things like lamb chops (preferably butterflied by the butcher), pork chops, sausages and steak can be cooked directly on the BBQ. Otherwise pork, lamb, chicken and beef is best cut into smaller portions and cooked directly or on skewers as kebabs.

Unless chicken is cut into small bits and cooked that way, or as kebabs, larger chunks take quite a while to cook right through. With larger pieces you could microwave them or maybe partially cook them in the oven, but in practice you just need a bit of patience and to accept that barbecued chicken takes a bit longer.

Fish is best barbecued wrapped in aluminium foil. Before you close up the packet sprinkle a bit of oregano or thyme over the top. You can also put some tomato slices or strips of green or red pepper on the top as well. Fish shouldn't need long before it is cooked.

Homemade beefburgers are just so good compared to those in franchised fast food joints.

Makes 6 burgers

500g minced beef

6 cream crackers or 1 cup breadcrumbs. Put the crackers in a plastic bag and break up into small bits like breadcrumbs

½ onion finely chopped

Handful of parsley finely chopped (alternatively chives finely chopped or leave out if you can't get either)

1 tbsp Dijon mustard

Salt and pepper

6 hamburger buns

- Combine all ingredients in a bowl and mix with your hands until all the ingredients are mixed through. Apparently if you put beef burgers in the fridge for half an hour they will stick together better. Cook on the BBQ, otherwise in a hot pan with oil.

- In the bun put lettuce and sliced tomatoes as a minimum. New Zealand burgers always have sliced cooked beetroot in them and this makes for an excellent Kiwi-burger. In addition gherkins and maybe a slice of cheese work well. I like ketchup as well.

MARINADES

Most meat should be marinaded for at least a couple of hours before barbecuing. To some extent it depends on the size of the meaty bits: chicken bits like thighs, breast and legs, steaks or bigger chunks of pork are better marinaded longer than if they are cut up into kebab-sized bits. It's also useful to score the top of the meat with a few crosscuts for the marinade to 'get in'.

You can marinade in some sort of bowl with cling film on the top or use a sealable freezer or zipped plastic bag. Put the marinade in the bag, then the meat, jiggle it all around and then seal before putting it in the fridge.

You can make up your own marinades from what you have. Generally a bit of oil, lemon juice or balsamic vinegar, something a bit sweet and something a bit sour and away you go. When I make the marinades below there are often variations depending on how I feel the mixture is going. As long as you make it up in a mug or glass and can taste it after you have whisked it together then you can use it or add something else to make it better.

Portions below are for 2 hungry people. Adjust accordingly for more.

Chicken with 'slightly spicy' marinade

Simple marinade Mix up 3 tbsp olive oil, juice of 1 lemon, good glug of soy sauce, 1 tbsp Dijon mustard and 1 tbsp of honey. Good with chicken, beef and pork.

Slightly spicy Mix up 3 tbsp olive oil, juice of 1 lemon, good knob of grated ginger, finely chopped half a de-seeded chilli and 1 tsp brown sugar. Good with all meat.

Yoghurt marinade Cup of plain yoghurt, some mint finely chopped or 1½ tsp mint sauce, ½ tsp cumin, ½ tsp coriander and 1 clove garlic crushed or ½ tsp Easy Garlic. Especially good with lamb but works for all meat.

Mediterranean marinade Mix 3 tbsp olive oil, juice of 1 lemon, 2 cloves garlic minced, 1 tsp oregano (or mixed herbs), and 2 crushed bay leaves. Good with lamb and pork.

BBQ sauce Mix 2 tbsp olive oil, 2 tbsp tomato ketchup, 1 tbsp honey, 1 tbsp sweet chilli sauce, 1 tbsp soy sauce, 1 tsp Cajun seasoning (or mix 1 tsp paprika, a bit of cayenne pepper or a pinch of chilli flakes and salt and pepper). Good with pork and beef.

Sticky sweet marinade Mix 1 tbsp sesame seed oil (or vegetable oil), knob of ginger grated, 1 clove garlic minced (or ½ tsp Easy Garlic), 1 tbsp honey, 1 tbsp soy sauce, 1 tsp Chinese five spice (leave out if you don't have it), 2 tbsp marmalade (or apricot/peach/fig jam), some orange or lemon zest (use a vegetable peeler). Good with chicken (including wings), beef and pork.

Beans and pulses

You can be forgiven for thinking of a lot of bean dishes as not being proper food, a bit like eating cardboard with some sort of sauce. Beans are great on board because they are tinned and a number of the other recipes here use beans and pulses in conjunction with fish, chicken, sausages, etc. The recipes here only use beans or pulses to make the dish.

Many dried beans need to be soaked for 6–12 hours, pulses for less time.

Bean burgers with carrot salad and rice

Anyone who has been to Turkey will recognise it as a staple in local restaurants there.

For 2, with some left over for lunch

1 tin (400g) borlotti beans (or try haricot or cannellini beans)

1 tin chopped tomatoes

2 fresh tomatoes diced

2 tbsp olive oil

2 garlic cloves finely sliced or 1 heaped tsp Easy Garlic

2 onions sliced

2 tsp brown sugar (or white)

2 celery sticks finely chopped (or chopped parsley stalks)

1 tsp dill seeds (or fennel seeds)

1 cup chopped parsley or coriander (or add 1 tsp coriander seeds or dried parsley)

1 tbsp lemon juice (half a lemon)

Salt and pepper

- Sweat onions, celery and garlic in a pan with the oil.
- When soft add the dill seeds and coriander seeds (if using), tinned tomatoes and sugar. Cook for a bit.
- Add the drained can of beans and 1½ cups of water and maybe a pinch of stock and fresh ground pepper. Cook for 10 minutes.
- Add chopped fresh tomatoes and lemon juice and cook for another 5 minutes or so.
- Garnish with fresh chopped parsley or coriander if you have them. Serve with rice or couscous or fresh bread.

CHICKPEA CURRY *Up to Force 6*

For 4, good for lunch the next day if just 2
1 tbsp vegetable oil
1 onion sliced
1 carrot sliced
1 clove garlic crushed or level tsp Easy Garlic
Small knob ginger grated
1 tin (400g) chickpeas
1 tin (400g) chopped tomatoes
1 tbsp lemon juice (half a lemon)
2 whole dried cloves (optional)
1 tsp ground cumin
1 tsp ground coriander
Pinch chilli powder, cayenne pepper or hot chilli sauce

- Put oil in a pan and sweat onions, carrot and garlic.
- Add ginger, cloves, cumin, coriander, chilli and lemon juice. Mix into onion and garlic.
- Add chickpeas and tomatoes and a little water and cook gently for 10–15 minutes.
- Serve with rice or couscous.

BEAN BURGERS *Up to Force 4–5*

For 4
1 tbsp vegetable oil
2 tins (800g) kidney, haricot or borlotti beans
1 small onion finely diced
1 carrot grated
½ cup breadcrumbs
1 egg (optional)
1 tbsp tomato paste
Salt and pepper

- Mash up the beans with a fork or potato masher.
- Add onion, carrot, breadcrumbs, egg, tomato paste and salt and pepper to taste. Mix up with a fork until all ingredients are mixed through.
- Form into patties with your hands and stand on a plate. You can dust them with plain flour if you want.
- Heat oil in a pan and over a moderate heat cook patties.

Best served in a bap if you have them, but are fine on their own with a salad and sauce of choice (ketchup is good or sweet chilli sauce).

RECIPES

For 4, good for lunch the next day if just 2

2 tbsp olive oil

1 onion sliced

2 cloves garlic crushed or 1 tsp Easy Garlic

4 rashers bacon cut up or lardons

1 chorizo skinned and cut into slices.
   Alternatively half a salami sausage, skinned and sliced

1 carrot sliced

1 tin (400g) haricot or other white beans or 1 cup of brown lentils

1 bay leaf

1 tbsp paprika

250ml chicken or vegetable stock
   (1 cube dissolved in a big mug of hot water)

- Heat oil in a pan and gently fry bacon or lardons with the bay leaf.
- Add onions and carrots and sweat until onions are soft and clear. Add paprika and stir through for a minute or two.
- Add garlic, chorizo or salami, beans or lentils and stock and cook gently for 20 minutes.
- Serve with bread, rice, couscous or mashed potato.

Spanish bean stew with lentils

Lentil soup is common fare throughout the Middle East and I always ask if mecimek is on the menu in Turkey. The basic broth below can be enlivened with other ingredients.

For 2

1 tbsp olive oil

1 tin (400g) lentils (or 1 cup of yellow or red dried lentils)

1 small onion finely chopped

1 carrot grated (optional but good)

1 clove garlic crushed or ½ tsp Easy Garlic

2 bay leaves

1 level tbsp paprika (black Turkish paprika is good)

1 tbsp lemon juice (½ lemon)

1 litre chicken or vegetable stock
(2 cubes dissolved in a litre of hot water)

- Heat oil in a pan and sweat onion and garlic.
- Add bay leaves, paprika, lemon juice and grated carrot and mix in with onion.
- Add lentils, and stock and put a lid on the pot and cook gently for 30–40 minutes.
- When cooked mash lentils in with a fork or potato masher until minced up. If you have a blender then blend.
- To serve you can add fresh chopped tomatoes, chopped parsley or coriander, a drizzle of olive oil. Traditionally served with a wedge of lemon which you squeeze over it. Fresh bread goes well with it.

RECIPES

Anton often makes this for lunch, but it's a satisfying evening meal as well.

For 4

Large onion sliced quite thickly

4 cloves of garlic chopped coarsely

Dollop olive or vegetable oil

1 tsp cumin

1 tsp garam masala

½ thumb ginger grated or 1 tsp dried ginger

1 tsp coriander

1 tsp turmeric

1 tsp chilli powder, preferably harissa powder

1 cup red lentils

Tin (400g) of chopped tomatoes or fresh equivalent finely chopped

4 medium carrots sliced

1 large potato or 2 medium cubed

2 vegetable stock cubes

About 3½ cups of water (750ml)

2 cups rice (preferably basmati)

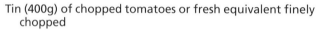

- Sweat onions gently in oil until translucent. Add garlic towards the end. Add spices and sweat a little more mixing spices onto onion.
- Stir in lentils. Add tomatoes, two thirds of water and crumble stock cubes in. Bring to boil and add carrots.
- Simmer for 45 minutes, avoiding burning by adding water as required.
- Add potatoes and continue until cooked.
- Meanwhile, when potatoes go in boil basmati with water (2 cups rice to 4 cups water) until most of the water is absorbed. Turn off heat and leave with cloth under the lid until rice is light and fluffy.
- Serve with minted yoghurt, popadums and chutney of choice.

BEAN DIP

This dip is good with drinks of an evening. It looks a bit gooey brown but is delicious with taco chips, crisps or chunks of bread.

Enough for 6
2 tins (800g) cannellini beans (or haricot or other white beans)
Grated rind and juice of 1 lemon
2 tbsp olive oil
2 cloves garlic, finely chopped or 1 tsp Easy Garlic
2 tbsp parsley, chopped
Squirt of Tabasco or chilli sauce
Salt and pepper

- Drain and rinse the beans. Mash or blend them to a coarse paste.
- Add lemon juice and rind, garlic, parsley and a splash of olive oil and mix well.
- Season with Tabasco, salt and pepper, transfer to a serving bowl and garnish with a splash of olive oil and a sprig of parsley.

HUMMUS

Enough for 4–6 as a dip
2 tins (800g) chickpeas
Juice of 2 lemons
2 cloves of garlic, finely chopped or 1 tsp Easy Garlic
150ml tahini paste
Pinch of cayenne pepper
Salt and pepper
Olive oil
Parsley garnish

- Drain and rinse the chickpeas. Mash or blend them to a coarse paste.
- Add lemon juice, garlic, tahini, cayenne pepper and a splash of olive oil and mix well.
- Season with salt and pepper, transfer to a serving bowl and garnish with a splash of olive oil, a pinch of cayenne and a sprig of parsley.

RECIPES

There are lots of vegetarian dishes scattered through the recipes for pasta, risotto, beans and pulses, eggs, salads and snacks. All of these recipes are marked with the symbol. Consequently I've just included a few additional vegetarian recipes here.

VEGETABLE CURRY *Up to Force 7–8*

Good re-heated for lunch the next day

For 4

2 tsp vegetable oil

2 potatoes peeled and cut into bite-sized chunks

1 tin (400g) chopped tomatoes

1 courgette sliced (you can leave the skin on)

1 onion sliced

2 cloves garlic minced or 1 tsp Easy Garlic

1 pepper diced

3 tbsp medium curry paste or 2 tbsp medium curry powder

1 mug vegetable or chicken stock (dissolve 1 cube in a mug of hot water)

2 bay leaves

2 cinnamon sticks or 1 level tsp ground cinnamon

1 tsp coriander

1 tsp tamarind paste (optional)

Plain yoghurt and chopped parsley or coriander to garnish

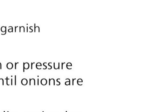

- Put a good glug of oil into a high-sided pan or pressure cooker and sweat onions with bay leaves until onions are translucent.

- On low heat add curry paste or powder, garlic, coriander, cinnamon, and tamarind and stir into a paste.

- Add stock, tomatoes, potatoes, courgette and pepper to the pan and cook over low heat for 40–45 minutes or 30 minutes in a pressure cooker, until potatoes are cooked through. Add a bit of water if it starts to dry out.

- Lots of other vegetables work well: cauliflower florets, mushrooms, sweet potato, diced squash, spring onions, whatever seems to go together.

- Serve with plain yoghurt and chopped parsley or coriander on rice. Naan bread goes well with it if you can get them.

CABBAGE WITH POTATOES AND COCONUT
Up to Force 4–5

This is an adapted Gujarati dish as they don't normally eat onions or garlic. It might sound a bit weird but tastes great as a main or a side dish.

For 4
500g potatoes chopped into bite-sized bits
New potatoes are good just chopped in half
1 onion finely chopped
2 cloves garlic crushed or 1 level tsp Easy Garlic
2 tbsp vegetable oil
1 tsp mustard seeds
1 tsp cumin seeds
1 chilli, deseeded and finely chopped
½ green cabbage, finely shredded
Juice of ½ a lemon
2 tbsp desiccated coconut or small tin of coconut milk (200ml)
Small bunch of coriander (or parsley) chopped

- Cook potatoes for 10 minutes until tender. They don't want to be squishy. Drain and return to pan and crush with the back of a spoon or fork until scrunched up but are not mashed.
- Heat the oil in a high-sided frying pan and sweat the onions for 5 minutes or so. Add the garlic, mustard seeds, cumin seeds and chilli. Cook over a low heat stirring into a paste.
- Add the scrunched potatoes and cook for a few minutes so they are coated with the spices.
- Turn up the heat and add the cabbage and cook for 5 minutes stirring all the time.
- Stir in the lemon juice and coconut and serve with freshly chopped coriander scattered over.

SPICY POTATO CAKES *Up to Force 4–5* Ⓥ

For 2

3 large potatoes peeled and cut into chunks
1 egg
Handful of coriander, chopped
6 spring onions chopped or small onion finely chopped
Zest of 1 lemon
Big handful of grated cheese (any hard, yellow cheese like Cheddar, Edam, Gouda)
1 red chilli, seeded and finely chopped
Small cup breadcrumbs
Vegetable oil

- Cook the potatoes until tender and drain.
- Mash the potatoes and add the egg, coriander, spring onions, some salt and pepper, the lemon zest, cheddar and chilli. Mix well and shape into 6 medium cakes.
- Cover the potato cakes in breadcrumbs.
- Heat 1 tbsp vegetable oil in a non-stick frying pan and brown the cakes on both sides.
- Serve with a green salad and mango chutney, sweet chilli sauce or ketchup.

Can be a main with rice or couscous, or a vegetable accompaniment to other dishes. This is a good pressure cooker dish. A lot of recipes call for salting the aubergine to take the bitterness out, but the sugar or peanut butter variation means you don't have to.

For 4
Several big glugs of olive oil (around 4 tbsp)
2 large onions sliced
4 cloves garlic crushed or 2 tsp Easy Garlic (less if you are not a garlic fan)
2 aubergines cut into bite-sized bits
3 tomatoes chopped or 1 tin (400g) of chopped tomatoes
3 courgettes sliced
2 peppers (red, green or yellow) cut into bite-sized bits
Handful of fresh basil chopped (optional)
1 tbsp brown sugar (or white)
Juice of 1 lemon or good glug of balsamic vinegar
Salt and pepper to taste

- Put a high-sided pan or the pressure cooker on low heat with several big glugs of olive oil and sweat the onions until translucent.
- Add the garlic, aubergines, courgettes and peppers and sweat over low heat for 5–10 minutes until soft. Add tomatoes, sugar, lemon juice or balsamic and salt and pepper and put the lid on and cook over low heat for 30–40 minutes. Top up with water if needed.
- 5 minutes before the end add chopped fresh basil.

Variations
- Leave sugar out and add two heaped tbsp of peanut butter. Sounds weird but it's excellent (thanks Pru).
- Add a small chopped chilli with the onion if you like it hot.
- Add a tin of chickpeas or a tin of baked beans for a sort of vegetable bean ratatouille. Baked beans sound naff but work incredibly well.
- If a main serve with rice or couscous.

Eggs

We tend to eat more eggs on board than we do on land and we always carry lots of eggs for fry-ups, scrambled and the recipes below. Scrambled eggs are one of our stand-bys for really rough weather. When it's rough don't bother mixing the eggs up in anything, just put some oil in the bottom of a pan and break the eggs in with a bit of salt and pepper, a dribble of milk or water, a bit of chopped fresh parsley is good as well, and mix up with a wooden spatula while it cooks. See the recipe for Menemen, a sort of Turkish variation on scrambled eggs as well.

OMELETTES *Up to Force 4–5*

Ⓥ

For 2

Olive oil

½ onion finely chopped

4 eggs

Salt and pepper

Additional ingredients: chopped fresh tomato, chopped pepper, grated cheese, bacon bits, chopped salami or chorizo, chopped fresh parsley.

- Break eggs into a bowl, add a glug of olive oil, a bit of water and salt and pepper to taste.
- Whisk mixture with a fork (or a proper whisk). The idea is to get some air into the mixture.
- Put a little oil in a frying pan and sweat onion (and bacon if using it) for 4–5 minutes.
- Pour mixture in. Other ingredients like tomatoes, pepper, cheese, salami or chorizo can be sprinkled on top. Cook slowly on a low heat then cut in half and fold over for serving.
- Just before it is cooked add chopped parsley (recommended).

Simple omelette but tastes so good when it's a bit bumpy on board

A tasty Italian omelette (similar to the Spanish tortilla de patatas) ideal for using leftover cooked potatoes.

For 2

2 tbsp olive oil

1 small onion, finely chopped

250g boiled potatoes, cut into bite-sized pieces

3 medium tomatoes, chopped

4 large eggs, beaten

Salt and pepper

Optional extras

150g leftover broccoli cut into small pieces

150g leftover peas or small 150g tin of peas, drained

100g cooked salmon

4 rashers bacon chopped or lardons

100g chorizo sausage

75g feta cheese or other cheese grated

1 tsp dried oregano or thyme

- Add the olive oil to a large frying pan and gently sweat the onion until soft.
- If using bacon or lardons remove the onions and cook these separately.
- Add in the potatoes and cook until they are slightly coloured.
- Add in the tomatoes, and any other ingredients you fancy, and cook gently for a few minutes. Season with salt and pepper.
- Pour the beaten eggs into the pan, covering all the other ingredients. If using cheese sprinkle it over the top just after you pour in the eggs.
- Continue to cook slowly until the sides are firm.
- Put the pan under the hot grill and cook until the top is firm.
- Serve cut into wedges with a green salad.

Leftover frittata will keep in the fridge and can be served cold the next day.

RECIPES

A Turkish take on eggs

For 2
Olive oil
4 eggs
1 onion finely chopped
½ green pepper, diced
1 chilli, de-seeded and finely chopped
2 medium tomatoes, chopped
1 tsp sugar
Small bunch of parsley chopped if you can get it
Plain yoghurt (optional)
Salt and pepper

- Glug a bit of oil into a frying pan and sweat onions, peppers, chilli until soft.
- Add tomatoes and sugar and let it simmer for 10 minutes or more until reduced.
- Make 4 hollows in the mixture and break the eggs into each. Season to taste. Let it all cook gently until the eggs are cooked.
- Serve with eggs intact. Put a dollop of yoghurt on it and scatter some parsley over if you have it.

ERIC'S HUEVOS RANCHEROS *Up to Force 4* Ⓥ

This Mexican dish is good for brunch, lunch or dinner. Eric lives on his boat in Los Angeles (though we met in Cochin) and this is his recipe.

For 2

Olive oil

1 red pepper (or green if you don't have red), finely diced (If you like, stick the pepper over a burner until the skin burns and then remove skin and dice)

1 onion finely chopped

2 tomatoes finely chopped

1 chilli de-seeded and finally chopped

1 clove of garlic minced or ½ tsp Easy Garlic

4 eggs

- Put a glug of olive oil in a frying pan and sweat onions, chilli, pepper and garlic, about 5 minutes.
- Add tomatoes and cook for another 5 minutes until mixture is mushy. Add a little water if it gets too dry.
- Make 4 hollows in the mixture and break eggs into hollows. Cook gently until eggs are cooked.
- Serve with mixture underneath and eggs on top. Good with crusty bread.

EGGS BENEDICT *Up to Force 2–3*

For 2

2 English muffins or bagels, even hamburger buns at a pinch

2 eggs

Vinegar

Hollandaise sauce (I buy it in a jar, in extremis add a tsp of whole grain mustard to some mayonnaise)

4 slices of ham or 200g chopped cooked spinach (tinned is OK here just)

Salt and pepper

- Put a pan of water with a splash of vinegar on to boil.
- When it is boiling lower eggs into the water to poach.
- While this is going on slice muffins, bagels or other buns in half and toast.
- Put ham or spinach on the muffins/bagels/buns and when the eggs are cooked gently remove and put on top.
- Spoon some Hollandaise sauce onto the top and put the top muffin, bagel or bun on.

I used to get a sort of egg curry as a kid. It was awful, but this one tastes better and it's quick and easy to make.

For 2
Vegetable oil
4 eggs hard-boiled
1 onion finely chopped
1 tin (400g) chopped tomatoes or two large tomatoes finely chopped
Small tin (about 250g) peas or same of frozen if you have them
1½ tbsp mild curry paste or 1 level tbsp curry powder
Cup of plain yoghurt
Handful of chopped fresh coriander or parsley

- Put a glug of oil into a frying pan and gently sweat the onions.
- Add the curry paste or powder and mix until onions are coated with curry mixture.
- Add the tomatoes, a cup of water and cook over a moderate heat for 10 minutes or so until you have a thickish mixture.
- Add the peas and yoghurt and over low heat simmer gently, stirring, for 3–4 minutes.
- Halve boiled eggs and put into the mixture on low heat for another 3–4 minutes.
- Serve with rice and chopped coriander or parsley over the top and chutney of choice.

Salads

We eat a lot of salad on board. We even have a mini salad whizzer that we found in New Zealand. You can make salad dressings or buy ready-made ones. You can always make up a larger amount of dressing than you need and keep it in a container in the fridge. Below are a few basic dressings, but there are a lot more you can experiment with.

Drizzle Cabernet or other drizzles are well worth using with some of these dressings.

Simple balsamic Salt and pepper the salad then drizzle olive oil over and then drizzle a lesser amount of balsamic vinegar. Toss.

Basic vinaigrette Put 1 tbsp Dijon (or other) mustard, ½ tsp Easy Garlic or 1 crushed clove garlic, pinch salt and pepper, 1 tbsp balsamic and 2 tbsp white wine vinegar, 6 tbsp olive or vegetable oil in a cup and mix. You can make bigger amounts and keep.

Honey and mustard As above but add 1 tbsp honey.

Yoghurt and sweet chilli Put a dollop or two of yoghurt on top and drizzle some sweet chilli sauce over. Good with things like avocado salads and green salads with things like apple.

Mayonnaise Buy it ready made.

Salads can make up a main meal that is not as stodgy as heavier meals in hot climes

BASIC GREEN SALAD ⓥ

If you don't have a whizzer wash the salad leaves and dry on a tea towel. To the basic salad you can add all sorts of other ingredients you might have: tomatoes cut in segments, sun dried tomatoes cut up, grated parmesan cheese on top, apple cut up, orange or pamplemousse cut up, sesame seeds, chopped walnuts or almonds, grated carrot, really anything that seems sympathetic with what is in there.

RECIPES

For 2, as a main course

Salad greens

2 tomatoes chopped

1 carrot grated

3 small potatoes boiled and cut into slices

Handful of green beans chopped and blanched
    for 5 minutes in a cup of boiling water (optional)

Small (200g) tin of tuna

Small (100g) tin of anchovies (optional)

Heaped tbsp capers

Half handful chopped olives (optional)

2 hard-boiled eggs sliced

Wash greens and add tomatoes, grated carrot, sliced potatoes,
green blanched beans, tuna bits, chopped anchovies, capers
and olives and mix with simple balsamic or vinaigrette dressing.
Arrange egg slices on top. Eat with crusty bread.

RECIPES

This is a good accompaniment to other dishes.
I only call it Moroccan because it sounds as if it should be.

For 4
Big mug (around 250g) couscous
½ onion finely diced
Handful of chopped dried apricots, dates or dried peaches
Small handful of currants or raisins
Handful of slivered almonds, chopped walnuts, pine nuts or pepitos
3 tbsp olive oil
1 lemon
½ small cucumber, finely diced (optional)
Small handful of chopped parsley or coriander (if you have it)

Make couscous by adding equal amount of boiling water to it.
When the couscous has absorbed all the water (about 10
minutes) put in a bowl and mix in the diced onion, apricots or
other dried fruit, currants or raisins, cucumber if you have it.
Put juice of lemon and oil in and mix up. Put slivered almonds,
walnuts, pine nuts or pepitos on the top and sprinkle chopped
parsley or coriander over.

Variations Sometimes
it's good to add a bit of
vinaigrette, Cabernet
or other drizzle or a bit
of sweet chilli sauce
when you add the oil
and lemon juice. Taste
it and see if it needs a
bit more dressing. You
can also grate a bit of
the lemon zest into the
salad. Other
ingredients that go
well in this salad are
chopped sun-dried
tomatoes, chopped
spring onions, chopped
celery, sesame seeds,
whatever you think is
going to mix and
match.

RECIPES

For 2

½ mug basmati rice
1 small onion finely diced or
    6 spring onions chopped
1 large carrot grated
Small handful of raisins or currants
Zest and juice of 1 lemon
1 tbsp honey

- Cook rice with two parts water to one of rice.
- Let it cool and combine onions, carrot, lemon zest and raisins or currants and mix through.
- Mix honey and lemon juice together and pour over rice mixture.

POTATO SALAD *Up to Force 6–7* ⓥ

For 4

6 medium potatoes peeled and boiled
½ onion finely diced or
    4 spring onions chopped
½ lemon squeezed
2 tbsp paprika
Mayonnaise
2 tbsp sour cream or cottage cheese
    (optional)
Salt and pepper to taste
Handful of chopped parsley (if you
    have it)

Slice cooked potatoes into bite-sized pieces. Put in a bowl with onions or spring onions, and sprinkle paprika over. Add a few tbsp mayonnaise, lemon juice and sour cream or cottage cheese if you have it. Mix around and add more mayonnaise if necessary. Add salt and pepper to taste and throw chopped parsley over the top.

Variations Add 1 apple peeled and chopped, 1 chopped tomato, a small handful chopped walnuts, chopped chives.

For 2

1 tin (400g) cannellini beans, or tin of three-bean mix, or other white beans

2 sticks celery chopped

Handful of chopped green beans and blanched for 5 minutes in a mug of boiling water. Otherwise small tin (150–200g) of green beans drained

½ onion finely chopped

1 small carrot grated

2 tbsp olive oil

Splash of balsamic vinegar

Juice of 1 lemon

1 tbsp sugar, preferably brown but white is fine

Small handful of chopped parsley if available

Combine salad ingredients then mix olive oil, balsamic, lemon juice and sugar and mix into salad. Throw chopped parsley over the top.

Variations Chopped chives, ½ pepper finely chopped, 2 slices of roasted pepper chopped, ½ small chilli seeded and finely chopped if you like a bit of heat, small apple peeled and chopped, orange chopped.

RECIPES

COLESLAW   *Up to Force 6–7*   ⓥ

Cabbage keeps well on board so you can produce this after a week or two at sea. See Introduction for how to look after your cabbage on passage.

For 4
½ cabbage finely sliced
½ onion finely chopped
2 carrots grated
1 apple peeled and diced
Mayonnaise
1 tbsp Dijon mustard
Juice 1 lemon
2 tbsp plain yoghurt (if you don't have yoghurt use more mayonnaise)
Salt and pepper to taste

Mix sliced cabbage, chopped onion, grated carrot, and diced apple. Mix mustard into 2 tbsp mayonnaise and add to salad with lemon juice and yoghurt. Mix through and add more mayonnaise if necessary. Season with salt and pepper.

Variations Finely chopped pepper, currants or raisins, chopped walnuts, slivered almonds, chopped cashews. You can make a variation on a Waldorf salad by just adding chopped apple, 2 sticks chopped celery and a handful of walnuts to the cabbage. Proper Waldorf doesn't use cabbage or carrot, but I think it tastes the better for adding them.

CARROT SALAD   *Up to Force 4–5*   ⓥ

For 2
2 carrots grated
1 apple, peeled and chopped
Juice of ½ a lemon
1 tsp honey
Small handful slivered almonds

Combine carrots and apple in a bowl. Mix honey into the lemon and mix through salad. Sprinkle slivered almonds on top.

Variations Chopped spring onions, chopped walnuts, even ½ a chilli de-seeded and finely chopped can work in this salad.

Ⓥ

This is basically Alex's recipe from the Ev Zin restaurant in Greece.

For 2

Lettuce or other greens

Avocado peeled, pitted and cut into bite-sized bits

Yoghurt

Sweet chilli sauce

Juice 1 lime or ½ lemon

Handful of toasted pine nuts, pepitas or crushed walnuts

Salt and pepper

- Wash lettuce and chop or tear up and combine with avocado in a bowl. Scatter nuts on the top.
- Pour lemon juice over and then put a good dollop of yoghurt on the top and make a hollow in which you can pour a good glug of sweet chilli sauce.

Variations   Sprinkle sesame seeds over, peeled and chopped apple, orange bits, chopped celery.

RECIPES

For 2
Olive oil
2 medium potatoes, peeled and sliced
Several handfuls of lettuce leaves
Sweet chilli sauce
1 tbsp lemon juice
Small pack (200–250g) halloumi
Small bunch chives
Dressing like a simple vinaigrette

Cook potatoes until just done. Wash salad leaves and chop chives into a bowl. Put potato slices into bowl and add a good splosh of vinaigrette and mix through. Put a frying pan on moderate heat with a glug of olive oil in it. Slice halloumi and fry either side until golden, usually a few minutes each side. When the second side is cooked add a glug of sweet chilli sauce and the lemon juice to the pan and heat gently for a minute or two until the halloumi is coated with mixture. Arrange halloumi on top of the salad.

RECIPES

For 2

Lettuce and salad greens – whatever you have

2 tomatoes chopped into thumb size pieces or handful of cherry tomatoes halved

Handful of chopped sun dried tomatoes

Handful of green beans cut into three or cup sliced beetroot (bottled or canned)

200g chicken, breast, thighs, etc. cut into bite-size chunks.
Can be leftover roast chicken

Marinade for chicken: make it up yourself from oil, lemon juice, soy sauce, sweet chilli sauce, honey, whatever takes your fancy

Glug of olive oil

Vinaigrette for dressing or olive oil/balsamic vinegar/salt and pepper to dress salad

Hot chicken salad and sautéd potatoes

- Marinate chicken for at least an hour in the fridge then heat oil in a pan and cook chicken over medium heat until browned both sides and cooked through. Or tear up roast chicken.

- Chop lettuce and salad greens roughly and put into a salad bowl with tomatoes and sun dried tomatoes, beans and/or beetroot.

- Mix through with vinaigrette or olive oil/balsamic and put hot chicken bits on top. Good with a baguette if you can get it.

Variations Use strips of beef marinated in soy sauce, sweet chilli sauce and a bit of hot chilli sauce and cook in a hot pan instead of chicken.

RECIPES

This is a rag-bag of entries with suggestions and demi-recipes. It includes suggestions for lunches and snacks, even for a light dinner.

Lunches can be an easy mix of cold cuts and salad

CROSTINI (OR BRUSCHETTA)

Baguette or bread slices. Even slightly stale bread can be used. Ciabatta is best if you can get it or make it.

Olive oil

Tomato paste or sun dried tomato paste

Spread olive oil on the sliced baguette or sliced bread, wipe over a good smear of tomato paste and sun dried tomato paste if you have it and arrange any of the following on top.

Tinned sardines with sliced tomato on top

Mozzarella with sliced tomato on top

Ham with grated parmesan

Sliced tomato and olives or capers

Stick the finished article under the grill until lightly toasted on the top. If you want to you can toast one side before starting, but thin slices of bread will be a bit hard if you do.

Everyone guffaws when I mention this, but when it's really bumpy at sea crew are more than grateful that you venture down to make it. It's best served in big mugs. We have big insulated mugs with plastic tops.

For 2

1 packet instant noodles, any flavour

Sweet chilli sauce

Hot chilli sauce

Soy sauce

Any old greens you have like celery, bok choi, even lettuce, chopped up

- Put pan on to boil two mugs of water – measure it out in the mugs. Before opening noodles crunch up the packet a bit to break them up. Take out flavour sachet(s) and empty into water. Add a good dollop of sweet chilli, a little hot chilli, a glug of soy sauce and the chopped greens into boiling water and cook for 3–4 minutes or until noodles are cooked.

- Cut up any bread or get Ryvita type crackers to eat with it. In bad weather it's a life saver.

BLTs

Lu has a really neat way of making BLTs on passage (and on terra firma as well) that she learnt from the chef of a restaurant she used to manage.

Fry or grill the bacon as per normal and while it is cooking finely chop the tomatoes and lettuce (and anything else you want to put in it). When the bacon is cooked chop it up as well. Put it all in a bowl and mix the mayonnaise into it. Then just spoon it onto the bread or into a warmed pitta.

RECIPES

Bread

Whatever ingredients you like: cheese, chopped tomato, egg (beat it up in a cup as the little manual advises you to use cooked egg, but beaten up and poured in it worked fine), ham, salami, whatever you have lying around.

- When I was a kid we used to make toasted sandwiches with a cast iron sandwich maker over the fire. So when I saw one in a hardware shop I bought it straight away. Search for the Diablo on the internet (it even prints Diablo on top of the sandwich). It's ideal for no mess (or not much) lunches and can still be used when it gets a bit bumpy on passage. Of course the new one is coated in Teflon, but it still works the same way as of old. A slice of bread on either side, one side butter-side inside and the other outside. Then whatever ingredients you like: cheese, chopped tomato, egg, ham, salami, whatever you have lying around. Favourite so far is a simple cheese, tomato and ham.

- A few minutes either side on the burner and a wonderful toasted sandwich.

RECIPES

FRANK'S PIKELETS

Ⓥ

In New Zealand pikelets were common fare when I grew up and they are a good treat to make on passage. They are sometimes known as Scottish Pancakes, I guess they are effectively mini-pancakes. Frank made them for me on passage in the Indian Ocean on a slow day and eating hot pikelets with butter and jam in the middle of the ocean is just a great treat. They are also great for breakfast with maple syrup. This is Frank's recipe.

For 4 (or a very hungry 2)
2 cups flour
1½ cups milk (powdered made up is fine)
2 eggs
1 tsp baking powder
Dessert spoon of sugar

Mix all the ingredients thoroughly to a thick pouring consistency and leave to stand for 30 minutes. Heat a pan with a drizzle of oil in it and when hot use a big spoon to put a dollop of mixture in and cook 3 or 4 at a time depending on the size of the pan. Turn and cook on the other side when browned and bubbles pop.

This idea comes from Michael on *B'Sherrit* and I'm amazed – and happy (I love pizza) – that it's so easy and the pizzas taste just great. It uses tortilla bases that you can buy with long use-by dates so it's easy to keep a good supply of them on board. Try to get the thickest tortilla bases you can find.

Tortillas (two per person is about right for hungry people)

Olive oil

Pizza sauce or tomato paste

Grated cheese (Cheddar types, Edam, Gouda and the like or whatever you have are fine)

Toppings: salami, bacon, sliced tomatoes, olives, anchovies, capers – choose your favourites or use whatever is on board

- Lay out the bases and dribble some olive oil over them. We use a little brush to cover the top of the base.
- On the same side as the olive oil spread on some pizza sauce or tomato paste, add toppings of choice, and then grated cheese.
- Put the first one in a heated pan with a thick base and put the lid on. It should be cooked in 4–5 minutes, but take a peek every now and again.

Eat pizza while the next one cooks.

Buying ready-made muesli is not possible everywhere in the world and often it can be expensive to buy the ready-made boxes of the stuff. I always tend to make my own.

Rolled oats
Cornflakes (large)
Ready-made crunchy cereal
Nuts
Raisins, sultanas, dried apricots, dried figs

- Rolled oats. The vacuum packed cans of Quaker oats can be found almost anywhere in the world. I've found them in Yemen, India, Sri Lanka, all through Southeast Asia, all through the Mediterranean, Australia and New Zealand, many Caribbean islands and in the western south Pacific Islands (Tonga, Fiji, etc.) Being vacuum packed they occupy something like 2½ times the volume after they are opened (or so it seems). Take one can of Quaker dried oats.
- Cornflakes (large). Whatever the cheapest brand is – often not Kellogg's.
- A box of ready-made crunchy muesli (if you can find it) or some other munchy cereal like Weetabix (crunch them up), Rice Crispies, whatever you can get.
- Nuts. Whatever is available. Chop up into bits. You can be really flashy if you want and grill or roast them with a bit of oil and honey – shuffle them about lots so they don't burn.
- Raisins, sultanas, dried apricots, dried figs, dried any fruit just about chopped up (though I'm not a fan of dried bananas).

Put in a large container and shake it up so it all mixes together. Good with chopped fresh fruit and yoghurt.

Night watch goody bag

On watch at night you need goodies to munch on to get you through the watch. In lots of places you can buy mini chocolate and other bars like Mars bars, Yorkies, Twix, Bounty and sesame seed and honey bars. Apart from the chocolate/sugar rush our favourite is a nut and raisin/currant and dried fruit mix usually referred to as 'Trail Mix' or something similar. You can also put in some Ritz or similar little cheese biscuits and other biscuits like cookies, digestives and the like.

And if you are a crisps fan you will probably need a small packet of those in there.

Ⓥ

Gill: This recipe can be sweet or savoury. My mother used to serve the savoury version with bacon and eggs instead of fried bread. My daughter serves the sweet version with fruit and yoghurt. I like the sweet version with maple syrup and a squeeze of lemon.

Makes around 10
150ml milk
2 eggs
175g plain flour
½ tsp bicarbonate of soda
½ tsp of cream of tartar
2 or 3 tablespoons of sugar (optional)
1 tsp vanilla essence (optional)
Knob of butter or spoon of cooking oil
     (vegetable or olive)
Pinch of salt

- Mix the dry ingredients together.
- Beat the eggs with the milk. Combine all ingredients and whisk to get a smooth thick batter.
- Add knob of butter to a frying pan and heat until the butter is just bubbling. Lower the heat.
- Pour in a large spoonful of the batter to form two 10cm circles. Normally you can get three to a frying pan, but positioning can be tricky. Leave until bubbles form on the top of the batter and then flip. Cook until golden brown on both sides.

RECIPES

Provisioning for bread

In lots of places you can buy vacuum packed pittas (usually six in a pack) that have use-by dates of several months. They don't have to be stored in the fridge and to heat them up either put them under the grill for a while or put them on a stove-top toaster.

I don't know what they do to long life bread in the sealed packs that last for months. The bread tastes like soft polystyrene, but it's useful to have a few packs of it on board.

Tortillas also have long use-by dates and half a dozen packets for tortilla wraps or stove top pizzas are worth having.

Flour for bread making, and what is often called hard (or strong) flour, can be difficult to find. We usually carry a good supply of the stuff. Put the packets of flour in zipped plastic bags and then in Tupperware plastic boxes. If you put a couple of bay leaves in with the flour this is supposed to deter weevils but it seems to be as much a matter of luck as of good storage.

Where there is hard flour you will usually find packets of dried yeast. These usually have a use-by date, though sometimes you can use them after that date with success. Whether or not it's worth it after a lot of kneading and no success getting the bread to rise is another matter.

Bread making at sea

There's nothing quite like the smell of freshly baked bread – all the more so when you are several hundred miles offshore and not a bakery in sight.

Making bread is often perceived as being difficult or fiddly, with yeast to activate and lengthy kneading. With modern dried yeast things are much simpler and quicker.

the final wonderful loaf at sea ...

... or buns

RECIPES

500g strong flour

1 tsp salt

½ tsp sugar (optional for a crusty top)

1 packet dried yeast

300ml warm water

1 tsp olive oil

Flour for kneading (any type)

Oil for greasing

Flour and water and a bit of yeast

- Put the flour, salt, sugar and yeast into a large mixing bowl and stir to mix the dry ingredients. Make a pool in the centre of the flour and add most of the water and the oil.
- Mix to a dough using a metal spoon – if too wet add more flour, if too dry and flaky add a dribble more water.
- Form the dough into a single piece using one hand, and turn out onto a floured surface. The bowl should be almost clean.
- Knead the dough for 10–15 minutes until the dough becomes nicely elastic.

Now leave it to rise

- Brush the bowl with olive oil, put the dough back into the bowl, cover with oiled cling film and put in a warm place away from drafts.
- After 40 minutes, or when the dough has doubled in size (in cooler temperatures it takes longer), turn the dough back out onto a floured surface.
- 'Knock back' the dough (it will lose half its volume) and form into the shape you need – for a loaf make sure the 'join' is on the bottom.
- Put into a greased loaf tin or shape and put on a baking tray, cover again with greased cling film and return to the warm place to rise again for 30 minutes or so.

Then the kneading bit

- Turn on the oven to preheat to 200°C.
- When bread has doubled in size remove the cling film and put in the oven.
- Bake for 20 minutes, then turn the loaf front to back so it cooks evenly, and cook for a further 20 minutes.
- When the bread is cooked it should be browned on top, and when tapped on the underside it should sound hollow.
- Put on a wire rack to cool slightly – for as long as you can resist.

Flour

Strong flour has a higher gluten content than normal plain flour. It is not always easy to find, but it will keep for ages so when you find a supply you can stock up.

It is common now to find wholemeal, rye and granary bread-making flour as well as the white stuff.

Measure out your flour into 500g lots and put into individual zipped plastic bags to save having to measure out flour when underway. I make a 500g blend of white and granary flour and put it into a zipped plastic bag along with a teaspoon of salt so it is ready to use. I also add a bay leaf to the bag – an old wives' tale suggests it helps prevent weevils. Store the bags in a stronger bag or plastic container to protect from damage. When you want to make bread pick out the bay leaf and just add yeast and water.

In some places you can find commercial ready-mix bread packets which even include the yeast. Many of these work fine, but work out more expensive than DIY ready-mix bags.

Yeast

In places where you find bread-making flour you will usually find yeast. It normally comes in foil sachets which are suitable for a medium loaf or equivalent. Unlike fresh yeast, there is no need to 'activate' the yeast with water and sugar in a warm place for a while before using it – the warmth of the water in the dough mix will do the job. If the water is too hot, it may kill the yeast; if too cold it won't activate it. It should be just warm to the touch. Yeast should be stored in a cool dry place, and will have a use by date. Yeast which has been kept too warm or frozen, or way beyond the use by date will not be as effective. In this case the bread will not rise much, and will be heavy and dense.

Kneading

This is how the gluten in the flour is released, the yeast is activated and the dough becomes stretchy and elastic. Technique is not really important, but the aim is to push and stretch the dough, to work it gently but firmly in all directions. Use the balls of the hands to push part of the dough away from the body, then pull this flap back over on top of the rest of the dough, rotate through 90° and repeat. Bread which has not been kneaded enough may rise OK, but may shrink back during cooking to give a heavy and uneven loaf.

Proving

It can be difficult to find a safe warm place to put the dough to prove, or rise. If the engine is warm we have a cupboard next to it which is perfect. Some boats have a safe sheltered spot in a sunny cockpit. For the final proving I will usually have lit the oven and so I put the dough on the stove top while it is warming up. The size of the dough when it goes into the oven is about the size it will come out. You can prove the dough overnight in the fridge. Take the dough out at least one hour before baking it.

Variations

- Loaves and buns using a variety of wholemeal, granary and white flours give a bit of variation. I tend to use a blend of 40% white to 60% granary flour for my usual dough.
- Adding a ½ teaspoon of sugar will give a crusty top to the bread. Brushing the top with milk gives a glaze to buns. The oil in the mix helps the bread to keep a little longer without drying out.
- Use a basic white flour dough to make pizza bases. Just roll and press the dough out and place on a greased baking tray. For pizza toppings see recipe for stove-top pizzas.
- For foccacia press the dough flat, about 1–2cm thick onto a greased baking tray. Dimple with your fingertips and add rosemary or thyme, chopped olives, sliced onion, salt crystals and olive oil. Whatever combination you fancy.
- For ciabatta-style bread use 450ml of water. The dough should be wetter than for conventional bread. Fold it like an envelope rather than knead it.

- For French style bread try using 20% rice flour.

Desserts

We don't make a lot of desserts though I do like them when we have them. Here are just a couple of suggestions.

READY-MIX COOKIES AND MUFFINS

You can buy packets of ready-mix cakes, cookies and muffins in lots of places around the world. We always carry a few packs to cook at sea where chocolate slabs or muffins are a special treat and need to be rationed so they don't disappear in a day. You can add extra ingredients to the mixes. Chopped walnuts or peanuts to chocolate cookies. Currants and sultanas to muffins. Chopped dried apricots to cakes. Whatever seems to work.

BAKED FRUIT

Most of us have had apples baked in the oven with a bit of honey drizzled on top and a sprinkle of cinnamon, but there are all sorts of other fruit you can pop in the oven and adulterate with honey and spices. One of my favourites is figs which you cut a cross on the top and squeeze open, drizzle a bit of honey over, and then add a dollop of cream or yoghurt after it's cooked.

LU'S FRUIT CLAFOUTI

For 4–6

This simple pud can be made with most fruit, including tinned peaches which go well with limoncello. Adjust the sugar quantity depending on the sweetness of the fruit.

Fresh cherries or other fruit (400–500g)

4 tbsp castor sugar

4 tbsp kirsch (or liqueur of choice)

3 eggs

50g plain flour

150ml milk

200ml crème fraiche or yoghurt

1 tsp vanilla extract

Icing sugar for dusting

- Wipe a film of butter inside a shallow baking dish and preheat oven to 190°C.
- Pit the cherries and spread over the bottom of the dish. Sprinkle with 1 tbsp sugar and the kirsch. If possible leave for 1 hour to infuse the cherries.
- Whisk eggs until they are soft and foamy. Stir in the flour, sugar, milk, crème fraiche and vanilla.
- Pour the mix over the cherries and bake for 30–40 minutes until golden on the top.
- Sprinkle with icing sugar and serve just warm.

Tip: Use a paperclip to prise out the stone.

Putting a stores list together is much dependent on individual tastes. We have a freezer but do not run it as such. It is used more as a very cold drinks fridge than a store for frozen stuff, which on yachts usually means frozen meat. To keep meat frozen down in a Mediterranean summer or in the Tropics would entail running the engine (the fridge compressor runs off the engine to two big holding plates in the 'freezer') twice a day for around 45 minutes to an hour each time, which takes lots of time and fuel, and the noise will annoy others in an otherwise quiet anchorage. There is more than enough good food you can magic up from the galley without resorting to the 'meat and two veg formula'. Consequently *Skylax* carries little in the way of fresh meat on passages. We usually reckon on a frozen chicken or maybe two. We do carry vacuum packed bacon, sausages, salamis and chorizo.

We also carry a lot more food than we need just for the passage. This is partly because its good to stock up in places that have certain items that may be difficult to get elsewhere and also if, gods forbid, the rudder falls off or the mast falls down, then we will not starve on board. You may also have a wife, husband, lover or friend who can't stand certain things and so the stores list needs to be amended to take these tastes into account.

The list below is for two people and as I've mentioned, goes way beyond what you will likely use on passage. A lot of the items such as some sauces or herbs and spices you may already have on board and we really use the list as a checklist for a total provisions list.

Tinned stores

16 tins chopped tomatoes
12 tins tuna
6 tins sardines
6 small tins peas
6 small tins mushrooms
6 tins mussels in brine
6 large tins fruit (fruit cocktail, peaches, apricots)
6 tins dolmades (stuffed vine leaves)
6 tins Gigantes (large haricot beans in tomato sauce)
6 tins baked beans
3 tins kidney beans
4 tins lentils
6 tins other beans (cannellini, haricot, etc.)
2 small tins sweetcorn
4 tins chicken soup
4 tins tomato soup
6 tins coconut milk
3 tins meatballs

Bottles/tins/packs

4 ready made pasta sauces
6 jars pesto
3 jars stuffed olives
3 jars/cartons passata
2 tubes tomato paste
2 jars beetroot
1 sweet dill pickle
2 jars chutney
2 jars mango chutney
2 jars Dijon mustard
1 tin Colmans English mustard
2 jars sun dried tomatoes in oil
8 small UHT cream cartons

Dry stores

30 packets pasta (*Skylax*: 6 penne, 4 rigate, 2 spirals, 2 tagliatelle, 4 linguine, 4 spaghetti, 2 parpardelle, 2 farfale, 4 conchigle)
3kg parboiled long grain rice (when you put it into a container add a bay leaf or two to keep nasties away)
1kg basmati rice
½kg wild rice
2kg couscous
2 packets egg noodles
16 packets instant noodles
8 packets sealed long life pittas
4 loaves long life bread
2 kg sugar (we don't use very much)
2 packets sugar lumps (easier than spooning out sugar)
1kg plain flour
5kg strong flour (for bread making: re-bag it into 500g plastic bags which is about the amount for a good sized loaf of bread)
3 packets ready-mixed bread
10 packets yeast
2 x 2kg tins of dried milk powder (if you are making your own yoghurt

Oil, sauces, and spreads

6 lt olive oil
1 lt vegetable oil
1 lt white wine vinegar
2 bottles balsamic vinegar
1 bottle sesame oil
1 bottle soy sauce
1 bottle teriyaki sauce
1 bottle Worcester sauce
1 bottle tomato ketchup
1 bottle hot chilli sauce
2 bottles lime or lemon juice
2 bottles sweet chilli sauce
3 jars mayonnaise
1 jar mint sauce
1 jar sun-dried tomato paste
4 jars olive spread
1 marmite
1 peanut butter
3 jars of jam
3 jars of honey (you can often get plastic containers of honey which look a bit like a ketchup container with a flip lid and a small pourer – these are a lot easier to use on board than a jar)

Herbs and spices

(More a checklist than anything else although in hot climates herbs lose their taste after a couple of years and need replacing. Spices are longer lasting.)
2 ground cumin
2 ground coriander
1 coriander seeds
1 large mild curry powder
2 jars curry paste (like Patak's)
1 oregano
1 rosemary
1 thyme
1 mint
1 parsley
1 basil
1 fennel seed
1 caraway seed
2 turmeric
1 wasabi
2 paprika
1 chilli powder
1 nutmeg (preferably whole with a little grater)
1 large salt
1 ground black pepper
2 largish whole black peppercorns

Nuts and dried fruit

3 packets pine nuts/pepitas
1 large whole almonds
2 packets blanched almond slices
2 packets walnuts
4 large jars/vacuum packs peanuts
2 packets raisins
2 packets dried apricots
1 packet sultanas
1 packet dried fruit mix

Hot drinks

3 medium sized jars instant coffee (it congeals together into a gooey lump when left in hot climates)
2 packets real coffee
8 packets x 100 Earl Grey teabags
2 packets x 100 'builder's tea'
2 packets hot chocolate
2 packets instant soup (for colder climes a lot more)
4 cartons UHT milk (we don't take milk in tea or coffee so this is just for visitors. You can also get small Tetra Paks of milk, usually for the kids lunch box at school, which is a better way to go)

Cold drinks

2 bottles lime cordial
48 cans tonic
48 cans soda
24 cans iced tea
48 cans beer
12 cartons fruit juice
12 bottles white wine
6 bottles red wine
24 x 1½ lt or 5 x 5 lt bottles water. (We don't drink bottled water as a rule and these are just to go in the bilge as back-up in case the water in the main tanks is unusable for any reason or if we have abandon ship it can be slung into the liferaft.)

Biscuits and treats

12 chocolate chip
6 digestive
6 hob-nobs
4 fig rolls
4 cinnamon
6 cheese biscuits/crackers
6 large packs mini choc and nut bars (These are for the 'goody bag' on night watch.)
3 bars good dark chocolate

Fruit and vegetables

Fruit

20 oranges

15 bananas (don't buy a bunch like you see in all those how-to cruise articles: they will all go off at once and unless you make smoothies or banana cake, get just enough for the first 4–5 days)

16 limes (keep better than lemons) and 6–10 lemons

12 apples

12 passion fruit (keep well if you can get them)

6 kiwi fruit

Vegetables

5kg potatoes

3kg onions

Lots of garlic

2kg tomatoes

12 green and red peppers

1kg courgettes

6 aubergines

½kg carrots (usually don't keep well)

1 cabbage

1 lettuce

1 packet mushrooms

1 hand ginger

1 celery

½kg green beans

Fresh produce

(By sealed I mean vacuum sealed packs)

5 dozen eggs

3 chorizo

6 salami

4 sealed packs bacon

2 sealed packs ham (easy to find in Spain, but they are salty and often fatty as well)

3 sealed packs sausages

2 sealed packs sliced ham

2 sealed packs smoked salmon

2 sealed packs parmesan

1kg Edam/Emmental in smaller sealed packs

2 small sealed packs Cheddar

3 sealed packs feta

2 small sealed packs mozzarella

2 small sealed packs haloumi

8 packs La vache qui rit

6 large plastic tubs butter

4 small plastic tubs margarine

6 small UHT chocolate milks

Other stuff

2 dozen rolls toilet paper

1 dozen rolls paper towels (how did we ever survive without it?)

3 bottles detergent

6 large packs baby wipes (perhaps less for those with functioning watermakers though they are useful to freshen up anyway)

1 loo goo to keep it smelling nice

2 lt cheapest white vinegar (for 101 cleaning jobs)

1 lt bleach

Any other cleaning materials you need

USEFUL BOOKS

General reference

The Oxford Companion to Food
Alan Davidson. Oxford University Press.
The final arbiter on food.

Mediterranean Seafood Alan Davidson.
Prospect Books.

Curry Lizzie Collingham. Chatto &
Windus. An utterly fascinating history
of Indian food and how it evolved.

History of food

Food in History Reay Tannahill.
Penguin.

History of Food Magueilonne Toussaint-
Samat. Blackwell.

Cod Mark Kurlansky. Vintage.
Fascinating history of cod and
fishing fleets in general.

Salt Mark Kurlansky. Vintage.
The history of a substance we need
and which shaped parts of history.

Fish on Friday Brian Fagan. Basic Books.
History of the importance of fish in
Europe.

*In the Devil's Garden: A short history of
forbidden food* Stewart Lee Allen.
Canon Gate.

Mediterranean Food Elizabeth David.
Penguin.

History of exploration

Captain James Cook: A Biography
Richard Hough. Coronet.

*Discovery: The Quest for the Great
South Land* Miriam Estensen.

Arab Seafaring George F Hourani.
Princeton University Press.

Over the Edge of the World
Laurence Bergreen. Harper Perennial.

*Discoveries: The Voyages of Captain
Cook* Nicholas Thomas. Penguin.

*New Zealand and the South Pacific
Islands* John H Chambers. Windrush
Press.

Nathaniel's Nutmeg Giles Milton.
Sceptre.

Fossils, Finches and Fuegians
Richard Keynes. Harper Collins.

Beyond the Pillars of Hercules
Rhys Carpenter. Tandem.

General

Storms, Shipwrecks and Sea Disasters
Ed Richard Lawrence. Carroll & Graf.

The Adventure of Food
Ed Richard Sterling. Travellers Tales.

The Little Book of the Sea: Food & Drink
Lorenz Schroter.

Like Water for Chocolate
Laura Esquivel. Black Swan.

Cookbooks

Australian Woman's Weekly Cookbooks
Various titles. Lu laughed when I first
showed her one of these, but soon came
around when she browsed through the
recipes in AWWC *Meals in Minutes*. She
is now a convert. Browse through the
titles and try one or two. I swear
celebrity cooks nick lots of the ideas in
these books.

BBC Good Food series. Various titles
with good easy recipes and the books
are a convenient size on board.

Otherwise I mostly turn to Nigel Slater,
good down-to-earth recipes or to some
of Jamie Oliver's cookbooks.

INDEX

INDEX